AF290992

SCOTTISH WARLOCKS, WIZARDS AND MAGICIANS

Dedicated to my relatives in Scotland.

SCOTTISH WARLOCKS, WIZARDS AND MAGICIANS

A HISTORICAL QUEST

KEITH COLEMAN

PEN & SWORD HISTORY

AN IMPRINT OF PEN & SWORD BOOKS LTD.
YORKSHIRE – PHILADELPHIA

First published in Great Britain in 2026 by
PEN AND SWORD HISTORY
An imprint of
Pen & Sword Books Ltd
Yorkshire – Philadelphia

ISBN 978 1 03611 997 3

Typeset in Times New Roman 11/14 by
SJmagic DESIGN SERVICES, India.
Printed and bound in the UK by CPI Group (UK) Ltd.

The Publisher's authorised representative in the EU for product safety is
Authorised Rep Compliance Ltd., Ground Floor, 71 Lower Baggot Street,
Dublin D02 P593, Ireland.
www.arccompliance.com

For a complete list of Pen & Sword titles please contact
PEN & SWORD BOOKS LIMITED
George House, Units 12 & 13, Beevor Street, Off Pontefract Road,
Barnsley, South Yorkshire, S71 1HN, England
E-mail: enquiries@pen-and-sword.co.uk
Website: www.pen-and-sword.co.uk

or

PEN AND SWORD BOOKS
1950 Lawrence Rd, Havertown, PA 19083, USA
E-mail: uspen-and-sword@casematepublishers.com
Website: www.penandswordbooks.com

Contents

Illustrations

Map

Andro Man's world, the East and North-East of Scotland, p. 39

Plates

1. Fresco, possibly of Michael Scot, in the Spanish Chapel, Sancta Maria Novella, Florence. (Image from *An enquiry into the life and legend of Michael Scot* by James Wood Brown, 1897.)
2. Ritual magician summoning Mephistophilis. (Frontispiece to Christopher Marlowe's *Dr Faustus*, 1620 edition; public domain image via Wikimedia Commons.)
3. St Andrews. (Photo © Keith Coleman.)
4. James Stewart, Earl of Moray, regent of Scotland and foe of witchcraft. (Engraving, H. Robinson, 1827; public domain image via Wikimedia Commons.)
5. Title page of *The Daemonologie*, King James VI, 1597.
6. Botriphnie, Banffshire, home of the healer Andro Man. (Photograph by James Mark.)
7. Elf Hillock, Botriphnie. (Photograph by Anne Burgess. Creative Commons.)
8. Memorial of William Shaw, Dunfermline Abbey. (Photograph © Keith Coleman.)
9. John Napier of Merchiston. (Image from *Memoirs of John Napier of Merchiston, his lineage, life and times, with a history of the invention of logarithms* by Mark Napier, 1834).
10. The old tolbooth, Edinburgh. (Image from *Major Weir* by K. L. Mongomery, 1904.)

11. German engraving 1631, showing Mackay's regiment landing in Stettin (Szczecin). (Georg Cöler, public domain image via Wikimedia Commons.)

12. Ritual of allegiance. (Image from *Compendium Maleficarum* (1610) by Francesco Maria Guazzo; (ed.) Montague Summers; (trans.) E. Allen Ashwin, 1929.)

13. Sir George Mackenzie. *A Biographical History of England: from Egbert the Great to the Revolution*, James Granger, 1824. (Public domain image via Wikimedia Commons.)

14. *Pandæmonium*, Richard Bovet, 1684.

15. Home of Major Weir, West Bow, Edinburgh. (From Walter Scott's *Letters on Demonology and Witchcraft*, 1830; public domain image via Wikimedia Commons.)

16. Major Weir's spectral coach. (Alexander A. Ritchie; public domain image via Wikimedia Commons.)

17. Witches condemned at Newcastle. (Illustration from *England's grievance discovered, in relation to the coal trade; with the map of the river of Tine, and situation of the town and corporation of Newcastle ... by Ralph Gardiner, 1796.*)

18. The unidentified witch-pricker takes payment for his work at Newcastle. (Illustration from *England's grievance discovered, in relation to the coal trade; with the map of the river of Tine, and situation of the town and corporation of Newcastle ... by Ralph Gardiner, 1796.*)

19. Edinburgh from Calton Hill. (Engraving W. Tombleson; public domain image via Wikimedia Commons.)

20. The Laird o' Lag. (*The laird of Lag, a life-sketch*, by Fergusson, Alexander, 1830–1892.)

21. Adam Donald, Prophet of Bethelnie. (Engraving John Williams, *The Bee*, 1780.)

22. The water kelpie. (John Careless, *The Old English Squire*, 1905; public domain image via Wikimedia Commons.)

23. The Sabbat. ('La Danse du Sabat', Émile Bayard, from *The History of Magic*, Paul Christian, 1870; public domain image via Wikimedia Commons)

24. The other Major Weir.Illustration to 'Wandering Willie's Tale', Douglas Percy Bliss. Wood engraving from *The Devil in Scotland*, 1934 © Rosalind Bliss and Prudence Bliss.

Foreword

Threw bitters hed he bitten, with hart and tongue and eye almaist, and wheir thrie [bitters] boit may be, the father sonne and haly gaist…

Charm to take off witchcraft c. 1606.
Taught to Andrew Aiken by Thomas Ferguson.[1]

This book outlines some traditions of Scotland's notable men of magic and examines the record of some others who were accused of being witches or warlocks. Like the far greater number of women prosecuted, many accused males were not involved in any magical practices. Others believed that there was nothing unchristian in their use of spells, incantations, rituals, or the use of herbs and other materials to help people. Of these who did dabble in what were deemed superstitious and diabolic practices, such as folk healing, some were condemned to death even though there was no evidence that they had indulged in *malefice*, the committing of evil acts. I have concentrated on more substantial cases, but I hope the circumstances of ordinary men caught up in accusations of witchcraft have not been neglected and that comparisons between the real and legendary groups is at least interesting and sometimes useful. Scant attention has been given to folk tales about real and imagined warlocks.

The large body of academic work dedicated to witchcraft in Scotland is a boon to any writer, even if it feels like some more rarefied studies seem to depersonalise the human element of those unfortunates accused, tortured and often killed by authorities who believed they were doing their communities and their God a service in rooting out those who had made pacts with the Devil. The non-academic writer is painfully aware of the numerous pitfalls that must be risked and errors that can go undetected by the vigilance of peers in the same discipline. I am grateful to the authors of works cited in the bibliography and to many others. Special mention must be made of The Survey of Scottish Witchcraft (https://witches.hca.ed.ac.uk/); I have consulted this constantly, though have not always referenced it.

My thanks go to Anne Burgess. Also to Rosalind Bliss and Prudence Bliss for their kind permission to include the wood engraving of 'Wandering Willie's Tale' by their father, Douglas Percy Bliss. Thanks also to Dianne Mark, Secretary of Drummuir and Botriphnie Community Trust, and also to her husband, James Mark.

Introduction

A *boddach*, or wise-man, lives in a rock called The Raven's, in one of our woods. He frightens people extremely in the evening (the rock commands a long hill on the road), but there is no proof that he has killed anyone as yet.[1]

Whatever this sinister creature was, it was not human: not a mortal warlock, wizard, or male witch. But it opens the door to questioning what those terms mean. The word warlock has peculiarly Scottish connotations, used to denote various kinds of evildoers in the sixteenth century, before becoming restricted to male magic workers in the following century.[2] Like many things associated with witchcraft, the term is far older in origin. The Anglo-Saxon *wærloga*, signified traitor, deceiver, or oath-breaker. In its later reference to male magic workers it was popularly favoured in Scotland and northern England before entering general English usage via the works of Sir Walter Scott in the early nineteenth century.[3]

Some modern historians have sought to refine the terms and traits of magic workers. Charmers, blessers, and touchers are defined by some as basic workers, performing simple healing in humans and animals. Cunning folk (an English term) offered more comprehensive magical services, and in Scotland such men may have been called wizards, witches, sorcerers, canny men, wise men, spae men, skeelie men, warlocks or wizards. The whole Scottish group likely differed from practitioners elsewhere, and witchcraft and their magic could be deemed beneficial or evil. While there was an overwhelming emphasis in those who pursued suspected witches on their supposed acts of malice or on their spiritual treachery in making pacts with Satan, healers were also pursued in many cases. One reason they were prosecuted was because they were seen as abusers, preying on the gullibility of their clients. Whether accurate or not, the records of some of these beneficial healers shows them involved in fierce disputes with neighbours or associates.

Male witches did not have any marked distinctiveness in magical behaviour, compared with the women who were accused. This is in contrast with some parts of Europe where male witches' behaviour was sometimes tied in with localised legends which preyed on the minds of the population. In Burgundy, for example, many male suspects were also believed to be werewolves.[4]

But did Scotland have a prevalent mindset peculiarly beset by uncertainty, illness and fear? Despite a perception by some of Scotland as a particularly occult nation, there is no reason to believe that the country was more infected with uncanny practices or beliefs than elsewhere. This idea flourished in the nineteenth century, again popularised by Walter Scott, James Hogg, and other writers. It was largely a literary concept, though not only a native one. This idea had sporadically surfaced from foreign sources. The French author, Jean Juvénal des Ursins (1388–1473) wrote how a countryman who wanted to consult with Satan was advised to go to 'wild Scotland', the residence of the Devil. The seeker journeyed to the northern nation and consulted with an old (female) witch.[5]

Even before the Lowland Scots defined their Highland compatriots as both untamed and imbued with supernatural characteristics, the English were inclined to portray Scotland as a land of savagery, with the cartographer John Hardyng in the fifteenth century going so far as to officially map the far north of Scotland, where the 'wild Scotrie' hosted Satan's mansion. Northern Scotland shared a reputation for magic in common with the area Scandinavian Sápmi (Lappland); both areas viewed as savagely un-Christian by sophisticated southerners. The North, a concept as much as a real place for Europeans, was an indistinct peripheral region, a buffer between civilisation and the chaotic abode of monsters, and even in Norse sagas, it was a place of trolls, ghosts, death, magic.[6] The Highland Line broadly dividing Gaelic speaking people from Scots speaking people became a de facto border between civilisation and savagery sometime in the Early Modern Period.

The English scientific establishment began to take notice of the Highlands of Scotland as a repository for second sight at the end of the seventeenth century, spurred on by contact between the scientist Robert Boyle, co-founder of the Royal Society, and George Mackenzie, Lord Tarbat.[7] It is difficult to say whether the dark glamour of Scotland as somewhere uncanny continued unabated into the Victorian age, or whether it was rekindled Celtic romanticism. In either case, the French author Jori-Karl Husyman had one of his characters, Des Hermies, in his novel *Là-Bas* (1891) describe Scotland as the nation 'where sorcerers proliferate'.

There was little in the pre-Reformation record to suggest that Scotland was a hotbed of magic or witchcraft, and those who suggest that organised pagan activity persisted in spite of the all-pervasive Church have little firm evidence to support this. The one, outlying example in the records is unique and demonstrates more about the individual involved than any national characteristics. At Easter 1282, the English *Chronicle of Lanercost* informs us that the parish priest of Inverkeithing in Fife, named John, revived ancient pagan rites by:

> collecting young girls from the villages, [he compelled] them to dance in circles to [honour] Father Bacchus. When he had these females in a troop, out of sheer wantonness, he led the dance, carrying in front on a pole a representation of the human organs of reproduction, and singing and dancing himself like a mime, he viewed them all and stirred them to lust by filthy language… If anybody remonstrated kindly with him, he became worse [than before], violently reviling him.[8]

Later that year, Father John set some parishioners against others, and when secular officials complained, he defended his actions, but was killed that same night when he fell on his own knife, or so the story goes, proving the swift action of providence. Nowhere else do we hear of such a uniquely perverse Scottish cleric. Few else in Scotland would likely have heard of Priapus, let alone embraced his worship. This did not stop Margaret Murray citing the event as evidence of an enduring pagan cult operating in Scotland, a claim which has been dismissed.[9]

Most of the people who admitted charming, healing or other forms of occult activity were fully embedded in their communities and admitted the names of those who consulted them, who they worked with magically, and sometimes who they used dark witchcraft on and who they initially learnt their craft from. What is still undecided in academic circles is whether there was at any time an active and enduring cult of magical practitioners who built their practices on ancient rituals. In Italy, Carlo Ginzberg identified a cult named the *Benandanti* from Friuli, Italy in his influential book

The Night Battles (1983). In the sixteenth and seventeenth centuries this mainly female group engaged in nightly astral battles with evil witches who sought to damage their crops. Another similar cult existed in Sicily: the *Doñas de Fuera* ('ladies from outside').

The historian Julian Goodacre sought to identify a possibly analogous, though barely detectable group in Scotland named the *seely wichts* or *wights*.[10] This group was mentioned by the Aberdeen academic William Hay around 1535, possibly as a native version of European cults which honoured the goddess Diana. The cult, if it existed (and there is a question mark about this), may have been overwhelmingly female, but this is not to say there were no male participants, as Goodacre acknowledges.[11] We might sight those few men who admitted flying-type experiences during their interrogations, such as Dr John Fian of Prestonpans. The term *seely wights* may have included otherworldly beings, fairies or related beings, as well as their mortal followers.

While other experts have moved independently towards believing there was some shamanistic cult practice in Scotland, the case has not been proven. Ronald Hutton is one historian who has reserved judgement on Goodacre's theory.[12] For the purposes of this book, the theory of the *seely wights* remains a footnote, though a fascinating one, especially as much of what follows concerns fairy interaction with supernatural beliefs and practices. It also has to be said that the majority of witchcraft accusations and trials do not mention fairies and associated otherworldly beings (just as many of them do not mention the Devil incarnate). The interaction between mortal and fairy realms is a fascinating one, which is one reason it features so heavily in this work.

From the time of the Inverkeithing incident to the Reformation there were few recorded cases of witchcraft in Scotland. The nation avoided the short, but intense waves of persecution which occurred sometimes in mainland Europe, which were often linked to the authority's fear of heresy. The Reformation is where certain ideas about the identity of Satan and his plan to control Christendom through the agency of willing human confederates, female and male, began to take shape, in Catholic and Protestant nations alike. For Scotland, it involved a dark century and a half of accusation and persecution following the Witchcraft Act in 1563 until its repeal in 1736. Although the act was sponsored by a newly reformed Protestant parliament, it was only one element in their programme of governing the country's moral and religious behaviour.

Between 1563 and 1736, perhaps over 3000 people were condemned for witchcraft and maybe around half that number were put to death, though the actual figures may be higher.[13] Executions were three times as high as in England, through the Scottish population was a quarter of the size of its neighbour. The socially coercive control of the early Presbyterians in Scotland ensured that, while around 500 people were executed as witches in England, up to three times that number perished in Scotland. Brian Levack, reckoning from the difference in national populations, reckoned a woman in Scotland was twelve times more likely to be accused of witchcraft than in England.[14]

Accused witches in England were generally tried in court under two judges and their guilt or innocence decided by a jury made up of men from a wide area. In Scotland, local ministers and lairds often prompted prosecutions (though suspicion might be community based), prompting people to confess. Permission to prosecute was then sought from higher civil authority and frequently the local figures were given the power to decide the case. So many were effectively condemned before trial. The justiciary court in Edinburgh would hear some witchcraft cases from the regions, but did not have the capacity or inclination to hear all cases, so the Privy Council delegated authority back to the accusers. Those commissions which allowed local people to try other local people often included men with no legal expertise.

There were six major outbreaks of Scottish witch hunting: 1568–1569, 1590–1591, 1597, 1628–1630, 1649, and 1661–1662, though accusations, trials and executions continued between these years. Given the fact that people were targeted locally, particularly by Kirk sessions and powerful community figures, and that some records may have been lost, along with the probability that some witches were unlawfully killed, the number of actual deaths is unknowable. Several accused witches, male and female, are known to have committed suicide while imprisoned. Others died as a result of torture, mistreatment or natural causes worsened by incarceration.

Scotland's male witches probably made up ten to fifteen per cent of the accused. The proportion of men accused may have risen during times of high prosecution. Several modern writers estimate that up to twenty per cent of the accused in Scotland were male.[15] Either way, the figures are comparable with parts of Germany, France and Switzerland but slightly more than England. Some countries, like Estonia, Finland and Iceland, had extremely high numbers of males accused.[16] In other places, localised witch hunts threw up an abnormal number of accused men in short periods, such as in Salzburg (1675–1682), where seventy per cent of those on trial were men, or Freising (1715–1717), where ninety-seven per cent of sixty people accused were male.[17] Overall, the pattern of witch-hunting for Europe shows marked variation. Catholic and Protestant areas alike could show forbearance or savagery, and areas which had been subject to the Inquisition (Spain and Italy) showed little appetite for witch hunting. Witch panics in Europe seemed contagious from region to region.[18] On a smaller scale, suspicion and accusation could spread like wildfire between places, in Scotland as elsewhere.

The mechanism for Scottish witchcraft prosecutions was geared against the person accused. Accusations generally arose within communities and were picked up by local lairds, civil officials or Kirk officials and enquiries made. The person might be arrested and held until a commission was sought from the central Privy Council of Scotland, in many cases, then the person would be prosecuted locally by people who would have a prejudice against them, and then overwhelmingly found guilty, strangled at the stake, then burned to ashes. Some have argued that witch hunts were sponsored more by the impetus and fears of central government, especially in the witchcraft panic of 1597 when the king himself was seen as a target of the witches, but this does not seem to have often been the case afterwards.[19] In England, the legal system and selection of the jury from a wider area meant that witches had a better chance of acquittal.

Despite the high prosecution rate, those who were suspected of witchcraft, or who practised charming or healing, could sometimes survive for years, even decades, before they were brought to trial and prosecuted. Local rumour could stigmatise a person as a witch or warlock for many years before action was taken. Some accused, for various reasons, readily admitted long-standing allegiance to powers of darkness. One accused warlock named William Crichtoun, a vagrant beggar, examined in Dunfermline in August 1648, admitted he had been a servant of Satan's for twenty-four years. He was condemned and burned.[20] There was also, in many times and places, a difference in how charmers and healers were treated compared with witches. Although male charmers were sometimes executed, we can surmise that more men in this category than women escaped death.

Community slander and suspicion involved other crimes than witchcraft. While outspokenness by itself seldom saw men being punished, women who were troublesome, argumentative, or sometimes seen as too economically privileged compared to their peers, could be targeted as witches. It was less likely that males would be denounced as witches following slanging matches, *flyting* in Scots, with people in their local area. There are numerous records of women in local parish records who were accused of being a witch in conjunction with receiving other abusive terms designed to generally flatten the recipient's social standing rather than prove supernatural misdeeds. People who slandered, gossiped, *flyted*, scolded or who otherwise socially transgressed might be put on display and humiliated by means of having to wear the *branks* (scolds' or witches' bridle) or be placed in the *jougs*, an iron collar attached to kirk walls and the other buildings. The war on female social deviancy grew over time. During the sixteenth century there are cases of men being punished like this, but it was it was used mainly for women in the seventeenth century.[21]

Most social disputes, where women were on the receiving end of verbal abuse or slander, was by other women, though men were involved. Much less commonly, men were targeted by other men in the same manner. A few examples are worth citing. On 3 June 1603, a man named James Murdoche answered to a charge of not attending communion that he had been prevented from doing so because James Cok had bewitched him, 'and he houpit to get amendis of him'. The two men had previously been friendly, and the previous year Cok admitted to the session that he and Murdoche had visited a witch who was afterwards burnt.[22] John Wadie complained to the Kirk session of Carrington, Midlothian, in May 1657, stating that James Nisbet had called him a witch.[23] Also in 1657, a tailor named James Cock complained to Canongate Kirk session in Edinburgh that James Braidie had slandered his mother by calling her a witch and also threatened to break his head. Braidie was referred to the civil magistrate. Four years later, Haddington Presbytery heard Thomas Strong complaining that Robert Lindsay was defaming him as 'ane warla carill', saying he had performed some ritual with a sheet over his head that involved him turning around widdershins (anticlockwise) three times.[24] In December 1677, Andro Currie and his wife, Margaret Douglas, complained to the Kirk session at Dunfermline that Isobel Cuper had called him a warlock, her a witch, and had accused their daughter of theft. Cuper was found guilty of 'odious slander' and fined £6.[25] In some cases when men slandered each other, there was a keen economic imperative behind the accusations. In Aberdeen, in 1607, ship's skipper, James Mar, called merchant Andro Paull 'ane common witche, and cum of witchis, and not worthie to remane in ane civill tonne'. Mar was punished as a slanderer.[26] John Dawson from Alves, Moray, was punished by the session in 1653 for maligning John Fraser, saying that a corbie had flown from Fraser's house and interfered with his salmon net so that he caught no fish for many tides. The bird was supposed to have been Fraser.[27]

Patrick Lowrie of Dundonald, Ayrshire (executed in 1605), was accused of threatening John Andro's wife after arguing with her. He also quarrelled with John Forgushill over interest on a debt. Debt was also an issue between Patrick and John Gottray. Gottray received a horse from Lowrie in payment for a debt, but afterwards the horse ate his crops and his cows' health dwindled.[28] Some of the records show glimpses of domestic disputes which goes beyond verbal abuse and involve a supernatural element in male aggression or violence. A Paisley miller named John Stewart admitted, in 1677, that he turned to the Devil to seek vengeance on his enemy, Maxwell of Pollock, after Maxwell kidnapped his mother.[29] In those rare instances where we have a substantial surviving record of both husband and wife accused of magical work, it is interesting to view the dynamics behind both accusations, which give a glimpse of how men and women behaved socially and were regarded by their communities.

Thomas Paton and his spouse, Bessie Grahame, came to the attention of the Presbytery of Dumfries in 1649 following friction with their neighbours and acquaintances. Thomas was primarily implicated for malicious magic by his servant Jonet Ker, who stated that the couple had unnaturally extended lifespans: 'They were over lang Livand be Twentie zeir'. More damningly, she said that Thomas made anyone whom he hated ill through his evil-eye. One example she gave was a woman who laughed at Thomas who collapsed after he maliciously looked at her and was still affected by a physical and mental condition. A man who assaulted Thomas during some business dispute suffered the loss of his goods. Thomas's neighbour, Robert Heslop, suffered a worse fate. During an argument, Thomas cursed him and Robert cast aside his faithful wife, then his finances dwindled away and he contracted some loathsome disease which affected his leg, and he died in poverty, 'begging his breid'. Another neighbour who chased off Thomas's sheep which were eating his crops, and caused two of them to drown, was the subject of a curse (another witness said), so that his wealth diminished by £1000. Two of his horses became ill and there was uncanny strife within his family, where before there had been harmony. Another economic dispute occurred concerning the pasturing of a horse, which afterwards died in a pond. A man who consulted Thomas about his health was advised to conduct a ritual involving a black cow, which afterwards died. A woman who refused to sell Thomas ale went temporarily mad until her sister beseeched Thomas's wife to break the curse.

A dramatic tale was also recorded, again involving disputes with community members, which was obviously a feature of Thomas Paton's life. This time, he argued with a man named William Makburnie, and when William's heavily pregnant wife encountered Thomas while going to market, she became ill, eight weeks before she was due to give birth. William furiously accosted Thomas and threatened him with a knife, saying he would go to his grave if his wife died. Paton visited the woman and muttered some prayers or charms over her. But the woman immediately looked like she was going to die, at which the charmer was again threatened. He stated that the woman's fever was turning and said some more prayers. This time the whole house and the bed violently shook, and the pregnant woman recovered. If Thomas was a healer, he was a singularly ill-tempered and unpopular one.

Bessie Grahame readily admitted being a healer when questioned. She was sought out by mothers of small ailing children, who usually recovered with her aid, though in several instances a child died (after Bessie pronounced that they would do so). A woman with a sick child sent her nurse to ask Bessie for help. She was given a charm to repeat, but the nurse refused to repeat the words and the infant died. One witness recalled an ancient complaint from some twenty-four years before, when one of her late husband's servants was deprived of a cloak by Thomas Paton. The two women had words and the witness afterwards fell ill for three months. Bessie was sent for, but refused to touch the woman, saying those who laid on the wrong could not then take it off. A man admitted that Bessie cured his sick cow without seeing it, and afterwards cured two of his horses which were also ill. Two men who were unwell were cured by Bessie without her having seen them in person. Thomas and Bessie were subjected to pricking by their examiners. Bessie had a long pin inserted into her left shoulder, but she did not bleed or feel anything, though she felt it when a finger was placed in the same spot. Her husband received the same treatment and he feigned pain, but could not precisely identify where the pin had been inserted.[30]

John Rind of Elgin had a reputation as a charmer and healer and the Kirk session in 1661 heard that he and his wife had cursed Thomas Gray when the horse Gray sold him died. He and his family fell into misfortune and other witnesses spoke against Rind. Rind scornfully attacked key witness, Bessie Alwas, because she was a whore and a thief and the session had therefore to juggle the testimony of mutually slanderous people. The matter was deferred to the Presbytery. Rind and his wife were found guilty of charming rather than witchcraft and sentenced to appear in sackcloth, then both were banished.[31]

Sometimes particular men found themselves being defamed by women, such as the case in 1694 when John Gray from Pencaitland, East Lothian, complained that a mother and a daughter harassed him by calling him 'witches gett' and wishing that his soul was soaking in hell's cauldron.[32] When defending themselves against ill-chosen and inflammatory words, which they may have issued in anger, women were more susceptible to being brought before civil and religious authorities. Men were expected to settle their disputes without recourse to the indignity of public arguments. When they did get pulled up for verbal offences, they frequently blamed alcohol for their misdemeanours. Perth Kirk session in March 1631 heard that David Duff had visited a woman named Isobel Hunter and had ungraciously said that her husband had 'the picture of death in his face'. He qualified this by adding that, if the man survived for three weeks, he would live for three hundred years more. Isobel accused her visitor of ill-wishing her husband, who was obviously sick, and said, 'David, are ye a witch, that ye can discern upon life and death, and time thereof?'

Duff angrily answered, 'You and your mother have witched him to lie pining in his bed till he die'. He followed this with a litany of slanderous accusations against Isobel and her mother and was forcefully ejected from the house, still mouthing off at the inhabitants. When Isobel pursued an accusation of slander against David Duff, he blamed his angry words on having been drunk. He was warded and fined for slander. It was interesting that neither he nor Isobel were actively investigated for witchcraft. Presumably both were known to the session members and there was no corroboration from anyone else in the community who would have cast doubt on either party.[33]

Many men resorted to soliciting the services of charmers and other magical workers to heal sick animals and humans, and to ensure the abundance of their crops. Charmers can be defined as people who answered queries or solved, through divination or spells, to give people answers about their concerns. Women of course would also be inclined to seek help in matters like ensuring their own fertility. Many men, while not witches themselves, indulged in rituals designed to ensure their material wellbeing. The 'heathenish' practise of raising need fires, to ensure the success of crops, was condemned by Church authorities but was widely practised by multiple men in the same community, none of whom would had considered themselves pagan in any way. Sometimes, however, such rituals were co-ordinated by a local wise-man. This seems to have been the case at Grange, in Banffshire, where the local population repeatedly indulged in the ritual. Eight men hauled before the Presbytery in May 1649 said they had only acted under the order of a James Duncan from Keith.[34]

The penalties for using charms and consulting witches or charmers were severe in theory, but many people escaped with warnings, censure, or other relatively mild punishments. Urquhart man, Finlay Macconnichie, and his wife Shiack, brought before the court at Dingwall in 1650 for employing a charm to remedy the supernatural theft of their milk, said that it 'took effect to their mynd', and escaped imprisonment.[35] Another example is Robert Shortus from Dunfermline. In June 1643 he was summoned for consulting and seeking charms for his sick wife. He showed due repentance and was ordered to sit in sackcloth for two successive Sundays in the kirk. The records add a note of leniency: 'he should have sittin before ye pulpett bot he was pittied'.[36]

Particular communities and areas were sometimes more prone to witchcraft and associated practices, for reasons not always altogether clear. The upland area of Glenesk and Lochlee in Angus was Gaelic speaking into the seventeenth century and maintained a reputation of apartness from the rest of the county. Together with some other parts of Angus, it remained resolutely Episcopalian and a hotbed of Jacobite dissent into the eighteenth century. The area possesses a store of unique folklore and was a very different place from lowland Angus. In 1649, a man named John Donaldson of Lochlee came to the attention of the Presbytery of Brechin, and was rebuked for charming, that is, using spells or devices to bring about a desired outcome or ward off evil. Donaldson admitted his sin, and 'casting the Shemfur', which was a traditional method of divining fortune by using scissors and a sieve. He was sharply rebuked and asked who taught him that skill. A man who was now dead, he said, and when he was pressed further said there were others in Glenesk who did the same as him, and he named four others, all men. The Presbytery was unhappy with his answers, as he had given more ample ones.

By June the following year, three of the men he had named (John Chrystison, Thomas Kyneir, and James Shanks) were brought before the Presbytery and sharply rebuked, all admitting their sin in casting the *shemfur*. They were made to appear in sackcloth on four successive Sundays before the congregation of Lochlee and were not to be absolved until the minister found signs of repentance in them. Further, the men 'wer strictlie inhibited to use the arte of charming in casting the Shinfur in tym with certification they shall be esteemed Sorcerers'.[37]

The same district was home in the late sixteenth century to Robert Murray, who came to the attention of the civil authorities in 1588. He too seems to have been involved in magical practices and made mention of the murdered David Riccio or Rizzio, secretary to Mary, Queen of Scots, who had died twenty-two years previously. Murray claimed some supernatural connection with Riccio, but the details are obscure. Was there something in the local environment here that gave rise to witchcraft and superstitious practice? If so, the actions of the Presbytery seem to have effectively stamped it out or at least drove it further underground.

Many other places seem to have been particularly afflicted with witches, female and male, at least in the minds of local prosecutors who were keen to root out harmful magic, which they believed was dangerous to humans and their wellbeing. Most of these places displayed a spike in accusations and prosecutions during regional or national panics. Large burghs, interestingly, showed comparatively fewer accusations and prosecutions.

The role of gender in magical power has long been discussed and sometimes disputed. One interesting belief is that certain charming and related powers could only be passed down within families from one gender to the other, from father to daughter for example. This was noted in the Scottish Highlands. It was also documented in Cornwall by Charles Thomas, in the case of modern 'blood-charmers', and Thomas also observed that it had been a tradition in the Isle of Man.[38]

What, if anything, stood men apart from women in the eyes of the authorities when they were rooting out witchcraft? The debate to which witch hunting can be equated with women hunting has continued among scholars for several generations, with no definitive resolution, though it may be fair to say that most experts would postulate there were a variety of reasons why more women were accused. Some accused men were guilty by association with women who were suspected of witchcraft. While the great numbers of actions against women involved females who were not otherwise different from their friends and neighbours, it could well be that men had a greater chance of being targeted if they were vagrants, involved in begging, or were even members of certain professions, like millers. The link between accusation and begging/vagrancy is something to be explored later.

Perceptions of specifically male roles within groups of witchcraft practitioners were skewed by perceptions of those combatting the supposed powers of darkness. There was likely no conspiratorial network of witchcraft covens (a Scottish term invented in the late seventeenth century) hellbent in overthrowing the Kirk and secular state. But this did not stop accusers imagining an elaborate, sometimes formal organisation of evildoers existing just beyond the brink of civilised society. Modern attempts to formalise male participants' roles in covens are based on the premise that such gatherings regularly occurred, which is a dubious proposition.[39] Male members of covens were often allotted specific important functions, reflecting the patriarchal view of those who imagined this shadow network. Most famously, John Fian of Prestonpans was cast as clerk to Satan and register keeper at meetings. At the other end of the scale, and reflecting his life as 'ane auld sely pure plowman', Grey Meill acted as the doorman at meetings of witches.

In the 1660s, the extravagant confessions of Isobel Gowdie included the information that a coven member named John Young was then officer, and one part of the role was calling in all the witches when the Devil had marked their presence. Janet Breidheid, an accomplice of Gowdie, mentions that two men, Alexander Elder and Walter Ledy (her own husband), were officers but when coven numbers fell, she and some other women would rule the rest. Other trials mention men as being rulers of their covens, whose other members were twelve women.[40] Rob Grieve of Lauder, convicted in 1659, was supposedly the Devil's officer in his home district for eighteen years, rounding up fellow acolytes to meetings when Satan summoned them.[41] In 1629, the warlock Andrew Hamilton mentioned under questioning the Devil's 'heid man' in Berwickshire, John Smith of Duns. At one meeting of witches, Satan copulated with all the women present. Smith then did the same and 'usit them all behind, and raid them lyk beastes'.[42] The legend of sabbats may have been based on some folk practices. As late as the turn of the eighteenth century a correspondent was complaining about the frequency of men and women resorting to abandoned (Catholic) chapels and cavorting all night with sex, music and associated frivolity. There is no mention however of witchcraft rites being performed.[43]

Warlocks as leaders of sabbats are also found in other countries. The French magistrate Pierre de Lancre, who wrote a treatise on Basque witchcraft in 1612, described Petri Daguerre, 73-year-old man executed as a wizard, as master of ceremonies and governor of the sabbats.[44] Men also provided entertainment for dark gatherings. John Douglas of Tranent (1659) and several others were named as pipers to the Devil.[45] John Douglas, active at Tranent in the 1650s, was told by Satan to play his bagpipes at meetings of witches. At one meeting at Brae Green, between Seton and Tranent in East Lothian, he played the tune 'Hulie, the bed will fall' ('beware, the bed will fall'), a hint at the bacchanalian activities there. One of the Forfar witches accused in 1661 was Andrew Watsone, a blind man. Despite his disability 'yet he daunced alse nimblie as any of the company and made alse great mirriement by singing his old ballads'. Less jovially, at one meeting of the coven he dug up the body of an unbaptised bairn and ate part of its body.[46] A Highland warlock, Donald McIllmichael, played the pipes at another supernatural gathering. Thomas Leys of Aberdeen (tried in 1597) was in charge of the dancing at sabbats and punished those witches who did not perform well. Occasionally the Devil deigned to entertain his acolytes himself. He is recorded at Culross in 1675 playing the pipes for his witches.

There are some traces of women being accorded specific roles within covens when they met. There are mentions of females acting as *furriour* (quartermaster) to the Devil, and occasionally maidens of the coven are mentioned, who were younger, attractive women within each group that Satan paid particular attention to. Yet women were rarely accorded elevated positions. In 1590, one witch in Scotland was described as being the admiral of her group, a rare title which also occurred in records of the Scandinavian area of Finnmark in 1621.[47] While female witchcraft confessions, reflecting the predilection of interrogators and prosecutors, readily concluded that female witches frequently enjoyed sexual congress with Satan, and that sex was part of their ritual induction into his service, there was no suggestion that male disciples of the Devil were obliged to do this. The demonic pact sometimes involved kissing the Devil's backside, but that was as far as it went. A few men were enticed into illicit liaisons with female demons (or possibly Satan) but not direct intercourse with the Devil in person. Homosexuality was not an accusation commonly made against male witches.[48]

The place of men in the sabbats or within covens appears ill-defined, and in many accounts they seem like interlopers who have gate-crashed the devilish festivities, always heavily outnumbered by females. Whether at sabbats or elsewhere, the notion of a pact, selling oneself wholly to Satan, was an integral part of the relationship between the fallen individual and the enemy of God. In Scotland, as it became common elsewhere, the fallen man or woman was given a mark or a wound by Satan to signify the infernal bargain. The whole subject of whether these gatherings ever took place, or whether they were inventions of either the social elite (interrogators) or the common people (victims) remains open to debate.[49]

Male witches (and male otherworldly beings) sometimes wielded symbols of power, such as a wand or staff. The Ayrshire witch, Bessie Dunlop, had a ghostly attendant called Thom Reid, whose authority as an intermediary with the fairy realm was signified by him carrying a white wand. When the male witch, John Stewart, encountered the fairy king in Ireland, this being struck him on the forehead with a white wand, which gave him second sight but also deprived him of the sight in one eye.[50] Alexander Hamilton of East Lothian met the Devil in 1630 and took part in a supernatural passing of the baton, giving him authority. Satan had 'ane battoun of fir in his hand [that] the devil than gave the said Alexr command to tak that battoun quhan evir he had ado with him and therewt to strek thruse upone the ground and to charge him to rouse up the foule theiff'. Repenting his allegiance, Alexander cast the baton into a fire, where it made a dreadful noise which alarmed those who heard it. The warlock was later beaten by the Devil with another baton for missing a meeting.[51] Shetland warlock Andrew Ratter, accused of witchcraft along with his two sisters in 1708, was accused of intimidating the local community and harming humans and animals. The records emphasise that he 'leaned on his staff' when performing a particular act of magic.[52] The Devil appeared to John Fian of the North Berwick coven in the late sixteenth-century carrying a white wand, which was later broken when Fian renounced his allegiance and this power was withdrawn.[53] Notorious wizard, Richie Graham, once showed the Earl of Bothwell his magical weapon, a carved staff decorated with human hair.[54] The worldly Bothwell claimed not to be impressed with this implement. More outlandish still was the staff owned by Major Weir in the seventeenth century, which was reported patrolling the streets and wynds of Edinburgh by itself, sometimes carrying a lantern and undertaking chores for its master.[55]

The record of people accused of witchcraft is full of unfortunate gaps. While it is safe to admit that most of those who were prosecuted were found guilty, the fate of many in local and national documents is unknown. We know little of the fate that awaited those who were discharged, though likely many would have been uneasy under the continuing suspicion of their communities. Banishment was sometimes used as a punishment, and this was perhaps no better than a long drawn-out sentence which ensured vagrancy, starvation, and eventual death. The details involved in acquittals are seldom recorded. Even the record of local legend and folklore is sparse concerning this class of accused person.

One exception is Watty Bryis or Bryce of Dunblane. Despite the fact that he confessed to local clergy and the Bishop of Dunblane in 1615, he apparently escaped execution. Action against him was taken five years after another local man, Morreis Scobie, was accused by the Presbytery of Stirling of charming. Scobie was not prosecuted, but consultation with charmers was still noted as a problem here on 22 July 1612, when it was recorded:

> The brethrein undirstands that charming is varte frequentlie
> vsit in thir bounds, for removing q^r of the brethrein ordanis
> ilk eldarship w'in thir boundis to tak Inquisitione quhair any
> sic thing is comitted and as thay find to tak ordur q^r with as
> apperteinis and to dischairge ye samin publictlie in pulpet.[56]

In April 1615, Johne Gentilman was summoned by the Presbytery after being accused of sending his servant, Elizabet Crystie, to ask the healer, Watty Bryis, on her knees, to heal his unwell wife. Bryis had allegedly made the woman, Margaret Duncansone, ill in the first place. Gentilman denied it, but said he confronted the healer about his wife's condition. Crystie admitted her fault and did public repentance, but Gentilman refused to accept his punishment. The following January he appealed to the Bishop of Dunblane and only admitted again that he had sought out Watty Bryis and pulled the man off his servant when he assaulted her. He was threatened with excommunication if he did not comply with the original sentence of public repentance and a fine.[57]

Bryis had admitted consulting the witch, Jonnet Murriache, who had recently been executed. A commission against Bryis averred that he had done great mischief by his witchcraft and sorceries. One of the men overseeing the process, the Laird of Kerr, suggested that the accused man should be present to confront those who were testifying against him. He was supported by some, but the bailies of the burgh opposed this. When allowed to speak, Bryis said he had been deprived of sleep for three nights and assaulted with knives and other sharp weapons. This was not denied by the officials. A witness named Elspat Whirrut said that Watty had appeared to her in a dream some thirty years before and urged her to leave her husband and run off with another man. She followed this advice and had suffered for it ever since, which she blamed on the bewitchment of the accused. On the basis of that and other similarly weak evidence, Bryis was discharged. Several of the bailies were themselves executed shortly after for other offences.[58]

Chapter I

Primal Men of Power

Michael Scot and Thomas of Erceldoune

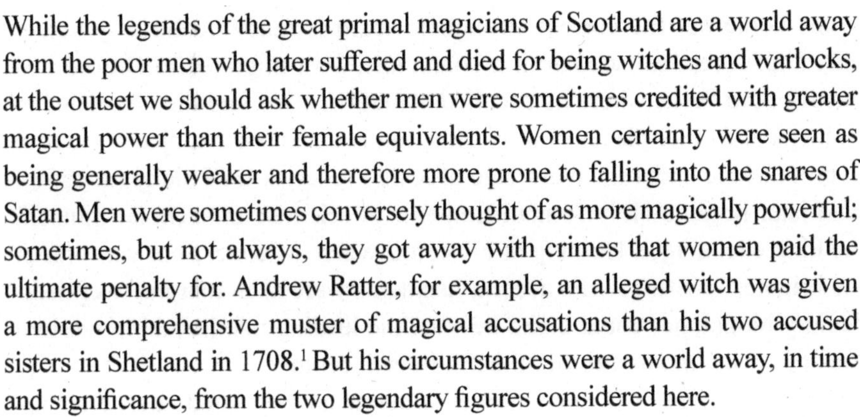

While the legends of the great primal magicians of Scotland are a world away from the poor men who later suffered and died for being witches and warlocks, at the outset we should ask whether men were sometimes credited with greater magical power than their female equivalents. Women certainly were seen as being generally weaker and therefore more prone to falling into the snares of Satan. Men were sometimes conversely thought of as more magically powerful; sometimes, but not always, they got away with crimes that women paid the ultimate penalty for. Andrew Ratter, for example, an alleged witch was given a more comprehensive muster of magical accusations than his two accused sisters in Shetland in 1708.[1] But his circumstances were a world away, in time and significance, from the two legendary figures considered here.

The two great medieval magical men of power in Scotland have had different fates in the national imagination. Thomas the Rhymer, or True Thomas, had a dual role in legend as a magical patron of the national identity, a kind of semi-occult patron saint, and as a prophet whose predictions involved the interminable wars of independence fought by Scotland from the late thirteenth century onwards. In later folklore he was remembered for more homespun predictions associated with a variety of places in Scotland. Michael Scot, absent for much of his life from Scotland, had no such place in the Scottish consciousness, though for centuries his overpowerful shadow was reckoned a force which could mould the very shape of the land. He was also a noted mystical figure famous in Italy where he spent most of his adult life.

A summary of Scot's life, published in 1707, based on a biography written a century earlier by the Italian cleric Bernardino Baldi, gives a good precis of his career:

Michele Scoto, that is Michael the Scot, was a Judicial Astrologer, in which profession he served the Emperor Frederick II. He wrote a most learned treatise by way of questions upon the Sphere of John de Sacrobosco which is still in common use. Some say he was a Magician, and tell how he used to cause fetch on occasion, by magic art, from the kitchen of great Princes whatever he needed for his table. He died from the blow of a stone falling on his head, having already foreseen that such would be the manner of his end.[2]

Long after his death, Scot's fame grafted him onto a family of that name from Balwearie in Fife, but he probably born somewhere in the eastern Borders in the late twelfth century. Aikwood Tower near Selkirk is sometimes claimed as his home but the current stronghold there is many centuries younger than him. A reputed scholar at a young age, Scot migrated to Oxford and then went to Paris, where he excelled at mathematics, and then travelled to Bologna and other places in Italy, studying law and other subjects. He rose to prominence under the patronage of King Frederick II of Sicily (d. 1250), who later became Holy Roman Emperor. A scientist and scholar himself, the king encouraged learning at his court, where Michael Scot was one of the brightest courtiers. His accomplishments were such that his twentieth-century biographer could claim he was 'the leading intellectual in western Europe during the first third of the thirteenth century'.[3]

Scot's international reputation as a magician circulated soon after his death. A tract written between 1450 and 1500 advertises his 'necromantic experiment' and expounds his fame. Like his patron, Scot was notably accomplished in languages and certainly acquired proficiency in Greek and Arabic. Among works composed by Scot, there were several which were dedicated to Frederick, including the *Astronomia*, in which he is described as astrologer to the king. Another of Scot's works, which earned him renown, was *Physionomia*, a treatise on the spiritual meaning of physiognomy. His large work, *Liber Introductoris*, deals with astrology and related subjects and contains information on specific demons – the names by which they may be summoned, and how they should be dealt with. If a demon is to be kept within a bottle, a sacrifice has to be made first. As demons have a taste for human flesh, the magician may have to supply this from a corpse or even from his own body.[4]

Like many contemporaries, Michael Scot's learning incorporated concepts regarded as esoteric and even occult. Interest in these areas, together with the fearsomely broad range of his learning, contributed to his reputation as a magician. He was certainly interested in aspects of magic, though as a cleric it is probably unlikely that he practised it. Some of his writings directly condemn magic, although he justifies interest in some arcane knowledge. Another ingredient in the spread of the legend of Michael Scot was his own far-flung wanderings. From residence in southern Italy, he travelled to Toledo in Spain, where he became immersed in further areas of learning, much of it influenced by Arabic knowledge. The fact that Scot's patron, Frederick II, was twice excommunicated and sometimes termed an Antichrist may have overshadowed his favourite scholar, if not his whole court.

With other medieval and later figures who researched into astrology, astronomy and alchemy, their reputations as uncanny magicians evolved over time as misremembered facts about their learning turned into legend. Scot's character as an occult worker seems to have developed in his lifetime. Soon after he died, Italian historians advised that he foretold the fate of several cities in that nation. In 1236, in a poem presented to the Emperor Frederick, Henry Abrincensis recalls Michael Scot issuing a prophecy about the emperor and cites the scholar as one 'who was a watcher of the stars, who was an augur, who was a soothsayer, and who was a second Apollo'.[5] In the manner of some other magicians, Scot also accurately predicted his own death, which he believed would be through being struck with a stone in his head. To forestall this eventuality, he took to wearing a protective iron helmet. However, one day at church he removed the helmet and was hit by a small pebble which had been dislodged by the action of a bell rope, with enough force to end his life. This may have been in the year 1235.

The European notoriety of Scot was cemented by his mention in Dante Aligheri's *Divine Comedy*, a century after the scholar's death. He appears in a miserable procession of other diviners, damned for their unholy earthly interests, whom Dante mocks for his lean looks.[6] The European legends of Michael Scot flourished for some centuries after his death, particularly in Italy, where he was a famed worker of marvels, astounding guests at dinner by producing foods from all over the known world or performing other acts of fairly innocuous wonder, sometimes at the court of the Emperor Frederick. Magical grimoires purporting to be authored by Scot were circulating in the fifteenth century, and the German abbot, Trithemius, had a volume composed by the wizard which instructed on the methods of summoning demons.[7] His name was still familiar to story tellers in Italy into the nineteenth century.[8]

Michael is said to have visited both England and Scotland in his later years and, like certain saints, his final resting place is claimed by multiple sites. These include Melrose Abbey, the abbey of Holme Cultrum in Cumbria, and (less probably) the fairy hill Tomnahurich, Inverness. A visitor to Burgh-under-Bowness on the English side of the Solway in 1629 was shown his grave there by a local guide, and saw Scot's huge spellbook nailed to a wall of the castle. No-one had summoned the nerve to open it since the magician deposited it there. The visitor, Walter Scot of Satchells, later wrote a fanciful metrical poem about his travels.[9] Wolsty Castle, near Holme Cultrum in Cumberland, was reputedly built to safeguard Scot's secrets. The Cistercian abbey of Glenluce in Wigtownshire was another reputed resting place. In the early nineteenth century it was said that a vault in the ruined abbey contained the lost magical library of Michael Scot, while nearly a century later James Maxwell Wood reported that a man who had the temerity to unearth Scot found his skeleton in a sitting position, the sight of which sent him insane.[10] The seventeenth-century Scottish Catholic writer, Thomas Dempster, repeated the fable that Michael Scot's magical books still existed somewhere but they could not be opened by mortals without simultaneously unleashing a host of demons. Some other writers asserted that the great man met his end while travelling with the emperor in Germany, with the assumption that he was buried somewhere on the Continent.

Despite Scot's reputation mainly being built abroad, legends about him in Britain which make him a semi-godlike figure, altering the very shape of the land for his own arcane purposes, have been in print since the seventeenth century. He magically tried to alter the course of the River Wansbeck in Northumbria; and near Carlisle he meddled with the shape of the coastline. Scot was also credited, along with the Devil, with creating the ancient causeway known as Watling Street, which believers in the tale called Mitchell Scott's Causeway (reflecting an English form of his name).[11] In the nineteenth century there were various tales about his building prowess associated with Hadrian's Wall. One story said that he had compelled Satan and other devils to build the wall in one night, or that he did it himself in the same period, though another version says he worked together with the Devil and they completed the task within two weeks.[12] He may also have been credited with building the Antonine Wall. In Cumberland, Scot was the collaborator with Satan in constructing the pikes on Carrock Fell.[13] He was also renowned for turning a group of witches into stone, where they remain frozen in a circle known as Long Meg and her Daughters, near Penrith. Similar magical manipulation of both waterways and the solid landscape was reported of him in Scotland. He tried to divert the River Clyde into the Tweed and also tried to bridle the Tweed with a curb of stone.[14]

Some of his land-shifting activities, in Scotland at least, were aided by three demons name Prim, Prig and Pricker, who had to be kept occupied with continual tasks or otherwise would turn on the magician. He finally got them to leave him alone by setting them a task of making ropes out of sand, a ruse also employed by other British necromancers. It may have been these demons who assisted Scot while he was living at Balwearie Castle in Fife. Nearby is the hill of Norrie's Law, formed, according to local folklore, by creatures in the employment of the great man. Michael had commanded the demons to flatten Largo Law, but while they were transporting material from that hill, they dropped a spadeful, which formed Norrie's Law.[15] An army of Scot's demons was also used in his plan to bridge the Clyde at Covington. While they were carting stones through the air, they heard the joyful news that he had died, so dropped their loads in the fields near Yelpin Craigs.[16] Michael also constructed a brazen man and used this artificial helper to carry the huge swathe of land known as Flanders Moss across from the Continent. But this helper was as incompetent as the imps and dropped the moss short of where the wizard intended, north of Stirling.[17] Scot was also reputed to have enslaved the Prince of Darkness himself and made him perform menial (but magical) tasks. While Satan was flying over Galloway, carrying a huge load of earth on the orders of Scot, he dropped the load and it became the hill known as Criffel.

Michael Scot's legend passed into Highland folklore, although the surviving tales of him there are modest in number, especially when compared with those of True Thomas. An oral tale recounted by John MacInnes of Eriskay in the twentieth century leaves no doubt about Scot's surviving reputation in the region. It begins with the statement: 'Michael Scot was an evil man. He had the Devil for a horse and acted in this way for a long time'. The story goes on to recount how a priest consulted the wizard about a problem he had, then visited his pre-made bed in hell. The priest later tended to Scot's remains; and the tale ends with Michael tricking another priest and taking his place in heaven. Traditions of his evading hell at his death were also featured in the Highland folklore.[18]

In another anecdotal tale, Michael mounts a 'fairy riding-filly' and magically flies to Rome to gain the date of Shrovetide from the Pope himself.[19] Some variants of the story aver that Michael's steed on this mission was the Devil, again signalling his ultimate authority over the forces of darkness. Another story from the Lowland which features Michael riding his supernatural steed has him on a mission to help the poor oppressed people who were straining under the weight of a tax which was imposed on them by (the Church of) Rome. This late tale was informed by Protestant sensibilities which would have been unknown by Michael in his own lifetime.[20]

The story's characterisation of Michael acting on behalf of the wider population, rather than following his own selfish magical agenda, goes against the usual tale-type associated with the magician. More usual is the theme of the tradition from the Highlands where he grandiosely tried to shape the Earth as he saw fit, building a natural bridge across the Moray Firth, which only his death prevented. Even in those later tales where Scot is involved in human disputes, the inference behind the humour is menacing, such as the following which envisages the lofty wizard arguing with a laird from Fife:

> There goes a story of his having made some sarcastic remark on the conduct of some harum-scarum Fife laird whom he had met one day at a hunt, and who, in resentment of the affront, told Sir Michael that his personal appearance would be vastly improved were he to bring his shadow along with him when he went from home. No sooner had the laird given utterance to this ill-timed sally, than he became sensible that his vision was growing dimmer, so that he directed his steps homewards; but before he had proceeded far he became stone blind, and was killed by falling over a crag.[21]

The second iconic pre-Reformation wizard is more indefinite in identity than Michael Scot. Despite the fact that he is not known to have ventured abroad, we know much less of him. Even his name is uncertain. To some he is Thomas the Rhymer, or True Thomas, while he is also called Thomas of Erceldoune or Earlston, Berwickshire. He was also dubiously given the surname Learmont, though this appears to be a later invention. The most intriguing legend associated with him links him to the landscape changing magician Michael Scot, a fellow Borderer. The triple peaked Eildon Hills in Selkirkshire, known to the Romans as Trimontium, was said to have gained its current form when Scot decided the previously unified peak should be split, in an act of godlike arrogance, and commanded his demons to do so. True to form, in the middle of this monumental task, his minions dropped a load of earth while flying through the air and this became a hillock between the southernmost and central peaks at Eildon, known variously as the Little Hillock, Devil's Spadeful, or most commonly, the Lucken Hare. One of the variants in the tale of the division of Eildon states that the Devil, to spite Michael Scot's command that Eildon should be split in two, scornfully divided the peak into three to demonstrate his superior power. The importance of this small landscape feature is that it links the place directly to True Thomas.

According to folklore, Lucken Hare was the portal which marked the entrance to the Otherworld beneath the peaks. The story states that a man named Canonbie Dick was returning from market when he encountered a strange old man who bought his remaining horses. They repeated the trade on several other occasions then, spurred by Dick's curiosity, the old man led him to Lucken Hare on Eildon Hill. The hillside opened and Dick was led into a deep chamber full of sleeping knights dressed in armour. He was presented with a horn or sword and asked to choose one. He chose the horn and then was transported in a whirlwind out of the place and onto the hillside, where he was found by shepherds the next morning; he told them his tale before dying. The mysterious guide was True Thomas and the sleeping knights generally reckoned to be King Arthur and his retinue, which links Thomas perhaps with Celtic British tradition predating Scotland. The tale has been known since at least the seventeenth century.

Apart from the Eildon location and tale, Scot and Thomas are linked together with prophesies regarding the death of King Alexander III. The most famous prediction tale about the monarch's demise came from True Thomas, according to Walter Bower's fifteenth-century *Scotichronicon*. At Dunbar Castle, the day before the king's sudden and untimely death, the Earl of March asked Thomas what the following day's news would be. The seer heaved a massive sigh and declared that the day was be a calamitous one and a wind would be heard in Scotland, the like of which had never been witnessed. It would dumbfound nations and make all who witnessed it senseless. The next day dawned bright and clear, so Thomas's obscure prophecy was ignored, until, just before midday, news was brought to Dunbar that the king was dead. He had been thrown by his horse near Kinghorn in Fife.[22] The doleful legend was so popular that it was repeated by John Major and Hector Boece in the sixteenth century. A lesser-known story states that Thomas foretold the king's death by stating that his favourite horse would cause it. The king heard the prediction and slew the horse. A year later, passing the spot where its bones were buried, his new horse reared up and threw the king to his death.[23]

Thomas the Rhymer may also have been a historical character, a man who lived in the Scottish Borders and died near the end of the thirteenth century. He was associated with Erceldoune, later Earlston in Berwickshire, where there are records of a father and son, Thomas Rymour de Ercildoun [*sic*], the younger of whom was alive around the year 1294.[24] Later antiquaries suggested that Thomas's name was Learmont, though Rhymer may have been his actual family name, implying some hereditary bardic or poetic role. True Thomas was a name which occurs in literature associated with him and may be fairly early. A fifteenth-century poem about this character, *The Romance and Prophecies of Thomas of Erceldoune*, details the meeting and intimate relationship Thomas had with the Fairy Queen, who took him into the elvish world for a number of years and gifted him the power of prophesy. The work also contains a lot of intensely obscure predictions and rhymes about the interminable wars between Scotland and England. Despite much analysis about the authorship of the romance (which is probably Northern English or Scottish in origin), neither the sources for the story, the meaning of the prophecies, nor indeed the ultimate identity of Thomas have been determined.[25]

Aside from the medieval poem about Thomas, there was also an oral ballad in circulation about the wizard, which was collected and printed in several forms in the nineteenth century.[26] The ballad relates how Thomas was lying on Huntlie Banks one day when he saw a fair woman ride by on horseback. When he greeted her as the queen of heaven, she identified herself as the Queen of Elphen, and when he kissed her he was obliged to accompany her to fairyland and stay there for seven years. In that place he was given an apple by the queen, and this gave him the dubious power of foresight. The poem ends with his return to our world after seven years. Included in the ballad are the famously threefold paths which mortals can choose to take, including the most beguiling but uncertain route which Thomas was led to:

> O see you not yon narrow road,
> So thick beset with thorns and briers?

> That is the path of righteousness,
> Though after it there's few enquires.
> And see ye not yon braid, braid road,
> That lies across yon lily leven?
> That is the path of wickedness,
> Though some call it the road to heaven
>
> And see ye not that bonny road,
> That winds about the fernie brae?
> That is the road to fair Elfland,
> Where you and I this night maun gae.[27]

The medieval poem has the same beginning, with Thomas lying in the countryside one May morning, spying the fair woman. He instantly asks to lie with her, despite her admission it will ruin her beauty, and immediately afterwards she turns into an old hag and he is committed to go to her realm. He is led underground, through terrible darkness and floods, until he enters a fair orchard, where his companion advises him not to eat the fruit, otherwise he would be damned to hell. After witnessing astounding sights and rich entertainment, Thomas is told to beware of the king, in case he guesses what happened between his queen and the mortal. Worse, Thomas was warned that the fiend of hell was due to come the next day to claim his tithe, and so the queen leads him back to the normal world. Thomas believes he has been there three nights, but is informed it has actually been three years. The queen then gives him a choice of gift: skill in music or the tongue that can never lie – and he chooses this prophetic power.[28] The remainder of the poem descends into a thicket of elusive prophetic rhymes about various events in Scotland, and we are left in the same puzzlement as doubtless Thomas was. A local tradition in Earlston says that the wizard was peacefully living in his birthplace in later years when a hind and hart appeared in the village. He followed them and was seen no more in the mortal world.

The origin, meaning and reality of Elfame, the fairy realm, is too large a subject to disentangle here. Suffice it to say that the fairies do not seem to have been ancestral members of a defeated race driven underground by the Celts, as Victorian anthropologists believed. Nor is it satisfying, in the case of Thomas's relations with them, to say that his encounter with the Fairy Queen and the elements such as the teind to hell were mainly fifteenth-century literary embellishments.[29]

The origin of Thomas, unlike those of Michael Scot, is hopelessly mired in legend. He was likely born somewhere in the eastern Borders, and the suggestion that he was actually born in Durham, given by the sixteenth-century antiquarian John Leland, is intriguing but likely untrue. Like Michael Scot, Thomas's name and legend were known in the north of England. There may have been localised prophecies associated with him in this region, as there were in many Scottish places, but if so they had all evaporated by the late nineteenth century.[30] In some Gaelic speaking areas he was known as 'the son of the dead woman', a reference to a number of birth tales. In one of these, he was taken out of his mother's side immediately after her death. Another story says he was rescued from his mother's tomb (or even her coffin) when his infant cry was heard. The strangest tale says that a woman whose husband was murdered and cut into four pieces engaged a tailor to sew him back together, which he did in two hours. The woman died shortly afterwards, and the woman's spirit led the tailor to her tomb, where he found the child who would become True Thomas. Like Michael Scot, Thomas was known further north than the Borders, residing in Dumbuck Hill near Dumbarton or the fairy hill of Tomnahurich in Inverness.[31] In the Highlands, the legend of True Thomas was notably more prevalent in those areas which were close to the Lowlands, Argyll and Perthshire.[32] His legend may have been carried from the Borders to the North-East when the noble Gordon family migrated northwards. Other Lowland families too may have carried his legend north.[33] Traditions of Thomas were certainly well entrenched in the North-East by the end of the sixteenth century, since the accused healer Andro Man of Banffshire knew legends about him. There is a trail of prophecies attached to localities, from the Lothians, up through Angus into the North-East of Scotland, and it is tempting to envisage these as markers in an itinerary made by the actual Thomas. Only a few of these traditions personalise True Thomas in each location, featuring the travelling wizard troubleshooting supernatural issues as he journeyed through Scotland. In one apocalyptic tradition at Fyvie Castle he appeared during a tremendous thunderstorm, and at Aikey Brae, also in Aberdeenshire, Thomas enacted revenge on an Earl of Buchan who had unwisely called him 'Thomas the Lyar'.[34] Later Highland tradition recognised his peripatetic nature.

Reflective of early (Lowland) tradition which cast Thomas as a national prophet, supernaturally supporting Scotland in the face of English aggression from the late thirteenth century onward, he also retained a political and martial aspect used in propaganda. The tradition that Thomas's obscure prophecies were circulating among the beleaguered Scots as they battled for their independence in the late thirteenth and early fourteenth centuries does not seem far-fetched. In the life of William Wallace ascribed to Blind Harry, Thomas is a spectral presence, delivering a prophecy of the thousands of enemy soldiers the patriot would cause to be slain, albeit through the work of a poet writing well after a century following Wallace's death.[35] Thomas was also written into literature associated with other Scottish patriots, such as Robert Bruce and the Countess of Dunbar. Bruce's supporters seem to have deliberately fostered a link with the legendary seer.[36] The fact that Thomas was renowned as a prophet was noted by the Englishman Sir Thomas Grey in the mid-fourteenth century.[37] In the ensuing centuries his distorted and arcane voice was added to the ranks of those other revered but obscure ancient prophets, such as Merlin and Bede.

Surprisingly, his first appearance in Highland Gaelic literature was in the mid-seventeenth century, when the celebrated bard Iain Lom Macdonald of Keppoch namechecked him in a verse which bolstered the Royalist cause of the Marquis of Montrose. Macdonald referenced an old prophecy of Rhymer's which foretold the coming of the hero to bolster Royalist hopes in Ireland.[38] The spirit of Thomas, supporting the righteous cause, was very much alive in native poetry right up till the last bitter failure of the Jacobite movement in the far north. Prose tales of him first appeared in the Highlands in the nineteenth century, and he was a presence in Scottish tradition throughout that century. Thomas only got displaced as a premier prophet in the Highlands when the legends concerning the predictions of the Brahan Seer were printed and gained popularity.[39] Mentioning the Brahan Seer allows us to briefly look at this triumvirate of seers in a national context. For several centuries after his death, True Thomas approached the level of Scottish national prophet, combatting similar, rival English claims to British sovereignty. In this sense he occupied the same lofty position as the iconic Welsh prophets, Taliesin and Merlin. It would be tempting to view Thomas in the lineage of those druids who were advisors to the early Celtic kings, but this line of enquiry has problems, not least a complete lack of linking evidence. Michael Scot, for all his prowess, did not occupy the same position in Scottish imagination, partly perhaps because of his time abroad. Coinneach Odhar, the Brahan Seer, despite modern renown, was always a regional seer famous only in parts of the Highlands and none of his prophesies aspire to national events. Thomas in particular lingers in some neglected recess of the national psyche, remaining something beyond his initial significance as a towering prophet who represented the fateful rights of Scotland.

Thomas of Erceldoune and Michael Scot serve as surrogate mythic figures for a nation which has no surviving mythology of its own. Both unwonted characters who superseded their own humanity to become, variously, prophets, Devil tamers, shifters of land, and ambassadors to a strange, familiar Otherworld. Apart from one extraordinary case, there was no link between these two figures and those unfortunates who were accused of witchcraft. But the link is there and it is a compelling one.

Chapter 2

Four Magicians and the King

The North Berwick witch hunts, which overtook the concerns of the kingdom of Scotland in 1590, centred on a supposed supernatural conspiracy to overthrow the king. On the face of it, this was merely a further in a succession of hurdles the king had to overcome. He had survived an exhausting childhood in the hands of a tutor who vilified his mother, then successive challenges, plots and conspiracies from the ascendant Protestant Kirk and the self-serving nobility. He may have derived some sour satisfaction in the detail of the witches' confessions that Satan had singled him out, from all the rulers of Christendom, as his primary enemy on earth.

Not initially credulous about the claims of the witches, he reluctantly accepted some of them were speaking the truth. It was convenient also to believe, after a prolonged personal battle, that Francis Stewart, his cousin and Earl of Bothwell, was indeed at the head of the conspiracy to displace him by magical means. Before the indolence of ruling the English overtook his senses, King James VI was a supremely adaptable, albeit devious ruler, capable of learning from the mistakes of others as well as himself to ensure his survival. If Bothwell was an uncertain antagonist in the king's mind, his supposed magical ally, Ritchie Graham, was a self-proclaimed warlock who openly admitted his occult lifestyle when questioned by the monarch. The other man who was implicated in the supposed plot against King James was a young schoolteacher, John Fian, who was improbably placed in the centre of a coven of witches and paid the ultimate price for it.

Accusations of witchcraft against high profile targets had occurred occasionally in the fifteenth and sixteenth century, albeit instances were as rare as records of witchcraft among the ordinary people. In England, the use or at least alleged use of witchcraft as a political weapon went hand-in-hand with poisoning and treason, and accusations of witchcraft were periodically used during the struggle between York and Lancaster in England, with accusations of sorcery thrown at high profile members of the nobility, usually females, from the fifteenth century onwards. And neither was it a uniquely British phenomenon, since King Henri III of France was cursed as a witch by his enemies from the Holy Roman Empire.

Direct violence among the nobility was more commonly employed in Scotland, and it took some time to catch up with English practice in this area of intrigue. In the reign of James III (1460–1488) that there are interesting traces of a struggle at the top tier of society involving supernatural forces. James coupled an unpopular personality with poor management skills, together with other failings. His two adult brothers were ambitious and in the traditional ruthless mould of the Scottish nobility. The elder brother Robert, Duke of Albany, allied himself with England and rebelled, but was forced abroad. The younger prince, John Stewart, Earl of Mar, was also rebellious, but ended his life in mysterious circumstances.

It is difficult to disentangle the facts around James III and his conflict with his siblings, since most historians were hostile to him. During his reign, prophecies abounded, and a witch alluded to the king being brought down by his family, and the king credulously listened to the dubious advice dispensed by a Flemish soothsayer. Some of his courtiers encouraged his suspicions. Young Mar was accused of trying to kill the king by making a wax image of him and melting it with fire. He was arrested and placed in Craigmillar Castle. Twelve witches and three or four warlocks were simultaneously executed, supposedly accomplices of the earl who were conspiring to slay the king.

One story states that Mar bled to death in the Canongate, Edinburgh, in August 1585, which may suggest that he was being treated by physicians as a remedy for some illness.[1] A further rumour also arose that he was drowned in his bathtub. Tales about Mar's end were clearly borrowed from stories surrounding the demise of his contemporary, George, Duke of Clarence, brother of Edward IV of England. He was convicted of treason against his brother and 'privately executed' in 1479; some sources saying he was drowned in a vat of malmsey wine.[2]

There were sporadic state-sponsored deaths in the sixteenth century, such as the supposed witchcraft-related accusations and execution of Janet Douglas, Lady Glamis, in 1537, which was part of King James V's vendetta against the Douglas family. The actual charges against Lady Glamis mentioned poison and treason, though chroniclers added witchcraft to her crimes. One notable example of a victim accused of magic was Sir William Stewart of Luthrie, Lord Lyon.[3] Previously holding the lesser heraldic post of Ross Herald, Stewart made an enemy of James Stewart, Earl of Moray, regent of Scotland, by displaying loyalty to his opponent, Queen Mary. He was accused of conspiring against Moray with others, including Patrick Hepburn, possibly the Bishop of Moray.[4] He was charged with 'conspyring to take the Regent's lyffe by sorcery and necromancy, for which he was put to death'.[5] Stewart was imprisoned in Dumbarton Castle before being executed at St Andrews on 16 August 1569. One source states that he was killed at the same time as a possible co-conspirator, a Frenchman named Parish. One of Stewart's more prominent occult companions was identified as Sir Archibald Napier, a prominent legal figure in Edinburgh.

Among the charges against Stewart was that he raised and worshipped a spirit named Obirion, summoned by means of writing his name on a lead tablet along with a Latin phrase. Obirion, or Oberon (in some literary sources the King of Fairies), was a name known to students of magic, and Napier and Stewart (if they were dabblers in arcane practices) may have obtained information on how to conjure the spirit from a book of magic. Stewart had allegedly also practised divination with scissors, through which he elicited information about the future. He also consulted two witches and found out that Moray would soon be dead, Queen Mary would return from exile and bear him, Stewart, children. One of the witches he patronised was Janet Boyman who confessed that she frequented with fairies, from whom she gained healing power. Boyman was herself put to death in Edinburgh in 1572, having unwisely forecast the death of Moray.

Another piece of political information magically obtained by Stewart was the identity of the killer of the queen's husband, Lord Darnley. He also visited a prophet, and used written rituals to summon infernal beings on Arthur's Seat in Edinburgh with several associates, a favoured location for different witches for their meetings. Here they practised arcane rights of ceremonial magic which were far removed from native witchcraft rituals. We don't know whether or not Stewart really attempted to perform classical ritual high magic in the European tradition, but it seems an unnecessarily elaborate accusation if there was no truth in it. Other high-profile people accused of magic and witchcraft in the latter decades of the sixteenth century were charged with slightly more run of the mill diablery.

The Earl of Moray was first a counsellor then an opponent of Mary, Queen of Scots – his half-sister, and a leader of the Protestant party. At the time, Moray was consolidating his power after Mary fled to England in 1568 and it is notable that there were a number of deaths supposedly related to witchcraft which may also have had secular motives. In the same year as William Stewart was hanged, another witch was burned to death. Several clergy in Fife were denounced as witches, while more witchcraft executions took place in St Andrews and nearby at Dundee. The fact that Moray was in the burgh when around ten executions were conspicuously laid on for him in the two towns suggests that he was making a political point against his enemies. But Moray was not the sole authority who used witchcraft accusations as a means of consolidating his power.

John Erskine of Dun, religious superintendent of Angus and the Mearns launched the nation's first large witch hunt through his territory in 1568–9, involving around forty accusations.[6] It has been seen as part of a wider campaign on morality and political enforcement organised by the regent the Earl of Moray, based on the principals of Old Testament morality.[7] The effects of the campaign, not so deadly as subsequent hunts, stretched up eastern Scotland, from Fife to Elgin. Details of this religious-political purge are sparse, but the theory that Erskine was the primary architect of the Witchcraft Act of 1563 makes his possible involvement in the matter intriguing. Erskine's character was a combination of contrary traits. He had to flee abroad in his early twenties, having killed a priest named William Froster, and absorbed Protestant influences in Europe. While John Knox was a close associate of Erskine's, his moderate nature made him a favourite of the beleaguered Queen Mary and a conduit for negotiations between all opposing parties in Scotland. Later, as religious superintendent of Angus and Mearns, Erskine oversaw the placement of ministers and teachers, and kept order, suppressing idolatry and vice. He and his fellow superintendents (five were first appointed in 1562) struggled with the huge responsibility, sometimes being censured by the General Assembly of the Kirk. Erskine was criticised for leniency in allowing Popish practises to continue.

The case for John Erskine of Dun being the principal author of the 1563 Witchcraft Act was made by Peter Maxwell-Stuart.[8] But Julian Goodacre has subsequently rejected this and states there is insufficient evidence between the choice of Erskine, John Knox and John Winram, Superintendent of Fife. All three may have had a hand in its composition.[9]

Several decades after Erskine's death his grandson, the proprietor of Dun, died, leaving his two young sons in the hands of an uncle and his three sisters, who determined to kill them. The sisters consulted a notorious witch and received some noxious herbs, which were steeped in ale and then administered to the children, one of whom died. Robert Erskine and his sisters were tried with murder in 1616. He and two of his sisters were beheaded, but the third, Helen, was banished for life.[10]

Erskine's friend, the renowned reformer John Knox, while acknowledging the threat of witchcraft, was not as preoccupied by it as some of his co-religionists. To Catholics, however, if Knox was not an actual devil, he was a close human incarnation. When Mary, Queen of Scots returned from France in 1561, she and Knox had a wary but cordial first meeting, although when Mary bluntly said that she had heard that everything he had accomplished to date was done by the power of necromancy, the good humour between the pair wilted. Knox accepted that he had been slandered by those accusing him of magic and necromancy, but strongly denied this, and asserted his opposition to all the dark arts that God had forbidden.[11]

Cruder accusations of diabolism continued, though they hardly deterred the determination of the upright reformer. It was whispered that Knox had attempted to raise 'some sanctes' in the kirkyard of St Andrews, but he accidently summoned up Satan himself, who appeared replete with huge pair of horns and presented such a terrifying visage that Knox's secretary, Richard, lost his senses and shortly afterwards died.[12] Similar stories were told about St Andrews' prelates Patrick Adamson, later in the sixteenth century, and James Sharpe in the seventeenth. When the 60-year-old John Knox married Margaret Stewart, the 15-year-old daughter of Lord Ochiltree, tongues wagged and some of his enemies wondered whether he had enchanted the young girl. This accusation possibly originated with the Catholic apologist Nicol Burne in his book *The Disputation* (1581). Lord Ochiltree's daughter was 'ane damosil of nobil blude and he ane auld decrepit creatur of maist bais degree of onie that could be found in the countrey'.[13] As intense as the political obsession with witchcraft and necromancy was for the reformers and, later, for the king and his ministers, it was based on a real prevalence of interest in magic among some middle and upper-class men. In the 1570s, the church minister John Kello of Spott was accused of using *igramancie* (necromancy), to rid himself of his wife. Kello readily admitted, and repented, the murder but denied using black magic. Stirred by avarice and thinking he would be better off single, he had tried to poison his wife, and when this failed he strangled her and he was executed for murder.[14] Catholic figures on the Continent gleefully made capital of this homicidal Protestant priest.

Upper-class families who resorted to using the services of witches and healers may have been more vulnerable to scrutiny than others at times, though their power may also have protected them from scandal and prosecution. There are several hearsay examples of the interplay between the witchcraft community and the nobility, most featuring the use of occult powers in political or dynastic disputes. Other legends too hint that it was not unheard of to use witches for purposes common to everyone. Margaret Maxwell, Lady Lothian, was rumoured to have consulted many witches and wise women, perhaps because of her fraught personal life. Her husband, Mark Kerr, 1st Earl of Lothian, had fathered thirty-one children by her but was still habitually unfaithful. When she became ill with breast cancer she consulted a warlock, whose pseudonym was Playfair. Playfair said he could cure her, but only if he was able to magically transfer the disease to one of her family. She began to convalesce, but her husband contracted a poisonous boil in his throat and he died in 1609. Playfair was soon afterwards locked up in Dalkeith steeple, where he confessed his magical crimes to the minister. News of his incarceration was brought to the attention of Robert Kerr, now 2nd Earl of Lothian, and he sent in some persons to speak with the prisoner at night. Next morning Playfair was found *worried* or strangled, with 'the point of his breeches knit about his neck; but never more inquiry was made who had done the deed'.[15] Robert Kerr himself committed suicide in 1624 by cutting his throat. It was said he had been affected by debt, or otherwise that he had been consulting with magicians and witches. There is some slight suggestion that the first earl was involved in witchcraft, but the details are vague, although the witches of North Berwick were active in and around some of his lands.[16]

The North Berwick witchcraft panic of 1590–1592 centred around the person of the king and differed from those previous threats to the king, such as the Raid of Ruthven, in that it appeared to be an unequivocal threat to the life of King James VI. There was also the factor that it came from a supremely powerful nemesis, whose agents were using horrific and novel tactics to eliminate the monarch. The treasonable intent by organised witchcraft to destroy the king was equally as heinous as the unnatural alliance between mortals and the ultimate force of darkness. The nebulous nature of the plot, the fact that it involved so many people, and that the participants ranged from servants to upper class women, a known necromancer and the king's own cousin, Bothwell, made the threat more sickening.

From our vantage point in time we can see that the activities of the group of witches was not invented by the king himself, though possibly some of his ministers may have exaggerated the significance of the witches' actions and turned them into a conspiracy aimed at James. James only gradually brought into the belief that the truth was being told by some of those accused, and that his cousin Francis Stewart, Earl of Bothwell, was at the centre of events.

Previous to the crisis and under pressure from his counsellors and others, James had been made to seek a bride and had found a match in Anne, daughter of the King of Denmark. Negotiations for the marriage were convoluted, as they were with all royal alliances, and James admitted, given personal choice (which was denied him), that he could have postponed matrimony indefinitely. Not that he was, in the normally understood meaning of the term, unready for marriage. As his later string of intimate male favourites proved, he was far more inclined to same-sex love rather than betrothal to a woman, however necessary that was, and however much he convinced himself that this was not so. The psychological strain of marriage to a woman, the perilous political state of the nation, the storm-crossed journey of the king's expedition to Scandinavia to fetch his bride when her voyage was delayed – all this contributed to the foreboding psychological atmosphere prefiguring the witchcraft panic.

Satan played his cards at a highly opportune time for ridding himself of his greatest enemy, the paragon of Christendom, James VI of Scotland. The conspirators, who hoped to kill both king and his new queen on their way back to Scotland, were a group of loosely associated individuals who lived around the settlements of North Berwick and other villages of East Lothian, near the nation's capital, Edinburgh. It was believed that a storm at sea, which had almost caused the king's ship to sink, was caused by witches using magical powers. The storm was blamed on the witches' malevolent actions, and this set off a wider investigation into witchcraft in the region.

As the trials progressed, more people were implicated, including prominent citizens, and the accusations grew more bizarre, with confessions being extracted under torture. Two men who were caught up in the East Lothian witch hunt, which centred around King James VI, had very different roles in the panic. Dr John Fian, also known as Cunningham or Sibbet, was a schoolteacher at Saltpans (now Prestonpans), and known to a number of the women accused of witchcraft. In the minds of the accusers he played a central role in the coven that were plotting against the king. Under prolonged torture, he admitted to being part of the supernatural conspiracy, but he later retracted his confession, along with others who were implicated.

The notorious wizard, Ritchie Graham, was outside the immediate circle of acquaintances in the East Lothian villages who were caught in the net of accusations. His world, both geographically and socially, was far wider than the schoolteacher's, and he was an admitted associate of Francis Stewart, 5th Earl of Bothwell. The first suspect was brought to light in November 1590. Geillis Duncan, a servant who had a reputation for her ability to heal people, began to be noticeably absent from her place of employment at nights. When questioned, she did not give satisfactory responses, so her employer, David Seton (a deputy bailie in Tranent), tortured her with thumbscrews and binding a rope tightly around her head. She later confessed to witchcraft and implicated many local people, including Agnes Sampson, Agnes Tompson, Dr John Fian, Robert Grierson, plus many others. She later retracted her confession, but it was too late and dozens of others, mostly women, were accused of or implicated in the organised witchcraft conspiracy. The revelations of this highly localised outbreak of malevolent witchcraft was centred on the East Lothian settlements of Tranent, Haddington, Saltpans and North Berwick, all settlements close to Edinburgh.

Worse elements than the usual *maleficium* were soon revealed. Not only were the witches intent on spreading mayhem in the general population, but they were also committed to ensuring that the king, who sailed to Scandinavia to fetch back his new bride in October 1589, was killed en route. The fact that the king and Anne landed safely at Leith on 1 May 1590, was a miracle, judging by the weight of malevolent supernatural power ranged against them.

Nor were the authorities blind to the fact that the black poison of magic had risen further up the social scale from that of a mere maid. Some of the female suspects were conspicuously respectable; John Fian was a schoolmaster. Most worryingly of all, several of the arrested women mentioned the involvement of Bothwell, who seemed determined to place himself on the Scottish throne. The horrific extent of the torture meted out to Fian is graphically illustrated in the pamphlet *Newes from Scotland* which was published in England in 1591, based on Scottish evidence. Fian was severely tortured on at least two occasions (as will be described below), but the female suspects around North Berwick were also similarly treated. Agnes Sampson is said to have suffered torture methods which were newly being introduced into the process of examining witches. Geillis Duncan was subjected to brutal physical torture delivered, under no legal authority, by David Seton of Tranent.[17] While these two linked cases may have involved uncommon violence by the authorities, torture was not unknown in other cases, and there must have been some torture and mistreatment sanctioned informally at local level by authorities throughout Scotland during the long history of witchcraft persecution, which largely escaped wider attention. Whatever Seton's inspiration for uncovering Duncan's 'crimes', he may have been partly motivated by jealousy and revenge in pursuing other witches. Euphemia MacCalzean, one of the richer accused, was related to him by marriage and had inherited some money that he had coveted.[18]

Of the several remarkable things about the dark saga of John Fian's questioning and imprisonment, was his capacity to endure the extremities of human cruelty without confessing his guilt of witchcraft. Partly this was because he was a young, healthy man who could tolerate torture physically better than many other suspects. But he was broken in the end, both physically and mentally, and confessed to what the authorities wanted to hear. In *Newes from Scotland*, the pamphlet perhaps authored by the East Lothian cleric and scholar James Carmichael, Dr Fian is the ultimate demonic hate figure among the exaggerated cast of witches hell-bent on magically murdering the king. A case could be made that some well-connected female protagonists in the North Berwick case, who were from relatively high ranks in society, may have made better studies for the propaganda pamphlet but were prevented from prominent placement because they were women. Nobody in Scotland would have credited the fact that the Devil's primary human vassal was not a man. We can also add here the question of why the Earl of Bothwell is not even mentioned in *Newes from Scotland*. Another male who might make a better satanic villain is Richard Graham, the enigmatic necromancer who was close to the nobleman and several of the witches.

Newes from Scotland has a subtitle which sets out its claim of revealing the crimes of the devilish protagonist at the heart of the witchcraft conspiracy:

> Newes from Scotland,
> declaring the damnable life and death of Doctor Fian, a notable
> sorcerer, who was burned at Edinburgh in January last, 1591.
> Which doctor was register to the devil that sundry times preached
> at North Berwick kirk to a number of notorious witches.[19]

Early in the tract, Fian appears in a list of the accused members of the East Lothian coven as 'Doctor Fian, alias John Cunningham, master of the school at Saltpans in Lothian'. (Another man mentioned in the trials was Robert Grierson, though his nickname was Rob the Rowar.[20]) Doctor was an honorific title given to Scottish *dominies* or schoolteachers. Fian was implicated by the word of the first identified witch, Geillis Duncan, and was in custody by 11 November 1590. At first, John Fian denied any guilt. The first recorded method of torture used against him to illicit a confession was *thrawing* his head, which involved binding his skull with a rope and tightening it, inducing agonising pain. He was then asked to reconsider his position and confess, which he refused to do. Then he had his legs crushed three times in the machine known as 'the boots'. Again, he obstinately denied wrong-doing. The other witches helpfully informed the authorities that Fian was prevented from confessing because he had two pins thrust beneath his tongue. When these were found and removed, the charm was *stinted* or broken. Fian was brought before the king and immediately admitted his guilt.[21]

The schoolteacher acknowledged that he was always present at the general meeting of the witches and that he acted as the clerk there, taking the oaths of all who swore allegiance to the Devil. He admitted maliciously bewitching a local man for the petty reason of loving a woman who he desired himself. The man fell into madness, and as proof of the matter the afflicted man was brought before the king on Christmas Eve, 1590. He impressed the court by screeching loudly, capering like a lunatic and behaving in such a manner that he had to be physically restrained. When he came to his senses, he asked how he had behaved, claiming he had been asleep the whole time.

It seems that Fian persistently pursued the affections of this same woman by various illicit magical means. The lady's young brother was a pupil of Fian's, so the schoolteacher asked whether he slept in the same bed as his sister, which he did, so he persuaded the young man to obtain some of her pubic hairs to include in a potion which would make her love him. While the brother was engaged in obtaining the items, the sister woke, complained to her mother, who beat the boy and obtained the truth about the diabolic ploy of Dr Fian. The mother, who possessed some witchcraft knowledge, made her son take hairs from a heifer back to the teacher, who then concocted his spell with them. At church the following Sunday, the congregation was astonished when the cow burst into the kirk, making towards Fian, 'leaping and dancing upon him'.[22] All of which reads more like a folk narrative of witchcraft than a plausible report of events. Fian was clearly more inclined to satyriasis than Satanism. His *dittay* contained the admission that he fornicated with a widow named Margaret Spens and, prior to his execution, he is supposed to have confessed adultery with thirty-two women. His promiscuity may explain why he was a conspicuous and suspicious figure in East Lothian, a notoriety which made him easy prey when suspected witches were under severe pressure to name associates the state could pursue.

Following his confession, Fian renounced his allegiance to Satan again and seemed to be a newly reborn Christian. But the day after displaying this religious piety he declared that the Devil had come to him during the night, dressed all in black and carrying a white wand (the symbol of authority). Satan asked if he would renounce Christianity and be true to the oath which he had formerly sworn to him, but Fian angrily rejected him. The Devil stated that he would once more be his, broke the wand, then vanished. The next day, the prisoner seemed very withdrawn and intent on his religious devotions, but he was evidently concealing something because, by some means, it was said, he managed to get the key to his cell and escape the prison.

How he managed to gain his liberty is a matter for conjecture. The official story is that he stole the keys, but he may have been helped by someone. The Earl of Bothwell bribed one of the officials of Edinburgh Castle to let him escape on 21 June 1591. John Fian may have done the same, supposing he had sufficient means. Yet, if he was helped by someone powerful (Bothwell himself?), why did he stupidly return to his own home, where he again met with the Devil, and then meekly remained until the authorities found him and took him back to prison? The supposition that the Devil at his home was actually Lord Bothwell does not make the matter any clearer, not even if we suppose Fian was some sort of satanic martyr who wanted to be recaptured and was willing to sacrifice himself for his beliefs.[23] A more prosaic explanation may be the poor security of makeshift jails in this period. Early in 1591, several witches from the area escaped captivity and fled to England. King James had to send a man to round them up. Michael Areskine was detained in Newbattle, Midlothian, in 1630 and the Presbytery of Dalkeith petitioned the Privy Council for his removal to Edinburgh because the building he was confined in was deemed too insecure to hold him, albeit he was guarded. Accused witch, Archibald Douglas, also escaped from a rough-and-ready jail in Douglas in 1650.

Whatever happened, Fian was transported back to prison, where he was carefully examined to see whether the Devil had made any new mark upon his body. It was believed that he had renewed his pact with Satan. He certainly refused to admit his own guilt again, so he was subjected to even more intense torture. All of his fingernails were removed by a *turkas* (pincers), and under every nail two pins were inserted up to their heads. This failing to elicit a satisfactory response, he was tortured with the boots again, his legs crushed and beaten until marrow and blood spouted out of them 'in great abundance' and he was permanently crippled. He still did not admit his guilt, but only admitted what he had previously confessed to, due to the fear of being tortured. Fian was tried, convicted and condemned. He was taken to castle hill in Edinburgh on a Saturday at the end of January 1591, then strangled and burned. The thoroughness of Fian's torture was probably due to the extreme and personal threat he was supposed to have represented to the king himself. Male suspects, through the period of prosecutions, were generally subjected to less torture, and less repeated torture, than women.

The *dittay* (indictment) against John Fian gives us further information about his circumstances. In the document (dated 26 December 1590), Fian implicated supposed fellow-witches Anges Sampson, Michael Clark and Robert Grierson, all of whom he claimed had been involved in witchcraft activities at North Berwick. Fian claimed he had first encountered the Devil while lodging in a house in Tranent and brooding negatively about his landlord, Thomas Trumbill. Satan suddenly appeared, dressed all in white, and promised him future prosperity if he would be his servant. Like some continental witches, Fian, by his own admission, travelled to sabbats in spirit form, while his physical body lay paralysed, travelling over mountains and the sea. This out of body movement was highly unusual for male witches in Scotland. Such activity, along with sexual activity with Satan and other practices, was described by the writer Jean Bodin in 1580. Other demonologists, such as Nicholas Remy (in *Demonolatry*, 1595), were not overly concerned about the gender of those who were ensnared by Satan.

Fian's admissions are marked by more imagination that was shown by many other contemporary witches. He memorably confessed that he heard the Devil 'making a sermon of doubtsome speeches' and enigmatically announcing, 'Many come to the fair and buy not the wares'. The black mass he described was illuminated by uncanny blue flames. Possibly influenced by the authorities, Fian admitted his part in trying to sink the royal flotilla carrying King James VI and his new queen back from Scandinavia. More routine satanic activity involved desecrating the graves at North Berwick, possessing people and performing sundry magical tricks like opening locks, foretelling deaths, plus malicious sinking of ships through magic. At a convention of witches in North Berwick, he sat proudly on the left-hand side of Satan.[24]

On the balance of evidence, it seems more likely that Fian's magical dabbling, if there was any, was largely confined to his efforts to obtain women. As a profession, schoolteachers were so closely monitored by local civil and religious authorities that transgressions were quickly spotted before they amounted to much, which makes us wonder why Dr Fian's supposed witchcraft activities went under the collective radar of his community, if he had been so active in supernatural circles as was claimed. Later *dominies* do not seem to have indulged much in dark arts, so far as we can tell.

Ritchie Graham, unlike Dr Fian, was undoubtedly involved in either magic or witchcraft and he seems to have been a larger-than-life figure, conspicuously seen in public with his magic staff, the symbol of his power. A note in one of the king's books describes him as 'fat and corpulent' and hints that he was one of those given over to the pleasures of the flesh and 'all kinds of merriness'.[25] It is apparent that he revelled in his notoriety and enjoyed worldly pleasures that may have been the fruits of his magical enterprises and contacts with influential people. There does not seem to be any analogous figure to him in Scottish history, which makes the lack of facts about him regrettable.

He was an associate of some powerful figures in the kingdom, including John Maitland, whom the Earl of Bothwell directly accused of orchestrating the story of him conspiring to kill King James by witchcraft. Maitland was chancellor of Scotland from 1587 to 1595, and a key figure in James VI's administration. When he was questioned at the chancellor's house in April 1591, Bothwell stated that Graham's allegations against him were made in consort with his own enemies, among the latter he claimed was the chancellor Maitland.[26]

Perhaps under pressure, or from some natural boastfulness, Graham accused both the Earl of Arran and some of the prominent Hamilton family of being witches. It was said that Graham himself had raised the Devil several times, once with Boswell of Auchinleck in Ayrshire, whose dabbling with supernatural forces brought him before the Privy Council. A story, repeated in the seventeenth century, states that Graham was consulted by Sir Lewis Bellenden (or Lewes Bellendine), Lord Justice Clerk of Scotland, who was curious regarding his powers. Graham raised a devil by magic in the yard of Bellenden's property in the Canongate in Edinburgh, which so terrified Bellenden that he took ill and soon died from shock.[27] Bellenden, according to sober sources, died on 27 August 1591, following eight days of fever. A career lawyer, he succeeded his father as Lord Justice Clerk in 1577, and he was involved with some of the political conspiracies during the early reign of James VI, and played a part in the downfall of the regent, James Stewart, Earl of Arran, who was deposed in 1585.

The legend of someone dropping dead after summoning a demon was ascribed to a number of individuals, including (as we have seen) to John Knox. A contemporary historian, David Calderwood, mentions the supernatural mud-slinging that involved several leading characters in Scotland at the time. Among the rumours was 'that Arran, Lord Farneyeere, was an inchanter; that the devil was raised at the Laird of Auchinfleck's dwelling place, and in Sir Leaves Bellendine, the Justice-Clerk's yaird'. He had also heard that the chancellor had mystical tables and images contained around his neck, which would save him from harm, but said the rumour had not come from Graham.[28] A similar fable was bandied about the Earl of Gowrie. The extent of Bellenden's connections with Ritchie Graham are unknown. Sir Lewis did have a servant in his household named John Graham, so this may have been a family link to the sorcerer.

The link between Richard Graham and the Earl of Bothwell was undeniably strong, which was unfortunate for the nobleman. Graham accused Bothwell of plotting to kill the king through magical means from Spring 1590, and added extra impetus to the hunt for the fugitive lord who was soon evading all attempts to catch him at the time. Graham would maintain the claims right through his own imprisonment and up to the moment of his own death, around the end of February 1592, after he had been convicted of witchcraft and was strangled and burned in Edinburgh, at the same time as other unidentified convicted witches.

Graham's origins are as mysterious as his career. Sir Andrew Melville calls Graham a 'westland man', which tallies with his activity in Ayrshire. There was mention of a man called Ritchie Graham whom the suspected witch Isobel Watson, tried by authorities in Stirling in 1590, states had been resorting with the fairies on multiple occasions.[29] It would seem that the notorious necromancer was active in different places. One recent historian associates him with the Grahams of Fintry, by Dundee in Angus.[30] An association with this kindred is possible since the head of that branch,

David Graham, was frequently in trouble with the Crown, although his execution in February 1593 was ascribed to his association with co-religionist Catholic lords in the north and he had no known connection to any wider political intrigue or dealings with the North Berwick witch cabal. Another historian has highlighted the similarly named 'ould Rich' Graham who lived in Eskdale in Dumfriesshire, possibly part of the Graham family based in Netherby.[31] An ally of Bothwell, Richie Graham of Brackenhill (1555–1606), lived just over the border in Cumberland. He was one of the party which Bothwell led in June 1592, besieging Falkland Palace in Fife.

Whether the mysterious Graham was from the Borders, Angus, or the west, he had a peripatetic lifestyle, suggesting a wide geographical spread of clientele and (in Ritchie's case) a substantial network of important people. Graham first came to Bothwell's attention when an unnamed third party asked for permission for the wizard to be given sanctuary on one of Bothwell's estates, evidently following some harassment Graham was facing, having been excommunicated by the Kirk. We do not know what prompted Bothwell to protect him, nor why he was being persecuted.

Ritchie Graham had been heard saying that he had a familiar spirit that could both do and tell many things, mostly against the Earl of Bothwell. He was apprehended, brought to Edinburgh, and soon examined before the king in an interview witnessed by Sir Andrew Melville. Graham admitted he had a familiar spirit which showed him many things, but denied he was a witch or had met them frequently. When asked why Agnes Sampson had declared that Bothwell had been sent to her by Graham as a client for witchcraft, he admitted the same and said he had been referred to the earl by Barbara Napier and Euphame MacCalzean. Then he was summoned by Bothwell and asked to make the king look more favourably upon him. He gave the earl some drug or herb to rub on the king's face. Somehow this was done, but it had no effect. Bothwell then asked to have the king wrecked but Ritchie Graham said he could not accomplish that, though advising that the notable midwife and witch Agnes Sampson could make that happen. The royal mind had already been enlivened with Sampson's testimony that a wax image had been paraded at a witches' meeting in the presence of Satan, and Sampson had told everyone, 'This is King James VI ordered to be consumed at the instance of a nobleman, Francis Earl Bothwell'. Graham was further quizzed many times by the Privy Council. [32]

Barbara Napier had confessed that she had consulted with Ritchie Graham, sending him a ring to enchant with and also seeking his help finding a cure when her son was ill. On this occasion, which took place in Edinburgh in early 1589, she asked Graham whether the king would safely return home to Scotland from his expedition to Scandinavia to bring his bride home.[33]

The question of what Ritchie's Graham's evidence against Bothwell contained and how it was obtained, was a matter of controversy at the time and subsequently. Graham was prized as a star state witness against Bothwell. King James had been vacillating over believing that his cousin Bothwell was indeed employing witchcraft to end his life, albeit there was ample evidence of Boswell's extreme violence and volatility. The earl had been notably violent in his personal affairs and reckless in his role of Admiral of Scotland. Sensing that he was losing the king's favour, he embarked on a haphazard campaign of intimidation again King James, which ran in parallel with his supposed witchcraft activities. In 1591 and 1592 he earned himself outlawry by attacking the king's houses at Holyrood and Falkland in Fife.

The belief that Boswell was actually a traitor and a witch was believed by many by the time Bothwell and Ritchie Graham were brought face to face at Edinburgh Castle in April 1590, a standard practice for witches who were accusing each other. We are not sure what level of conspiracy existed between the two men, nor of what each man believed they were doing in a supernatural sense. Once they met in a glen near Crichton, Midlothian, and Bothwell supposedly asked Graham if he knew any women who had the skill that would enable them to slay the king by witchcraft. Graham, at first, refused to answer the question, then he formed a magical triangle and conjured up his familiar spirit, which supplied him with the answer.[34] They met at least half a dozen times, in different parts of the country (though the earl tried to downplay the number of meetings), with Bothwell carefully sending his servant Ninian Chirnside ahead to a rendezvous to fetch the wizard and bring him to a meeting place nearby. The earl would question Graham about the current state of the king's opinion of him, or ask the wizard to devise fresh means to end the king's life. Graham would consult his spirit and give answers, though sometimes reluctantly.

There is no direct evidence about whether Ritchie Graham was tortured during his imprisonment, though there is a surviving, undated summary detailing complaints about the treatment during his confinement. Graham claimed he had received 'hard handling' while in Edinburgh tolbooth (where he had been held since 11 November 1590) and had been deprived of 'entertainment in meat and cloth'. His letter was passed to the king's Master of Works, William Shaw, and later read to the king.[35] The fact that this missive reached royal attention is significant. Graham alleged the treatment he received ran contrary to an agreement that was made with him. According to this arrangement, which has not survived, Graham understood he was to be safely confined to Stirling Castle, away from the violent attentions of the jailers and probably geographically removed from Bothwell's baleful reach. The king confirmed that Graham, initially at least, was to be handled significantly differently from the run-of-the-mill confined witchcraft subject. James wrote to Maitland in April 1591, telling him to 'garr see that Richie Grahme want not his ordinaire allouaince quhill I take farther ordoure with him'.[36] For a time, at least, he was pacified and well-treated.

The malicious intent or otherwise of Richard Graham's magical practice is open to question. While he was abroad as a young man, Francis Stewart had consulted with a seer or witch in Italy (the epicentre of forbidden magic in some Scottish minds) to gauge his future relationship with King James VI. The seer informed him that he have great power and possessions when he returned to his homeland, but that he would kill two men and would be accused of two capital crimes by the king, though he would be pardoned for the first and punished for the second. This is given by some as the motivation for the earl's increasingly volatile relationship with King James. If true, this would still be several steps removed from him being the architect of an occult plot to extinguish the life of the king. Graham's version of this tale is that the seer had told the young earl that his life would be in danger from the king. Either way, Bothwell was a man who hardly shrunk from direct, brutal violence against any man, whether king or commoner. Graham, too, does not fit the bill as a lynchpin in a tightly organised coven of witches centred in East Lothian. While he seems to have known some of the alleged female witches within that circle, there is no evidence for him being one of their leaders. He was too restless a character to have devoted his attention to the confines of a group of witches in one particular area. We might ask what kind of magic worker he was anyway? With his magical staff and habit of hobnobbing with well-connected members of society, he was perhaps a vainglorious, certainly a conspicuous individual. David Calderwood called him 'the great enchanter', a title which he would surely have been proud of. Graham's ostentatious nature is also demonstrated in his other magical implements, such as a ring he showed to Boswell which could predict the future and also ascertain the loyalty of the earl's servants. He does not fit the pattern of being a common wise man or charmer. One of his recorded actions, at the behest of Bothwell, was attempting to heal the seriously ill Earl of Angus (Bothwell's brother-in-law), and though he was also consulted by the accused witch Barbara Napier who wanted help healing her son, healing was perhaps a minor sideline of his magic. His alleged association with the fairy world gives yet another aspect of his otherworldly involvement. From his conjurations and showmanship, Ritchie Graham comes across more as an individualistic ritual magician rather than a lowly regional co-operative member of a village coven. He was undoubtedly one of the best-connected Scottish warlocks on record, and seemed to have contacts across the social spectrum. And he was notably affluent enough to employ a servant named John Fairlie, who sometimes acted as go-between with the East Lothian witches.

At Bothwell's trial in August 1593, the earl declared that Ritchie Graham had been strongly leaned on to provide false testimony against him, and that 'divers honest men of Edenbroughe ... deposed that Richard Greyme said to theme that he must eyther accuse the Erle Bothwell falselye, or els endure such tormentes as no man were able to abyde'. Graham's own brother said that Richard had told him many times that he had only given evidence against the earl 'for feare of maymynge with the bootes and other tortures'.[37] But Graham's brother could easily have been in the pay of Boswell as much as Ritchie was in the pay of the king. Bothwell admitted that Graham had gone to his death still damning him, yet claimed to have evidence that Ritchie Graham was only slandering him in the hope of saving himself from execution as a witch. This evidence was never produced.

The downplaying of the connection between himself and the warlock seem disingenuous, to say the least. His protection of Graham initially, he said, was only done to pay a favour to a friend of his. A further meeting was a mere chance encounter at Kelso. On the occasion where Ritchie Graham showed the earl his marvellous 'sticke with nickes in yt all wrapped about with longe haire eyther of a man or a woman, and said yt was an enchanted stick; to which speache I gave smalle regarde', he claimed that day he had encountered Graham while the wizard was with the chancellor, Maitland, and that the three men went out riding, another almost accidental social encounter.[38]

A letter addressed to 'the nobility', in defence of Bothwell, says that Ritchie Graham had either been threatened or bribed to make up witchcraft allegations against the Earl of Bothwell. Who was to be believed, the letter asked: a noble earl or a man who was not only low-born but also an infamous 'persoun moved by the dispositioun and humeur of his divilish natur,' who was 'pretended nigromancer bot in effect a lyer and a false abuser ignorant of that art that men wald attribut unto him'?[39] Against this may the claim by Graham that Bothwell had sent him money while he was in prison. Graham was kept alive far longer than any other of the witches accused of treason. The records of Ritchie Graham's trial are lost, but any agreement he had with the authorities was cynically disregarded when it became clear that Bothwell could be got rid of by one means or another, with or without Graham's damning evidence against him.

Ritchie Graham's involvement with the supposed witchcraft coven centred around North Berwick is clouded by competing interpretations of the reality of their magical practice and whether or not there was a substantial conspiracy to kill King James VI. The historian, Peter Maxwell-Stuart, believes that the conspiracy was real, that there was an active coven practising witchcraft. He sees Graham as one of the chief instigators in the witchcraft circle, arranging meetings between members, conspiring with the Earl of Bothwell, accompanying the witches to their sacrilegious meeting at North Berwick Kirk, and perhaps even playing the part of the Devil there.[40] He concluded in his earlier study of the case that the likelihood was that both the Earl of Bothwell and King James VI were played against each other by a masterful third party, each led to believe the other was maliciously plotting against him.[41] The truth may never be known, though what has to be admitted is the odd symmetry in character between the warlock and the nobleman, which parallels the antagonistic connection between the earl and the king. Both Richard Graham and Francis Stewart, within their own spheres, were exceptionally well connected. Graham was an admitted magician and Bothwell must have used this speciality in furtherance of his own means, to some extent at least. It was just one tactical weapon of many he aimed at the king. There was a convoluted atmosphere of intrigue between the two men, though it was this strained scheming which tied them in knots and let to their downfalls. Picture them huddled together, as they realised the circle of freedom was closing in about them, desperately trying to throw the scent off their guilt. One glimpse of this is when it became known through the evidence of the witches that Bothwell had been named as an accomplice. The witches then denied it and claimed instead that the English ambassador, Bowes, was the guilty party. Graham later said that Bothwell told him to slip Bowes's name into the mix as the witches might confuse the two similar sounding names. Luckily for the Englishman, he did not tally with the description given by the accused women, and even more lucky, he was not in Scotland when Bothwell and Graham suggested he might be cavorting at a witches' sabbath.[42]

Nearly a decade after the outburst of witchcraft near Edinburgh, John Ruthven, 3rd Earl of Gowrie, was killed in his own house in Perth in May 1600, along with his brother, in the presence of the king and his close associates. The 'Gowrie Mystery' has never been conclusively unravelled. The Ruthven brothers, to all appearances, were ardent allies of the Kirk, and the murderous incident was mostly seen either as a government plot to eradicate them, or a conspiracy by the brothers to entrap the king which went disastrously wrong. Either way, in the aftermath of the deaths, the state went to some length to hunt down Ruthven family members and associates and to comprehensively blacken the noble family's name and reputation. An officially sponsored publication, circulated soon after the incident, sought to exonerate James's role in the affair and castigate the Ruthvens. According to this, the king himself ordered a search of the earl's body, and there was found:

> a little close Parchment Bag, full of Magicall Characters, and Words of Inchantment, wherein it seemed, that he had put his Confidence, thinking him selfe neuer safe without them, and therefore euer carried them about with him; being also obserued that, while they were vppon him, his Wound whereof he died, bled not, but, incontinent after the Taking of them away, the Blood gushed out in great Aboundance, to the great Admiration of al the Beholders.[43]

Although some contemporaries also noted these charms, the earl's bag of magical papers may have been no more than notes for his 'memorial book' or journal, written partly in Latin and partly in Greek, which his tutor William Rhynd first saw when he was with the earl in Italy, saying that he kept them on his person until his death.[44] Rhynd's information about the matter was elicited with the aid of being tortured by a device called the boot, so is likely untrustworthy.

In 1713, George Mackenzie, Earl of Cromarty claimed that he had possession of these papers, which had been taken from John Ruthven's body by Thomas Erskine, who was present at his death. The writing was not in any intelligible form, and the document was not similar to anything found on his body, but 'sheets of paper, stitched in the form of a book, nearly five inches long, and three broad, full of magical spells and characters'.[45] After describing them, Cromarty contrarily stated he could not find the book when he had again searched for them prior to publication, but declared it was still in his possession.[46] Nobody has seen it since. There was another mysterious Ruthven document containing recondite material which ended up in the archive of an antiquarian society in Perth, confirming that the family did take an interest in hidden knowledge. This book had been the property of Dame Lilias Ruthven, an aunt of the first Earl of Gowrie, and was kept by the family. This volume too has vanished.[47] Following the earl's slaughter, further efforts were made to associate him with the occult. The earl's cousin, James Wemyss of Bogie, testified under pressure that Ruthven chastised him once for killing an adder while hunting, saying that he could make it dance to the tune of some Hebrew or cabbalistic words which he had learned from a noted necromancer in Italy. At another time, John Ruthven spoke to him of magical mysteries, and he responded to a man who spoke ill of him, saying he would hang, which came to pass.[48]

A proclamation issued by court chaplain Patrick Galloway firmly accused the deceased earl of transit with Satan. He stated that 'the Earl of Gowrie was plainly proved to have been a student of magic, a conjurer of devils, and had many of them at his command'. A broadsheet issued the following year confirmed the earl's alliance with Satan. The propaganda generated by the king reached far and wide. In England, Queen Elizabeth archly alluded to the Earl of Gowrie's alleged satanic associations and remarked to the king that she supposed hell must be empty of demons since Gowrie controlled a thousand familiar spirits. 'No infernal power bears any sway where a higher force makes defence', she added piously.[49]

Part of Gowrie's association with black magic was inspired by his sojourn in Italy, not only a Catholic realm, but somewhere notoriously supposed by northern Europeans to be a hotbed of the black arts. Ruthven had attended the university of Padua, and was part of the Scottish 'nation' there between 1596 and 1597. In later folklore, Padua was synonymous with black magic and a number of Scottish 'wizards' were reputedly students there. In Europe, the earl also stopped at Orleans and there, the Earl of Argyll illicitly viewed some of his papers. These documents contained a prognostication about his fate and said that the earl would fall into melancholy back in Scotland, despite being much loved, and more alarmingly, that he would die with a sword in his hand. The seventeenth-century historian William Sanderson mentions the Argyll story and says that the earl adopted as his device in Italy a symbolic picture of a sword aiming at a crown.[50]

Details of Gowrie's occult papers were supposedly conducted to the king and to the English ambassador Nicolson, who wrote of them to Sir Robert Cecil in November 1600. His source was a man named Colville who had been secretary to the outlawed Earl of Bothwell, and who had been pardoned after the latter's disgrace and exile. There is no saying if this document actually existed and, if so, if it was genuine. Nicolson's information about papers found on the earl's body states that the writing variously concerned spells for love, for blood, and against his majesty, King James. A contemporary publication supporting the Ruthvens admitted the existence of the spells on his body, but said the charms' purpose was to attract good and repulse evil spirits.[51]

Several commentators expressed shock at the death of John Ruthven at the time, including those he had encountered on the Continent. The Master of Gray, who met the earl in Italy, was perhaps close to the truth when he estimated him 'rather fashioned like a pedant than a cavalier'.[52] Gowie may have been drawn to some esoteric knowledge and learning out of intellectual curiosity in Italy, but probably not at the expense of endangering his own Protestant beliefs.

The occult slandering of the earl extended to his immediate forebears, though how much was invented retrospectively is unknown. The murdered third earl's grandfather (one of the murderers of Riccio) had given Queen Mary a ring which protected against poisoning. William, first Earl of Ruthven (father of the 3rd earl), also went to Italy and consulted with a wizard to learn his future. The historian, Spottiswoode, states that the first earl pried too much into forbidden knowledge, though he was not formally charged with necromancy or magic. His downfall and execution was due to the part he played in kidnapping and imprisoning the adolescent king after the so-called Raid of Ruthven and in a subsequent rebellion. William Ruthven, when he was being tried for treason at Stirling in 1584, was accused of consulting a witch named Maclean, but laughed off the charge and said a tenant was the guilty party.[53]

Where King James had been almost powerless to dispose of his truculent personal adversary, the Earl of Bothwell, he was ruthlessly adept in disposing of the Ruthvens, and spreading malicious rumours about the family. A primary reason for Gowrie's disposal seems to have been suspicion about the young earl's popularity with the militant Protestant party on his return to Scotland. If Ruthven was not then an ally of those in opposition to the king, he had the potential to be such, and he was snuffed out with ruthless efficiency.

Chapter 3

Andro Man and the Fairy Tradition

As a 70-year-old man who came before the authorities in Aberdeen in the dying years of the sixteenth-century, Andro Man must have caused them a mixture of emotions. Firstly, how could such a notorious servant of Satan, as they saw it, have eluded public attention for so long? Secondly, the wealth of material which Andro offered – healing of men and beasts, consulting with angels and dead men, casting spells, blessing lands, consorting with the Queen of Fairies – was so rich and varied that it must have strained their concepts of the geography of the shadowlands which threatened them. The surviving testimony of Andro has no equal in any other male witchcraft record and can only be compared in its complexity and imagination to the evidence given by women like Isobel Gowdie and Bessie Dunlop.

Andro's survival as a magical practitioner for decades rests in part on the beneficial view that secular society had of his services. As well as charming men and beasts, he seems not to have shirked accusing others of harmful witchcraft. These included Elspet Graye in Deskford, an old woman called Gray in Findlater, and a woman and her husband in Auchattye.[1] Another group that he accused included Gilbert Fidlar and his mother-in-law, Jonet Leisk. These two were blamed with causing a man's death but they were later acquitted.[2] Fidlar had earlier been accused of making Lord Erroll's wife ill and had been imprisoned by Erroll in Slains Castle for over a year. He was confronted by Andro Man (the details are meagre), which perhaps suggests that Andro was an associate of the Catholic Francis Hay, ninth Earl of Erroll. Such an association would not have endeared him to the Kirk.

Andro came from Rathven, Banffshire, and latterly lived at Tarbuckie (or Tarbruith) near the fishing port of Buckie. Andro's indictment was based on his confession, the latter following an unrecorded indictment of 21 October 1597. The year 1597 marked a rise in witch-hunting activity in Aberdeen. It is unknown what caused this sudden spike in official activity against witches, but in February and March there was a flurry of prosecutions which P. G. Maxwell-Stuart grouped into three sets of linked accused people.[3] One of the accused (later executed) was Thomas Leis (or Leyis). He had wanted to marry his mistress, Elspeth, but family opposition made them think of moving from their native area of Aberdeenshire, west into Moray. Elspeth worried how they would make a living there, to which he replied there was a hill on the route to Moray, and she should summon a man (in other words, a fairy) at the hill foot there, and if she did so she should never want. Elspeth refused, thinking she was being dragged into some devilish practice. The fairy hill may have been in Banff.

On 20 January 1598, Andro was put on trial and found guilty of most of the charges, and was almost certainly executed. During the proceedings it was heard that, some sixty years before, he had an unexpected inauguration into the unseen world when the Queen of Elphen, or Fairies, appeared at the door of his mother's house while he was fetching water, had a baby there, and told the young boy that he would have the power of foresight and be able to cure any kind of illness short of death, a skill which he used throughout his long career as a magical practitioner. In this way, Andro haplessly entered the profession of a cunning man, chosen by a supremely powerful (female) being and told what powers he had been assigned, a process opposite to those high medieval magicians who consciously strove to connect with elusive powers of the occult. By way of punishment for trespassing on her domain perhaps, the Fairy Queen slew one of the family's cows which was grazing on the aptly named Elf Hillock. There is a prominent mound of this name in the inland Banffshire parish of Botriphnie or Drummuir.[4] As an interesting aside, the Banffshire elven lore seems not to derive from Gaelic culture, which would have been prevalent in the area in the Middle Ages. Elf Hillock is a Scots name, and it has been pointed out too that the Elphen Queen, so prominent in Andro's life, is conspicuously absent from Gaelic folklore.[5] Botriphnie (*Both Draighnigh*, possibly a name with an ultimately Pictish rather than Gaelic origin) was likely the birthplace of Andro Man. Possible Victorian relatives with the same surname lie in the kirkyard there.[6]

Details of Andro's healing methods are given in his trial. One remedy he used employed the use of black wood and salt, and his cures were effective for both humans and animals. To cure Alexander Symsoun in Fordyce, who had been made seriously ill by witchcraft, Andro passed him through a bundle of yarn in a specific sequence and managed to transfer the curse onto a cat, which immediately died. The healer Thomas Grieve, prosecuted in 1629, also cured a man by passing him through some yarn which he afterwards burned.[7] Several others cured by Andro were in the record of his prosecution but there would have been many more recipients during his exceptionally long career. One power which could be readily monetised was giving magical protection to a farmer's growing crops. Andro would advise farmers to 'lay the harrowis on the land befoir the corne be brocht furth, and hald aff the crowis quhill ane rig be brockin... [and] say ane oration, quhilk thow hes perquier, nine sindrie tymes, and that being done, the cornis sall cum saiff to the barne that year'.[8] Another highly specialised magical ceremony he used involved sanctifying a specific piece of land which was set aside as a sacrifice to a supernatural being as an insurance that there would be fertility on the remainder of the farm:

> Thow hes mett and messurit dyvers peces of land, callit wardis,
> to the hynd knicht quhom thow confessis to be a spreit, and
> puttis four stanis in the four nokis of the ward, and charmes
> the samen, and thairby haillis the guidis, and preservis tham
> fra the lunsaucht and all vther diseasis, and thow forbiddis to
> cast faillor divett theron, or put plewis therin.[9]

Andro performed this rite on the Mains of Innes, the Mains of Caddell and many other farms, dedicating a plot on each to a being named the Hynd Knight, which the authorities equated with the Devil. This ritual of laying aside an untilled plot of land for the sake of the health of cattle (protecting from *lunsaucht*, lung disease, or other ailments) has been puzzled over by some.[10] But it is actually one of the first recorded instances of the Gudeman's Croft ritual which was practised all over Scotland, but particularly in the North-East (see chapter ten). It was mainly a male magical prerogative though there was at least one record of a female making a Good Man's Croft.

His skills also led him further afield. His trial heard that he attempted at least to heal:

> the Laird of Kynardis guidis, in Angous, quhilkis thow left
> bluid, quhilk bluid quhen the doggis had lepit theirof, they
> instantly deit...Lykas, thow heallit a woman of Angous, of kyn
> to the Ladie Kynard, of the falling seiknes, be thy devilische
> witchcraft and sorcerie'.[11]

Kinnaird, between Brechin and Montrose in northern Angus, is a considerable distance south of Andro's home ground in Banff. The estate had been held by the Carnegies since the fifteenth century, a widespread kindred in the district (who later became earls of Northesk and Southesk). The straight line distance between the Banff coast and Kinnaird is around 60 miles (96 km), and the actual journey in the sixteenth century must have entailed crossing the eastern part of the Grampians known as the Mounth. His journey can be compared with the 40 miles plus which supplicants for the services of male magic workers like Willox Macgregor were willing to undertake a century after Andro Man's time. This raises some interesting points. The first is that Andro's clientele included members of the upper classes from outside his native district. Around the same time that Andro was operating, we know of one Ayrshire witch/healer with female aristocrats, albeit they lived in their own area.[12]

Andro's reputation must have spread by word of mouth, and the Carnegies were unlikely to have employed his services solely on the recommendations of servants or labourers. The Carnegies, due to their position, may have been unwilling to risk their reputation to travel to the home of the magic worker or have a local healer visit them.[13] How much travel did Andro's occupation as a male witch/healer involve? He seems to have ventured often from Banffshire into neighbouring Aberdeenshire, and it would seem unlikely that the journey south to Angus was an isolated one. In chapter six I discuss the prevalence of *sorners*, beggars, bards and others who wandered through Highland and Lowland Scotland for centuries. We are reminded that True Thomas's sobriquet in the Gaelic world was *Tòmas Reumhair*, 'Thomas the idle wanderer'. Although occasionally legislated against by central and local authorities, these travelling men, along with the Scottish Travellers or Tinkers (*Ceàrdannan*) and ethnic Roma, continued to ply the byways. Most people in medieval and early modern Scotland were confined to their own village or parish. Even those men who would change farm employment at every term time, into the twentieth century, did not venture far from one farm to the next, though there was some migratory travel between regions at harvest time.[14]

Some individual male magical workers may well have been able to roam far beyond their native communities, a liberty that many female equivalents were denied. In the records, the geographical range of accused witches is limited. The mainly female witches brought to trial in Forfar, Angus, in 1661 confessed to having been active at a number of locations; none more than around 15 miles (24.1 km) away from the burgh.[15] Agnes Sampson, one of the North Berwick witches, seems to have been active in many of the surrounding local settlements.

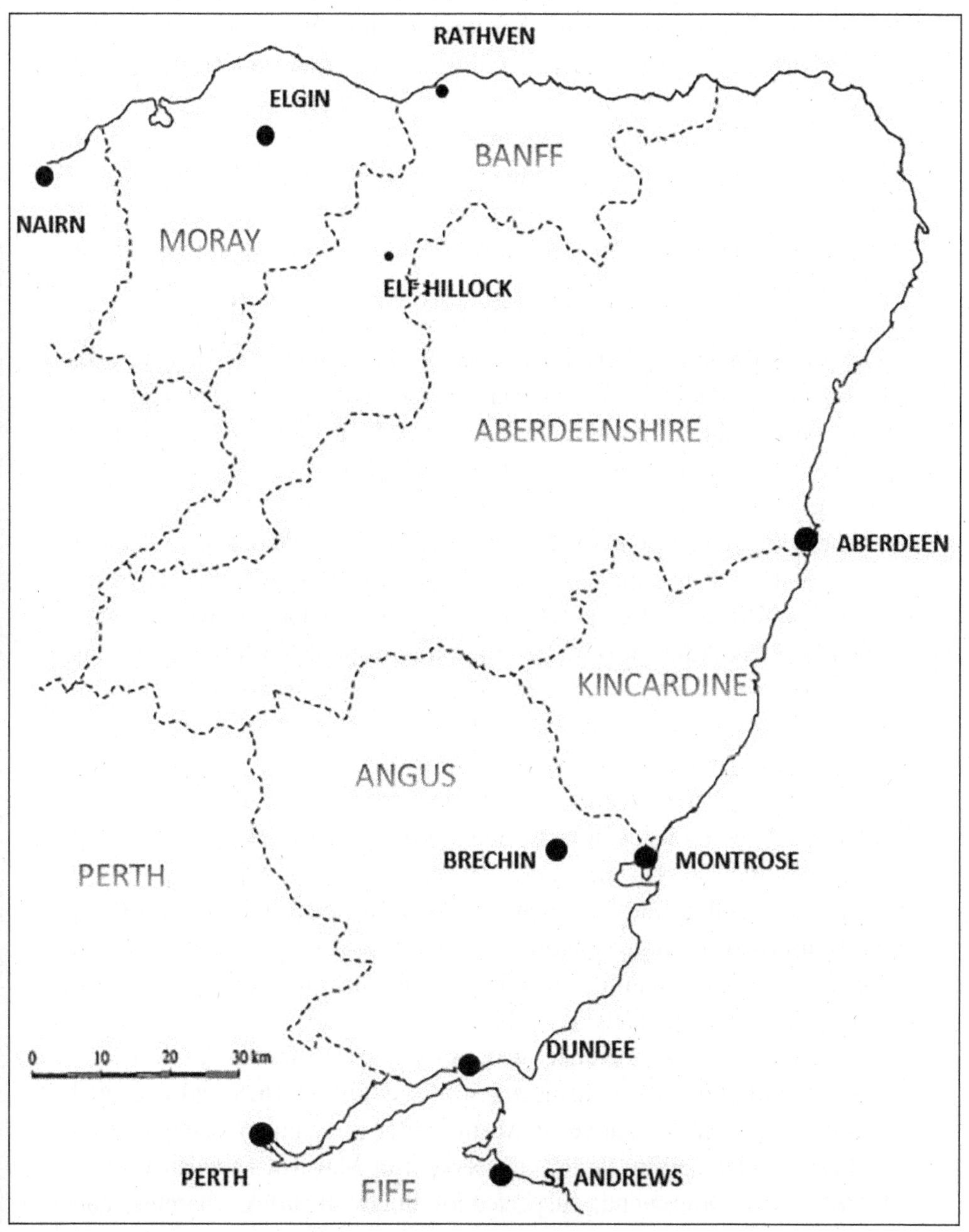

Map. Andro Man's world, the East and North-East Scotland.

Other healers, charmers and male witches plied their trade far and wide, such as the notable warlock, Ritchie Graham. John Neill, from Tweedmouth, Duns, worked all over Berwickshire in the late 1620s. John Brughe of Muckhart (historically Perthshire, now Clackmannan), brought to trial in 1643, had a range which encompassed fairly nearby settlements including Culross, Kinglassie, Auchterarder, Dunfermline, with one more distant outlier, Crieff. Whether there is any correlation between healers' travelling and the distances pilgrims travelled to holy wells seems doubtful, though there might be a link with travel necessitated through transport of cattle and the like.[16]

In Fife, a man named David Zeman was arrested in 1597, a year in which there was a heightened awareness of the dangers of witchcraft. In May, it was noted that this known warlock was active in south and east Fife, and had been seen to 'pas throght the cuntrie to do curis'. People seeking his services also visited him in jail. Two weeks later, it was reported that the bailies in Pittenweem had given license to a man named Walter Gourlay to take the warlock to help his sick son. A search was undertaken to root out others involved with Zeman, revealing some part of his charming activities. A Thomas Watson had employed the warlock to intervene with a witch named Beartrix Adie, who he believed was responsible for stopping his cow giving milk. Walter Gourlay stated he wanted Zeman to counter a curse laid on his son by the witch, Margrat Smyth. Others too consulted with Zeman. Although his fate is not known, he may have been one of a group of witches executed at St Andrews at that time.[17]

There may be a consideration of numbers of magical workers. In England, it was reckoned that charmer numbers were on a level with parish priests in the early sixteenth century and that nobody in Elizabethan Essex was more than 10 miles away from a charmer.[18] If that was also the case in Scotland, why did some male charmers venture very far and wide? Exceptional skill and reputation are the likely answers.

Another seasoned traveller was Alexander Drummond, who was tried at the High Court of Justiciary in Edinburgh in 1629 and executed in July of that year. A native of Auchterarder in southern Perthshire, he had been condemned by Perth Kirk session in May 1624, which warned of 'Alshander Drummond, suspected of unlawful airtes, charmes, and abuses of the people'. In the same year, authorities in Dunfermline noted his activities. Drummond challenged religious authorities by stating he was more powerful than Kirk ministers because he could restore people's health. The records detail his claimed skill at dealing with a diverse number of diseases:

> persones visseit wt. frenacies, madness, the falling evil, persones distractit in their wittis, and possessit with feirfull apparitiones, St. Anthone's fyre, the seikness or disease callit 'noli me tangere', [hidden cancer] and of canceris, wormes, glengores, and dyverse utheris uncouth diseases, all done and practized by sorcerie, incantations, devillyshe charmeing.[19]

Like Andro Man, Drummond claimed that he could cure every illness short of death. Equally as extraordinary as his proficiency of healing was the range of his practice, over mid, east and west Scotland. Among his patients was a man in Kirkcaldy, a merchant in Dundee, a burgess in Dumbarton, as well as many others in Fife and Perthshire. The court heard that he had cured hundreds of men, women, children and animals. Drummond was assisted in his cures by a familiar spirit who instructed him. He confessed that he was a healer but denied he used any incantations or charming. The prosecutors claimed that his healing was misleadingly 'falselie culloured under physicall meanes' but was actually done by 'charmes, inchantments and uthers devilish and unlawfull meanes'.[20] Two methods of healing he employed were, 'carding of ane quik cok in the grund, and of pleuch irnes upone merches betuix tua lords lands, for cureing of madness be sorcerie and witchcraft'.[21] He also attempted exorcisms of possessed people, and employed methods similar to other healers or un-witchers, including using efficacious south-running water and using the bewitched party's shirt to help diagnose and cure their condition. Like some others too, there is a flavour of Catholic ritual about his operations. He advised people not to eat meat on a Friday and termed his healing spells 'holy orations'.

Drummond, like Andro Man, was active for an exceptionally long time without incurring serious repercussions from the law. His career had lasted over fifty years by the time the Presbytery of Muthill appealed to the Privy Council for a commission to prosecute him in January 1629. As in some other cases, the clergy took the lead in first denouncing an accused witch rather than lay people in the community. A few months previously Drummond had been imprisoned at Stirling. The ministers complained that the manner of his confinement was far from secure or secret. Drummond was 'confirmed in his obstinat perversnes' and was resorted to daily by friends and those who believed in his powers.[22] He was sent to death on the pretext of his supposed use of diabolic powers. Under pressure, Drummond had admitted that an accused witch named Catharine Oswald had taken him to meet the Devil at a place near Niddrie near Edinburgh, appearing first in the shape of a foal, and then a man.[23] The case of Drummond was called to mind as being unusual by Sir George Mackenzie at the end of the seventeenth century, but there was also mention of him in several letters written by a lady to her brother, John Bannatyne, Justice Clerk, in 1643 and 1646, asking that Drummond be posthumously pardoned. The claim that he was 'ane notable Christian and did all his wondrous cures by lawfull meanes' echoed his own defence. The letters were equally ineffective, but they remain an unusual example of protest against the fate of an accused witch.[24] Drummond's prosecution signalled the growing national hardening of attitude towards charmers, that is those who used spells, incantations or magical objects to affect cures. The change has been seen as aligning with religious and social changes in Scotland. Many had signed up to the National Covenant in 1638 and the Solemn League and Covenant in 1643, pledging their personal commitment to godliness and strict Presbyterian precepts which focused on righteousness and the rejection of all sin in the community. If Scotland was going to be God's chosen nation, there was no place for those who meddled with the powers of darkness, whether they supposed it was for healing purposes or not. The growing prosecution of charmers in the 1640s and 1650s has been seen as a symptom of the growing power of strict Presbyterianism in the nation.[25] The General Assembly first prescribed charmers in legislation in 1640, when ministers were ordered 'to take notice of Charmers, Witches, and all such abusers of the people'. Further notices of charming were made in the next few years.[26] Other charmers prosecuted before Drummond include Thomas Grieve in 1629 and John Philip, who was executed in 1631.[27]

Stevin (Stein) Malcolme from Leckie, west of Stirling, also readily admitted his practice of healing people, which he said he had learnt from the fairies around the start of the seventeenth century. Fairies do not figure greatly in his interrogation record and Malcome (also called Maltman) seems ambivalent about them. He was examined by the Kirk session of Gargunnock for the charming of a cow in 1626 and then brought before the Presbytery of Stirling two years later. He seems to have confessed freely, another case where a healer believed he had not done anything unlawful. Aside from the standard acts of healing, he did confess unusual interaction with one prospective patient. He performed a ritual to heal James Glen which involved drawing a compass in the earth with a sword to hold off the fairies who had sickened Glen. When Glen withheld half of his promised payment for the healing, Malcolme told him he should put him in his own place, and that night Glen hanged himself.[28]

The distinction between legitimate healing and employing unlawful powers to heal was blurred. A late example of a man accused of magical acts who was known over a large area comes from Newtyle in Angus. Robert Small was a farmer who came to the attention of the authorities in 1665 when the Presbytery of Meigle investigated him for his curing diseases and finding lost and stolen goods. He denied this, but a paper was produced in his own writing. Small had given the document to a man named John Mencurre, who had been slandered with theft and also had a bad knee. The letter gave instructions to remedy both. The first part of the instruction contained nothing more sinister than making a concoction of salt and aqua vita. The second half made no sense to the Kirk committee who examined it, but seems to have implied the use of supernatural powers:

> Showing you the truth of this matter as farre as god hes given me grace, the partie being clear he durst not come in till my company, hearing the commendation of the man that I knuw the airt of the physiognome of a loun, for he knuw that a guiltie conscience bleaks the self of it, certainly this geir will come to light.[29]

Small dismissed this strange document by saying he knew no more than any other man about the person's guilt, but that he tried to find out as much about his enquirers as possible and this gave him the appearance of possessing uncanny knowledge. He promised to write no more such letters. It was found that Small had been similarly active in the nearby burgh of Dundee. Shortly afterwards, evidence came from Saline, a parish near Dunfermline in Fife, 34 miles or 56 km away across the River Tay, from John Mitchell, another of Small's clients. Mitchell had coveted a cow and accused two others of stealing it, which led to a charge of slander at a Saline Kirk session. Suspecting him further, the session enquired whether he had any contact with anyone suspected of sorcery. He unwisely replied that 'he would either go to devill or fiend that would tell him of his cow'. The session must have done some digging for they asked him if he had been to

Robert Small in Angus. He said he had done and would do so again in a similar strait, giving him a glowing reference: 'for he gave me a letter for getting of my cow, and I offered him a pynt of aill but he refused to have it, but said poor man it wer more alms to [give] the pynt of aill, for thou hes no more but ane groat to carry the home, and I had no more'.[30] It was implied that Small knew the sum of the man's worth during the visit.

Small denied guilt and also the charge that the letter to Mitchell had been dictated by him and written by his servant. He blamed Mitchell and then took the trouble to journey to see Mitchell, and confronted Mitchell before the Saline session, stating he had never met him and had not dictated the letter. The two men traded versions of the event (which may have occurred in December 1664), but no conclusion was drawn. Back in Newtyle, Mitchell stuck to his story. Mitchell travelled to Angus but refused to sign a statement giving his version of events. The session passed the matter to the Presbytery, who in turn passed it up to the synod of St Andrews. The latter found, in April 1666, that Small was 'by his owne confessione guiltie of drunknes prevaricatione and of pretending skill in divining when stollen goods are to be found. And finds him sensible of these sinns and sorrie for y^m promising through gods grace never to doe the lyke againe'.[31] The archbishop and the synod delated the matter to the Presbytery and Small did his repentance in his home kirk of Newtyle in June 1666, having escaped any serious repercussions.

While it is easy to see that Small used the psychological threat in his letters as a tool to induce the guilty parties to own up to various crimes, it is interesting that he was not motived by monetary gain for his services, or at least not in the case that brought him to public attention. The fact that there was no real hint or charming or diablery in the evidence presented doubtless saved him from the charge of witchcraft. The ecclesiastical authorities at all levels had a marked reluctance to pursue Small. He may have had good connections locally, but in fact he had been in trouble previously, In September1660, he was cited by Newtyle Kirk session for 'living in open constant malice', contempt of the communion and other sins. The following month, before the Presbytery, he was unrepentant and it was reported that his behaviour had been scandalous for several years. At a second meeting, he admitted fighting, slandering, and disobedience to authority.[32] It was true there was less distinction in Scotland between those who peddled 'good' magic with little hocus-pocus and for beneficial purposes and those who used 'bad' magic to harm people than, say, England. But it was a thin line and lives could be lost when the charmer had in fact healed rather than hurt. More men escaped than women.

The fear of strangers, and particularly those who travelled for a living, was a marked tendency in early modern Scotland. Drovers, as a class, were looked on with suspicion by many. Some individuals who were uncommonly mobile may also have attracted negative attention. A prime example is the East Lothian accused Andrew Hamilton, caught up in a local witch panic in 1628. There is evidence of him being active in Berwickshire as well as East Lothian. At one stage, he deserted his wife and moved to Holland before returning to Scotland. In his evidence, he also stated that he had worked in the English coal fields and had been a soldier in Sweden. Hamilton was accused of murdering Elizabeth Lawson, Lady Ormiston, and her daughter by witchcraft, in revenge for her refusing him the loan of a mare and for calling him names, and he fled to Newcastle-upon-Tyne, but was brought back to trial in Scotland.[33] Another accused, Sara Keith, said that she and Hamilton went with other beggars to Lady's Ormiston's home at Woodhead House. Elizabeth Lawson gave one of their party, a lunatic, a shirt. Hamilton was angry he received nothing and demanded the shirt. Lady Ormiston then scolded him and his companion for being beggars as they were able bodied. After Lady Ormiston was bewitched and died, Hamilton had Keith fetch some water and they used it to ritually wash the lady's body in her chamber.

Hamilton eventually confessed to numerous meetings with Satan around Haddington, accusing some prominent people from Lothian of witchcraft. There is some suggestion that George Home of Manderston, who was sent to arrest Hamilton in England, was using the suspect to blacken the name of his own wife, Helen Arnot. Under questioning, Hamilton stated that he had witnessed Arnot ask the Devil at a meeting in Coldingham for permission to slay her husband. The warlock later admitted that a servant of Home's came to him and told him what to say to incriminate his master's wife. Arnot had earlier petitioned for a divorce from her husband. Hamilton implicated over forty people for witchcraft crimes. Due to his unreliable and inconsistent testimony, many of those he named were never charged. Hamilton notably consulted Satan in healing cases, such as the time he had instructions from Satan about the ingredients needed for a potion which would cure Thomas Home of Clerkington, who had been bewitched by a beggar.[34]

In different ways, Drummond and Man were able to bolster their reputations. One means of magical self-aggrandisement Andro shared with others was linking himself with national figures in Scotland, trading on an arcane relationship with important figures who could liaise with the world of fairy and the dead. Evidence against Man stated that he had consorted with sundry dead men who happened to be guests or prisoners in Elfame. These human or former human inhabitants included the legendary True Thomas and the 'kyng that deit in Flowdoun', James IV. As I have shown in an earlier work, there were multiple, interlocking legends about the fate of King James IV, who ruled Scotland from 1488 until his demise on Flodden Field, where he perished in the front lines of a Scottish national army fighting the English.[35] The fact that James was an exceptionally accomplished monarch who died heroically, if needlessly, combined with the unprecedented scale of defeat, quickly engendered rumours that the king had not died. Contrary stories said that the king had been kidnapped by a disgruntled noble, or that he had gone in disguise to Europe or to Jerusalem. The additional tradition that King James IV had neither died in battle, nor fled abroad, but was a prisoner in fairyland, like Thomas Rhymer, is found in no other source than the passing comment in the trial of Andro Man.

Thomas was a legendary national figure, as we have seen, famous since the early fourteenth century. Andro would have known the national and local legends about True Thomas. In Banffshire, there are the Stanes of St Brandon, subject of a typically apocalyptic verse attributed to Thomas the Rhymer:

> At two full times, and three half times,
> Or threescore years and ten,
> The ravens shall sit on the Stanes of St Brandon
> And drink the blood of the slain![36]

Like Thomas, Andro was promised he would know all things (as well as being able to cure all sickness), but like the great seer he too 'wald seik thy meit or thow deit, as Thomas Rymour did', and beg his bread before he died. This accords with folk belief that supernatural knowledge came with a heavy price of forsaking worldly wealth. Other Scots individuals accused of witchcraft also entered into that shady bargain, obtaining supernatural knowledge via fairy contacts. Mostly these were women, but they did include at least one man, John Stewart (tried in 1618).

Did Andro get arcane information about the fairy captive monarch through his travelling network of contacts? The transmission of such underground information was one by-product of the roaming of healers and magic workers. There are various interpretations of why these high-profile Scottish national figures, like True Thomas, James IV, and the later Reverend Robert Kirk (who dared to write a treatise on the fairies), should be represented as undying inhabitants of a fairy afterlife. Serious modern occult tradition agrees that James IV did not die at Flodden. This conscious linking with famous figures may be, as Diane Purkiss suggests, the result of an 'educational protocol,' albeit an oral one, whereby Andro imbibed tales of True Thomas and King James IV and chose to associate himself with those at the highest echelon in the human-elven interface.[37] At any rate, this linkage seems to have been a mostly male one. There seems to have been an elusive masculine attraction to dangerous, famous dead men of the realm, and the connections were made mostly (but not always, as we will see) by males accused of witchcraft.

A suspected Angus warlock, Robert Murray of Glenesk, brought to the authorities in 1588, made a passing admission that he had 'falselie assurit that he wes Senyeor Davie's man'.[38] This was referring to David Riccio, the unfortunate secretary of Mary, Queen of Scots, murdered by a group of Scots nobles at the behest of her husband in March 1566. Riccio had not had the reputation of being a witch or necromancer during his lifetime, not even among his enemies, but the manner of his death, and its many dark associations spun him posthumously into an occult orbit.

Riccio had a possible oblique connection with a male witch named Damiet or Damiot. In 1597, an Edinburgh witch, Jonet Stewart of the Grassmarket, had been accused by a man named Andrew Pennycuick of making him ill through witchcraft. Some of her craft had been taught to her by the late Michael Clark, a smith of Laswaid. But she also worked cures by means of passing sickly people through a circle of green woodbine, a practice that she confessed she had learned from an 'Italian strangear callit John Damiet, ane notorious knawin Enchanter and Sorcerer'.[39] This figure is obscure. Some have suggested it is a folk or distorted memory of the notorious alchemist monk John Damian, Abbot of Tungland, an alchemist from the time of King James IV.[40] But he is more likely the French priest Jean Damiet, a confessor of the queen, reckoned also to be a magician, who had repeatedly warned Riccio about his safety, and specifically about a bastard who would slay him? Riccio disregarded the warning and did not flee abroad, as Damiet advised, and paid the price. He was indeed slain by a bastard, but not the one he had thought. Riccio had thought of the queen's bastard brother, the Earl of Moray, who was abroad. But the assassin who struck the first of many blows was George Douglas, bastard of the Earl of Angus.[41]

The accused witch, Alison Pearson, from Fife claimed to have seen several famous dead Scots in her trips to fairyland, most notably William Maitland of Lethington, secretary of Mary, Queen of Scots and a highly divisive figure in the latter part of her reign.[42] Imprisoned by Mary's opponent, the regent Earl of Morton, Maitland died in mysterious circumstances in Leith tolbooth, with one version of events stating that he poisoned himself in July 1573 to escape the humiliation of execution. The importation of Lethington into the cast of characters encountered by Alison in a parallel realm was probably untypical of female witch experience. But she moved in relatively important circles, counting the Archbishop of St Andrews among the clients who came to her for healing.

The sexual element in the tale was not a lurid detail invented by Andro Man's prosecutors. True Thomas famously also lay with the Fairy Queen, at least according to the fifteenth-century poem which detailed his adventures in the Otherworld. The theme was widespread in folk culture. Robert Glass of Kingarth, Bute, admitted in 1670 to scandalising his brother-in-law, James MacPhie, by 'saying he sould frequent the company of a lemman among the furies commonly called Fairfolks, quwich was a base and unchristian scandal'.[43] Sexual interplay between fairy and human was not all mortal man and fairy; it could be a woman and fairy man. Such was detailed in an Aberdeen witchcraft trial of 1597, when Isobell Strauthaquhin and her daughter were accused of witchcraft. The magical skills were passed down the female line of this family but were ultimately derived from a fairy man who slept with one of them.[44] And there were other examples of female-mortal/male-elven liaison. Janet Drever of Orkney was banished in 1615 for fostering a fairy child and for having sex with fairies. Women were sometimes evidently reluctant to have carnal relations with non-incarnate beings, and the element of coercion appears in some accounts. The identities of these shadowy male figures who came to women were not always clear cut. An Orkney wise woman named Elspeth Reoch confessed in 1616 that she was accosted by two otherworldly men, one in black and the other in green tartan, targeting her by a loch-side when she was twelve. Sometime later the black attired man appeared to her in her sister's house, 'And callit him self ane farie man quha wes sumtyme her kinsman callit Johne Stewart quha wes slain by McKy'.[45] He had been murdered at the going down of the sun, and this was the reason he was trapped in fairyland. After some persuasion, she submitted to sleeping with him. As they did in all cases, the authorities simply labelled the mysterious figure the Devil. It is interesting that the fairy man/ghost also met a violent end like some other such figures. Another point to note here is that sexual relations between Satan and witches is not a feature of early witchcraft accusations, though it did crop up more during the later seventeenth century. Another uncertain male ghost/fairy/familiar spirit who had relations with a mortal female was a figure named Thomas McRory, with whom the accused witch Isobel Watson (convicted in Stirling in 1590) had intimate relations. He gave her a mark upon her head as a sign of her pact with the fairies and was described as 'being with them'. In some sense he was present in fairyland, though whether this was temporarily (as a living human), permanently (as a ghost), or something else entirely is unknown.[46]

The presence in the fairy realm of dead people was common to near contemporary people accused of witchcraft such as Bessie Dunlop of Ayr, who met a deceased local laird and also Thom Reid (slain at the Battle of Pinkie in 1547), who became her intermediary with the Fair Folk (and who was also a lover of the Fairy Queen), or Alison Pearson of Fife, who met a William Simpson in that uncertain realm.[47] She also admitted that she saw many dead people in Elfame.[48] Highland folklore sometimes located recently dead people in Elfame. Though the reason for their transference there was not always plain, those who died before their time were deemed to be vulnerable to going there.[49] The Reverend Robert Kirk stated that seers frequently reported seeing those people who had died before the natural span of their lives with the fairies. They were not always contentedly held in that place. A widow who once asked a diviner named Alasdair Challum where her late husband was now, was told by him bluntly, 'He is a baggage horse to the fairies in Slevach Cairn, with a twisted willow tithe in his mouth'. Slevach Cairn, *Càrn na Sleabhach*, was a notorious abode of the fairies in Glen Erochty, Atholl.[50]

Males were less liable to be entrapped or led astray by fairy and otherworldly beings. The case of Walter Ronaldsone of Dyce, Aberdeenshire, involves the intervention of a 'spirit', though it might as well be a fairy man. The account in the Kirk records is a strange one:

20th November, 1601
The quhilk day, Walter Ronaldsone, in the Kirktone of Dyce…
wes dilate to haue familiaritie of a spirite, comperit, and being

> examinat, confessit that, upone a 27 yeiris syne, there came to
> his dur a spirit, and callit upone him, Wattie, Wattie, and this
> wes in the barley seid tyme, and thairfra removit, and thaireftir
> came averie yeir twa tymes sen syne, bot saw na thing, hot
> harde a voce as said is. In speciall at Michaelmes in 1600 yeris
> it came quhair the deponar wes in his bed sleipand, and it satt
> down anent the bed upoune a kist, and callit upone him, saying,
> Wattie, Wattie, and than he wakynnit and saw the forme of it,
> quhilk wes lyke ane litill bodie, haiffing a scheavin berd, cled
> in quhyt lening lyk a sark…[51]

The spirit advised Walter to go to a certain place where he would find gold and silver, and he did so, taking with him a spade and three men, but found nothing. Despite this, he still believed there was treasure to be found. His minister vouched for his Christian integrity and he seems to have escaped punishment. Walter was lucky in a sense that he was only repeatedly tempted by talk of an unreachable treasure and did not converse with the being on other matters.

Most of the figures from fairyland met by humans were male and sometimes these intermediaries (whether they were human, fairy or *other*) had a distinct role in advising or teaching the person they communicated with. John Gothray was a healer from Perth. He was kidnapped by the fairies at twilight (a dangerous time) and was helped by a young lad, himself an abductee, who instructed him there. When he came back to the mortal realm, Gothray was given the power of healing. The boy visited him each month and gave him herbs to assist his cures.[52] Another man contacted by the fairy world at twilight was Harry Wilson, brought before the Presbytery of Duns in 1669. He admitted to having stayed for nineteen days with the fairy folk and enjoyed their revelry. But he strongly denied that his magical gift of revealing secrets came from them. When pressed, he said a woman had appeared to him last Yule at twilight and communicated the gift.[53]

Overall, the insight into the elven world revealed by Andro chimes in well with other testimony. It has been pointed out that, generally, the role of some fairies in Scottish witchcraft trials took the place occupied by familiar spirits in English trials. When Andro averred that the fairy world is not dissimilar to ours, with fairies clothed as men, who danced and sang like us, but who were like strong, stark shadows, he was voicing a tenacious tradition which was also confirmed by the religious commentator Robert Kirk a century later.

Many similarities exist between the case of Andro Man and the Nairnshire witch Isobel Gowdie of Auldern, who was condemned in 1662. Both inhabited the same Lowland region bounded by the Highlands and the Moray Firth, Banff and Nairn being separated by the small county of Moray. Gowdie too may have been a healer (the evidence is not so clear in her case), and her confessions are as fulsome and remarkable as Andro's, with a number of similarities, notably her interface with the elven realms. Like Andro's entry point to fairyland, Isobel also accessed the realm via a natural feature in the landscape, the Downie Hills. Where Andro and Isobel differ is in her exuberant admissions of *malefice* against members of her own community, several of whom she gleefully admitted killing.

The Fairy Queen, via Andrew's evidence, is a major Otherworld power. She is 'verray plesand, and wilbe auld and young quhen scho pleissis; scho mackis any kyng quhom scho pleisis, and lyis with any scho lykis'. Andro's second-sight and healing powers came with a price to pay, as did many fairy gifts in traditional tales. The striking authority wielded by the Elven Queen, in Andro's testimony (as elsewhere), inverted the earthly order where males were overwhelmingly in positions of power.[54] Exactly the same transformation of beauty into hideousness is found in the story of Thomas the Rhymer, whose tale prefigures Andro's encounter with the same female being. True Thomas was lying on Huntlie Banks in the Borders when he saw the queen ride by, and he had sex with her immediately, after which she lost her looks. Andro, on the other hand was a boy, and seems not to have had congress with the queen until he was possibly in his thirties. His intimate relationship with her was intermittent, and he had fathered children with her. This sexual contact with an exalted spirit being is unique for the male witchcraft record in Scotland.

Although Andro was said to have the ability to summon her with a magic word, this is likely an interpretation of his prosecutors, for she was unlikely to be easily biddable. The power to summon supernatural beings, and particularly Satan, is never given in evidence against female witches and very rarely attributed to male witches. In 1629, Alexander Hamilton confessed his ability to summon Satan by striking a wand on the ground three times and shouting, 'Rise, foul thief!' And he could dismiss him by striking him on the head and announcing, 'Go away to hell, thief!' Such powers represent a residual tradition attributed to medieval ritual magicians.

Andro describes Christsonday as both an angel and the son-in-law of God. Christsonday was able to tell him secrets of nature, such as the crows bringing a magical stone from one district to another in order to hatch their young. Also, Christsonday was able to tell Andro that 1598 would be a bad year (presumably for the harvest), but the next fourteen years would be good ones. Not too far from Banff (at Methlick in Aberdeenshire), and not too long before, the accused witch Marion Grant had also been accused of having an attendant spirit called Christsonday, which sometimes appeared as a man and sometimes as a creature. She both danced and had sex with Christsonday while he was in human form, though he also appeared to her as a black horse and a black man. She promised herself as his servant and learned magic from him.[55] Andro, or his interrogators, seems to have confused the extent of Christsonday's powers. At one stage he is claimed to have all the power under God, but the subtext is that he played second fiddle to the Queen of Fairies. Possibly, Christsonday had the power over the mortal realm while the Fairy Queen ruled the elven world. In one passage, Christsonday is seen by the mortal in a startling vision, coming out of the snow on Rood Day in the form of a *staig*, a young male horse, and the Queen of Elphen was there, along with others, riding upon white hackneys and they progressed to Binhill. Bin Hill, or the Bin of Cullen, is a conspicuous hill not far from Rathven in Banff. Andro's interrogators typically cheapened the encounter with this fairy procession by stating that Andro had kissed the rear parts of both Christsonday and the queen in greeting.

Christonday is a confused amalgamation of figures. He made a mark on Andro's hand, just as Satan did to witches. And Andro states that he would be God's notary of Judgement Day, taking account of each person's book of indictments, and some other comments by Andro have him behaving like an avenging angel from the book of Revelations. Yet he is not credited with directly influencing the direction of Andro's magical abilities. The darker associations of the spirit were likely influenced by the religious conceptions of Andro's interrogators: 'he grantit that Chrystsondaye schew him the gryt fyre of hell, and that he suld get ane tuich therof, and that Chrystsondaye suld be put thairin him self'.[56]

A generation after Andro's death there was another man condemned for operating in a very similar way in the region, which shows the tenacity of magical practices in the face of fierce persecution. John Philip seems to have worked in Banff as well as Aberdeenshire, and he was censured and hounded out of at least five parishes for his healing which he performed on animals as well as humans.[57] He was put on trial at Banff in February 1631, accused of having been for a considerable time suspected of witchcraft, sorcery, enchantment, and of using devilish charms. Many of the charges relating to his charming detail his method of washing the afflicted person. In one case he cured a man and transferred his illness to an ox (worth forty marks), which then died. This was in the parish of Fintray, where John seems to have been particularly active, curing a number of parishioners of fever, perhaps during an outbreak of malignant disease.

Some of John Philip's methods appear to accord with those used by Andro Man. When he cured Gilbert Leslie, he put him 'throw ane hesp of yairne'.[58] He used the same method to heal some oxen. Andro is also recorded as having used this method in at least one case. He also used 'orisons' or prayers as a method to cure people. There was also some connection with the shadow world familiar to the earlier warlock. John denied some of the charges against him, but one of his admissions was that he 'confessit the charming of James Maltman in Banff for the feveris with the queine of fairies, quhilk wes verefeit be the said James Maltman himself'.[59] Unfortunately, the circumstances around this event are not recorded.

In August 1633 George Fraser and his wife, Giles Chalmer, from Itlaw, Banff, were charged with using witchcraft for curing animals. The indictment records that Fraser had fallen ill some years before and had recourse to the services of the warlock John Philip (who was executed) and later another warlock named Walter Baird, who had also recently been executed. Having been cured by magical means, it was alleged that George had learned healing acts from them, though he strenuously denied this.[60]

One thing barely described in the surviving record of Andro's prosecution is the description of fairyland itself. He stated that sometimes the fair beings would make it appear he was a guest in a fair chamber, and yet in the morning he would be left on a moor. Such mischievous distortions of the fabric of reality were one of the most disconcerting attributes of the elven race. Though Andro had enjoyed decades worth of acquaintance with these others, and seen sundry dead people and his own half-elven children in their land, he gave no detailed topography of the realm, apart from the fact he enjoyed their entertainment at times. Others were more forthcoming. At a somewhat opposite end of the scale from Andro Man is Donald McIlmichall of Appin, a vagabond who was arrested in 1676 along with an associate, and both were initially accused of stealing cattle and horses.[61]

Donald was charged with theft the following year and also for conspiring with the Devil in order to find information about stolen goods. Still more remarkable was his confession about encountering the Fair Folk. One night, travelling between Ardturr and Glackiriska, he saw strange lights on the hill. He went to this place and entered inside the hill and saw there a great many men and women with lighted candles. Some of the throng wanted to shut him out, though others drew him in. In charge of the gathering was an old man. Lizanne Henderson pointed out the likely site of the first encounter at Dalnasheen ('field of the fairy people').[62]

The authorities asked what he thought these beings were, and he answered he did not think they were worldly men and women. Later he encountered the fairies at other places including Shian of Barcalden. He broke a promise not to reveal the Otherworld beings to any mortal, but he told an associate and for this incursion he was assaulted by the Fairies, yet he still went to their gatherings, where he enjoyed the music they played on trumps. Donald was found guilty of theft and consulting with evil spirits and hung at Inveraray on 19 November 1677.

Another man who encountered the shadow realm under the hill was John Stewart, tried at Irvine in 1618.[63] Stewart became embroiled in a complex dispute between sisters-in-law, which led to one of the women, Margaret Barclay, being accused of witchcraft. Stewart was accused of having assisted Margaret in causing the shipwreck of a vessel whose crew included her brother-in-law. Like Donald McIlmichaell, Stewart was described as a vagabond, and this rootless manner of life may have been linked, in the eyes of some, to disrepute and witchcraft.

Poverty and begging among males who were perceived to be healthy was a mark of suspicion to authorities in Scotland through the centuries. In May 1662, James Welch was accused of witchcraft by Janet Wast in Haddington. He was examined and several witch marks were found on his body, after which he was sent to the tolbooth in Edinburgh, where he confessed almost immediately. James admitted meeting the Devil in various places and that his witchcraft was encouraged by his mother and his grandmother. His first supernatural encounter happened when he was urinating in a stream and met a pretty girl who offered herself to him, which he refused. A short time later he met a man who offered to make James his servant, and he met the man the following night. The 'man and women' were both the Devil. Around eighty people were delated by James for their involvement in witchcraft.

At some point James, to the frustration of his questioners, refused to say more. He was still imprisoned and the authorities fretted about how much his incarceration was costing. They could not make him pay anything because he was a beggar. There was also a question about how to proceed with the case against him because he was a minor (though we do not know his exact age). He was deemed to be too young to stand trial, so he is likely to have survived.[64]

Patrick Elles, a common beggar from Strathdon, came to the attention of Alford Presbytery several times. In January 1676 the minister of Auchindoir reported him as one who was conspicuously part of a dangerous class of:

> seducers, [who] under pretence of transes, or converse with familiar spirits, there is none yet knowne to be within the bounds of this Presbytrie, but one Patrick Elles, within the parochine of Auchindore, wherfor the minister of Auchindore is appoynted to cite him befor their Session, and question him therupon, and if he deny it, and be not convict, to warne him to bewarre of the lyke in all tyme comeing, under the pain of censure, but if he be convict to charge him befor the Presbytrie, that he may receive sentence accordinglie.[65]

Several weeks later, the exasperated minister could not locate the man in order to summon him, though he was exhorted again to try to find him. Elles presumably was helping clients to answer questions or locate lost or stolen goods while in a visionary state, which seems to have been known in Aberdeenshire but may still have been a fairly niche magical activity in Scotland, but the exact details will never be known.

It was said that Stewart was also claimed skills in juggling and palmistry. After Margaret had cursed her sister and brother-in-law and hoped the latter's ship would sink, Stewart went to the house of Andrew Train, Provost of Irvine, and told his wife that the ship had indeed foundered. Train had been on board. The only two survivors of the wreck later returned to Scotland and said that the ship had been lost near Padstow in Cornwall.

Stewart was arrested and he implicated Margaret Barclay in destroying the vessel. He said that Barclay had applied to him to teach her the magical arts, 'in order that she might get gear, kye's milk, love of man, her heart's desire on such persons as had done her wrong, and, finally, that she might obtain the fruit of sea and land'.[66] He denied to her that he possessed such arts or had the power to communicate them. Possibly influenced by torture, he claimed to have visited Margaret Barclay's house by night and saw her and two others maliciously form a clay model of Provost Train and also of the doomed ship. Satan came among them in the shape of a handsome black dog. The party then went to the shore and cast the clay images into the water, at which the waves boiled and became as red as blood.

When asked where he had gained the power to foretell future events, Stewart attributed the gift to the fairies. He had travelled in Ireland and, twenty-six years before on Halloween, he had been travelling at night between towns in County Galway when he met the King of Fairies and his company. The king gave him a blow on his forehead with a white rod, which robbed him of his speech and the sight in one eye. Three years later in Dublin he met the same company and his eyesight and speech were restored. Since that time, he had met the elven company every Saturday night at seven o' clock and remained with them all night. He also met the fairies at Halloween at Kilmaurs Hill, Ayrshire, and another hill, and was instructed by them there. His interrogators pricked the spot on his forehead where he had been stricken and found it was insensible to pain. He declared he had seen many people at the fairy court and that it was the fate of all those who died suddenly to migrate there.

John Stewart was put in very secure bonds in the tolbooth, for fear he would harm himself, and just before trial was visited by two ministers who exhorted him to renounce the Devil and call on God for mercy. He prayed with them and said of his condition that, 'I am so straitly guarded that it lies not in my power to get my hand to take off my bonnet, nor to get bread to my mouth'.[67] The ministers left him and when Stewart was called for shortly afterwards, he was found hanging by a noose of hemp (possibly drawn from his bonnet or garter) attached to the door, his knees drawn up about four and a half centimetres from the ground. He was still breathing, but he could not be revived. A group of other women, besides Margaret Barclay, were drawn into the accusations, questioned, and sometimes tortured. The co-accused, Isobel Inch, was on the point of giving a confession when she escaped from the belfry where she was being held, falling from a height and suffering injuries, which led to her death five days later. Before she died, she retracted all admissions of guilt. Margaret Barclay was tortured by laying heavy metal bars on her legs, which led to her confession. Despite retracting her confession she was found guilty, strangled and burned.

Other male accused Scottish men described as a vagabond were Alexander Hunter and William Scottie.[68] There are continental parallels of men who became suspicious in the eyes of the law because of criminality, and who were then moulded into witchcraft suspects. One such destitute, an unmarried man in Germany in 1615, was initially accused of sodomy and theft, but was afterwards prosecuted as a witch.[69] Rootless males were just as ill-favoured as flighty or wanton females. The fact of poverty also shows that, for a good many witches or healers, there was not enough money in their specialised careers and they often had to supplement their income with begging or other pursuits.

Like the St Andrews witch, Alison Pearson (put on trial in 1588), a healer and diviner, was not accused of malefice against anyone in her community. Like Andro also, she had prominent connections, in her case the Archbishop of St Andrews who was a client of hers. She was a resident some time in fairyland, though she complained of mistreatment from the inhabitants there. Another female accused who had dealings with fairies of a non-sexual nature, and who also had a ghostly male intermediary with the fairies, was Isobel Haldane (tried in 1622). She was kidnapped by the fairies and rescued from their realm by her male spirit guide.

Bessie Dunlop's connection with fairyland was also initiated by an abrupt face-to-face intervention. She met a mysterious man who offered her help for her earthly worries, and on his third appearance he was in company of twelve unearthly beings who were revealed to be the Good Neighbours, elven folk.[70] The man, Thom Reid, stated that he had died in battle thirty years before and then called on Bessie to remember an incident from her past when she had been in childbed and a stout woman came to her door and asked for a drink. She was the Queen of Fairies and it was she who sent Thom Reid as an emissary between the worlds. A healer like Andro Man, mention of the elven folk only compounded her guilt in the eyes of the prosecutors and she was executed in November 1576. Although she gives tantalising glimpses of the fair folk, such as them riding into Restalrig Loch, near Edinburgh, we could wish for more details to be forthcoming. The same is actually true of that most remarkable female witch trial, that of Isobel Gowdie.

Unlike many poor wretches who were caught in the witchcraft net but had no stake in supernatural trade, Andro and those like him were a different matter. A self-avowed and life-long healer, he used exact magical formulae to heal men, women and beasts. He set land aside to the Gudeman to insure the fertility of farms in the North-East. It is highly unlikely (as in some other witchcraft cases) that the bulk of his testimony about elven queens, uncertain beings, dead kings and other uncanny things was the invention of his interrogators or judges. Willingly or otherwise, he gave this information, which he believed to be true. What, then, did it mean? The complex alternative world may have been a fantasy comprised of folk beliefs and aspects of his own unconscious. Some of his outlandish visions have been suggested as the hallucinatory side-effects of sleep paralysis.[71] But the paucity of Andro's testimony, as well as its content, hardly supports this.

More fruitful is Emma Wilby's citation of the three classifications of false confessions which were identified by two American psychologists in 1985. These were 'voluntary', 'coerced-compliant' and 'coerced-internalized'.[72] Voluntary confessions may be made on the basis of protecting someone else, or because of mental illness. The second category, 'coerced compliant', involves the accused admitting a crime without memory of having done it, either to give their accuser what they want or because they simply cave in. The third, most sinister category occurs when the massive pressure of questioning (and sometimes torture) generates a false memory within the accused person, who previously believed their own innocence.

Modern scholastic debate on witchcraft has included a facet which argues whether or not there was an element of active shamanism in Early Modern western societies, wherein some of those accused of witchcraft were following elements (or degraded traces) or ancient, pre-Christian practices. Margaret Murray, in the early twentieth century, propounded the view that there was an active and enduring cult of witchcraft which survived from pre-Christian days to the modern era. This wholesale survival theory withered away towards the end of the twentieth century. But the presence of some shamanic cults in scattered areas into the Early Modern age was propounded by Carlo Ginzburg, who highlighted the extravagant and imaginative confessions given by the Elgin witch Isobel Gowdie and also mentions Andro Man as being symptomatic of beliefs that predated the formalisation of Christian beliefs equating witchcraft with satanism.[73] More recently Emma Wilby authored a remarkably comprehensive study of Gowdie's case and followed Ginzburg's thinking.[74]

Otherwise, attempts have been made to fit the more dazzling fairy-related confessions of Andro and his female counterparts within a framework of modern psychological analysis.[75] But shoehorning inexplicable historic experience into the confines of modern thought is always going to be an uncomfortable fit.

Andro's cultural background and place of origin doubtless fed into his belief system. Banffshire, like some areas of Aberdeenshire, retained substantial minority Catholic populations after the Reformation, bolstered in the seventeenth and eighteenth centuries by an underground network of Catholic clerics fed into the area by the European Church. Around 1720, there may have been around 600 Catholic in the parish of Rathven, out of a population of roughly 2500.[76] An estimate for the end of the eighteenth century has Catholics comprising almost a third of the parish population. If Andro Man himself was not a Catholic by the time of his trial, he was still living in an area rich in continuing Catholic heritage. Moreover, if he was born in the 1520s, he would have grown to manhood as a member of the old religion. This explains Andro's designation of the powerful male spirit Christsonday as an angel rather than a male fairy (or Satan, as the Kirk described him), and his usage of invocations to St John in his magical work, as well as some of the pseudo-Latin words he used in his spells. He was able to summon Christsonday with the word *Benedicte*, 'bless you', suggesting some lingering Catholic association in Andro's mind.

There may have been some recusant atmosphere about the parish of Botriphnie itself which lingered after Man's time. In the mid-seventeenth century, the Presbytery of Strathbogie had dealings with another local man whose behaviour bordered on religious irregularity. In February 1651, the Kirk brethren heard there were instances within Botriphnie of those giving or taking oaths of indemnity for witchcraft, and that one John Anderson of Westertoun was present. He was summoned to appear next day to answer but evidently did not appear, nor when ordered to do so the following month. He had a history of defying convention, for in 1649 he refused to sign the National Covenant, and in 1650 he was deemed a malignant and removed as an elder from the Kirk session. In 1651 he was punished for accusing the minister of adultery. Later, he seems to have fallen back into doctrinal and social regularity.[77] In Rathven too, where Andro Mann latterly lived, there was also late occurrence of that irreligious impulse which invoked unseen powers. The Kirk session in 1725 heard that Katharin Symson had prayed that Janet Forbes might get a cold armful of her husband, and two years later that Marjorie Wilson had turned her face to the sun upon a Sunday and evilly cursed Patrick, her son, wishing him sudden death, which then happened.[78] The old beliefs were a long time dying here.

Chapter 4

The Anti-Witches

Prickers and Persecutors

The forces which allied themselves against witchcraft were not just ordained ministers and members of Kirk sessions, Presbyteries and the general assembly of the Kirk. Nor were the secular authorities confined to elite members of the Privy Council. Local lairds and merchants in small communities were key partners in forcing through investigations and prosecutions of suspected witches. And their motivations were not always a strict desire to identify those who caused harm by magic. A web of social and economic forces may have been behind the motivation of these powerful men. Their role in driving witch trials has not been fully explored in Scotland or elsewhere.[1]

In Scotland, often the most conspicuous, certainly the most fearsome representative of the drive against witchcraft was the witch-pricker. Scotland did not invent the peculiar trade of witch-pricking, identifying a witch through piercing with a pin, but it could fairly be said that the nation professionalised the activity. The most usual practices of witch-prickers were to find moles and other blemishes on the body of a witch and test whether they were insensible to pain, supposed proof that they had been caused by the Devil. Satan habitually sealed a covenant with a witch by nipping the human who had entered a pact with him, leaving the tell-tale mark after the encounter. The usual method was to test the place with a pin or other implement. If the spot did not bleed and if the accused did not react to the examination, this was taken as proof that they had been satanically marked.

There may have been a dozen or more active witch-prickers in Scotland in the seventeenth century, though biographical details about the members of this profession are scanty. Was it a full-time, well-paying profession for some? Almost certainly it was, though there may have been others involved for the power and control as well as financial reward. The first examiners of suspects for these marks seem to have been ministers, since there are records of several of these stating their involvement in pricking suspects. The reverends John Aird and John Bell were enthusiastic early testers of this method of uncovering the guilt of accused women. But the opportunity to professionalise, and monetise, the practice soon attracted non-clerics. An interesting query is to ponder how many healers, charmers or male witches may have indulged in identifying others (rivals perhaps) in their own profession, whether they resorted to physical pricking or not. One such was a folk healer called Alexander Fortune, who testified against a suspected witch named Isobel Young, in Duns, Berwickshire in 1619. He had been asked to heal a wound that Isobel had under her breast and, because it could not be healed by him, he assumed that it was a Devil's mark.[2]

One early pricker was John Balfour of Corshouse, who, in February 1632, was brought before the Privy Council and accused of being a malicious charlatan. 'Upon the presumption of, he goes athort the country abusing simple and ignorant people for his private gain and commoditie.'[3] He declared that the first time he had acted as a pricker had been when the minister of Tranent had him examine a gardener's wife. The lords found that 'his knowledge in this mater hes onelie beene conjecturall and most unlawfullie used within Gods kirk, and tharfoir discharges him of all forder exerceing of that art and trade in tyme coming as he will answer upon the contrarieat his perell'.[4] He was not the last of his profession to be accused, yet the practice continued and thrived.

Insight into the local operation of a secular witch-pricker is detailed in George Sinclair's *Satan's Invisible World Uncovered* (1685). A woman named Bessie Graham from Kilwinning had, in 1649, sworn at her neighbour, who shortly afterwards died. She was taken into custody but the local minister was unconvinced of her guilt and reluctant to get a civil warrant to send her to assize.

> At this nick of time one Alexander Bogs skilled in searching the Mark, came, being often sent for, and finds the Mark upon her ridge-Back, wherein he thrust a great Brass Pin, of which she was not sensible: neither did any blood follow, when the Pin was drawn out. I lookt upon this but as a small evidence, in respect of what I found afterwards, yet this some-what inclined the Judges to send the Process to Edinburgh, though there were small hopes of obtaining a Commission for putting her to an Assize.[5]

A prominent local man was unconvinced of her guilt, but the legal process was permitted and she remained in custody, reluctant to voice her guilt, although the minister and others heard her converse with Satan in her cell, which contributed towards her being found guilty and executed. Prickers were often evidently drawn in from the local community and examined suspects without any legal sanction; even then, their findings were not universally believed by ministers and laity without other evidence to substantiate guilt.

The actual operation of puncturing the witch with an implement was often no quick matter, lengthened possibly by sadism more than professional thoroughness. During the order of Janet Barker in Edinburgh in 1643, a pricker named James Scobie from Musselburgh was sent for and embedded a pin in a suspect mark on her back for forty-five minutes, during which time Janet demonstrated no sensation of pain, and nor did the spot bleed. Another man, George Cathie of Lanark, was sent for by the authorities and pricked eleven suspects who were jailed in the tolbooth of Lanark in November 1649, by their consent, and none of them demonstrated pain. The freedom of the consent may be doubted.[6] Upsurges in witch-hunting inevitably brought opportunities for those who could convince local Kirk sessions and Presbyteries that they were adept in detecting witches. Following his pricking of a suspect named Janet Coutts in Peebles, she confessed to witchcraft and accused some eighty others. But the Kirk authorities were unconvinced by the speed of proceedings and Cathie was ordered to appear before his home Presbytery of Haddington. He failed to appear and only did so when threated with the magistrate, and in May 1650 he was accused of striking some sort of deal with Coutts 'so that he might get his implyment'. This he denied and the matter was taken no further even though he was due to be sent to another Presbytery. Coutts was still executed, though those she accused were exonerated.[7]

The most notorious Scottish witch-pricker was John Kincaid.[8] He came from Tranent, East Lothian, where he conducted most of his early business, and there is scant details about his life though he was advanced in years when he found his witch-pricking vocation. Despite illiteracy, he soon convinced authorities he could detect witches by examination. An early notice of his activity was in summer 1649 when he was summoned to prick two people at Dirleton Castle, North Berwick – Patrick Watson and his wife, Menie Haliburton.[9] Interestingly, these subjects had asked that Kincaid prick them, 'of their awin frie will uncompellit', possibly believing that Kincaid would find nothing and they would be freed. In his testimony to local officials, Kincaid swore that he had found incriminating marks near the left shoulders of both man and wife, 'whairof thay wer not sensible, neither cam furth thairof any bloode after I had tried the samin as exactlie as ever I did any uthers'.[10] The couple were executed.

Kincaid's name afterwards appeared fairly frequently in trial records. He was mainly active in Lothian, but sometimes employed in more distant areas. He worked in Aberdeenshire and was even hired in Newcastle in 1649, which suggests that his reputation had built up for a considerable period and spread to the north of England. He enjoyed the same sort of professional mobility as the most elite, sought after charmers. Kincaid's services were rewarded well, though they were not without controversy. When he declared that the marks on a woman named Barbara Cochrane were witch's marks in front of magistrates, she angrily proclaimed him a deceptive liar, suggesting that Kincaid had been paid by her to prove her innocence. She had voluntarily submitted to examination, stating she would be content to admit to being a servant of Satan if any incriminating mark was found on her. The same year, 1659, he was prominent in examining many of the eighteen people executed for witchcraft in East Lothian.

He seems to have been particularly busy in this part of his career, the earliest recorded, in 1649–50. On 2 September 1649 Kincaid was in the village of Stow, Midlothian, swearing before the Kirk session that he had examined a man named Harrison and his wife and found evidence that both were 'great witches'. The minister and elders awarded him £6 Scots for 'brodding' or pricking another suspect, Margaret Dunholme, and Kincaid and his entourage were awarded more money for food and drink. Apart from the lucrative monetary reward for his expertise, Kincaid also gained official recognition in some places, such as Forfar, where his efforts were rewarded with the freedom of the burgh in 1661.

Around the same time the Kirk session of Corstorphine had him examine two female witches. He found two on one woman, to the satisfaction of the session, but the Presbytery was unsure and had the two women pricked anew in the presence of their ministers. On this occasion, Kincaid's efforts did not provide satisfaction. The women 'cryed pitifully and the place qr the prins were put in uped with blood a little'. In the summer of the following year he was operating much further north, at Brechin in Angus, where he examined a witch named Catharine Walker and found incriminating marks on her. The same year he found the marks on a witch in Selkirkshire, in the Borders.[11]

There are some hints that authorities, both secular and religious, were watchful about the integrity of the witch-finders and considered them at best a regrettable necessity. In 1661, a minister and magistrate, who had called him in to examine Janet Cock, warningly 'charged the said Johne, vpon his great oath, to goe about his office faithfullie, and to do nothing theirin but what sould be of trueth'.[12] Kincaid performed as expected and found two suspect marks on the woman, which did not bleed even after his pin was removed and the open wound remained visible.

Kincaid was accused of cruelty in his dealings and was sought for arrest by the Privy Council in January 1662. When asked, he claimed that his skills were simple and could be mastered by anyone. He claimed that he could recognise the marks of the guilty by sight and that he gained some of his knowledge from witches themselves. He was a prisoner a few months later, but after an appeal he was able to claim that he was elderly and so ill that he would die soon. He was released after nine weeks' incarceration, on condition of giving £1000 as bail and swearing that he would not take part in any unauthorised torture or pricking of witches. The huge sum evidences his earnings from his shadowy trade. One further intriguing accusation against Kincaid was laid in April 1662 by a young vagabond named James Welch, who accused Kincaid of meeting with the Devil at the muir brae in Tranent.[13] Welch's claims do not seem to have been taken seriously. He was himself released after some time in prison.

Six years later, John Kincaid's pupil, David Cowan, was similarly brought to justice, having been complained against by an accused witch, Catherine Liddill, who said that she had been foully tortured by him, pricked multiple times until her body bled profusely and her whole body swelled up.[14] She was declared innocent and freed. Cowan was detained at the Privy Council's pleasure. The same chicanery had been practised by other witch-finders. In August 1661 the Privy Council ordered the arrest of 'an ordinary pricker of witches, to answer for the pricking of Margaret Tait, who immediately thereafter died'. Some control was imposed on the activities of prickers. In 1679, David Cowane, a drummer from Tranent, was allowed to use pricking only on licence from the Privy Council.

The notoriety of Scottish witch-prickers even crossed the Atlantic, highlighted by the New England Puritan, Increase Mather, in the late seventeenth century. His account is revealing on the malign reputation

Scottish witch-prickers had gained, even among those who ardently believed in the reality and danger of witchcraft.

> I have heard of an enchanted Pin that, has caused the Condemnation and Death of many scores of Innocent persons. There was a notorious *Witchfinder* in *Scotland*, that undertook by a Pin, to make an Infallible discovery of suspected persons... If when the Pin was run an Inch or two into the Body of the Accused party, no blood appeared, nor any sense of Pain, then he declared them to be Witches. By means hereof my Author tells me no less than 300 persons were Condemned for witches in that Kingdom. This Bloody Jugler after he had done enough in *Scotland*, came to the town of *Berwick* upon *Tweed*. An honest man… saw the man thrust a great Brasse Pin two inches in the body of one … The Accused Party was not in the least sensible of what was done... Only is so happened, that Collonel Fenwick…was then the Military Governour of that Town. He sent for the Mayor and Magistrates… [and] he told them it might be an Inchanted Pin, which the Witch-finder made use of. Whereupon the…ordered that he should make his Experiment with some other Pin as they should appoint. But that he would by no means be induced unto, which was a sufficient Discovery of the Knavery of the Witch-finder.[15]

The method of using a retractable pin to fool witnesses and condemn witches seems widespread. A further account from the north of England concerning a Scottish witch-pricker relates how, in 1649 or 1650, two officials from Newcastle invited a Scottish witch-pricker to the town, promising him twenty shillings for each witch he uncovered. A bell-man went through the streets asking for people to report witches and around thirty women were brought to the town hall, stripped, and examined by the Scot. Most of them were denounced by him, but his efforts to condemn one woman were disputed by a local official. He then went into Northumberland and was paid to discover more witches. A suspicious member of parliament tried to pursue him, but he escaped into Scotland. However, the law there caught up with him and he was condemned to death. He confessed on the gallows that he had caused the death of 120 women for twenty shillings a piece, and begged forgiveness. All of which makes for a good tale, if it's true.[16]

Towards the end of the seventeenth century, some legal officials voiced doubt about the validity of witch-prickers and other fundamental aspects of witchcraft as a whole. Sir John Lauder, Lord Fountainhall, the judge and commentator, expressed misgivings about witchcraft trials. In particular, he railed against the testimony of witches transforming into the shape of various animals. In one case in Haddington a woman confessed and accused five other women and men of witchcraft. Lauder witnessed the man examined and tested by pricking. The examiner was hardly professional in his business, as Lauder remarked: 'I remained very unclear and dissatisfied with this way of trial, as most fallacious: and the man could give me no accompt of the principles of his art, but seemed to be a drunken, foolish rogue'.[17]

The advocate, Sir George Mackenzie, was equally disparaging of the witch-pricker profession, stating:

> This mark is discovered amongst us by a Pricker, whose Trade it is, and who learns it as other Trades, but this is a horrid cheat … there are many pieces of dead flesh which are insensible, even in living bodies: And a Villain who used this Trade with us, being in the year 1666 apprehended for other villanies, did confess all this trade to be a meer cheat.[18]

Some mystery remains about the medical aspect of the witch-pricker's 'art'. Not all prickers used a retractable pin to fool the authorities. And those who employed genuinely intrusive pins and knives to probe suspects did not exclusively violate victims via moles and similar points on the body which were known to be insensible to pain. The mystery of why so many suspected witches did not react in agony to being prodded has never been satisfactorily resolved, though expertise on behalf of the prickers and shame, shock and the wish of victims to get the legalised ritual over as quickly as possible may have been factors.[19]

Beyond the basic motivation of witch-finders for monetary gain, plus influence in the community and power over individuals, some of course had a sexual motivation for the intimate examination and torture of captive subjects. One of the most extraordinary examples of a witch-finder within this category found a geographical gap in the market. In March 1662, a Mr Paterson, known as the Pricker, came to Inverness. This witch-hunter was already widely renowned and had 'run over the kingdom for triall off witches'. Like other prickers, Mr Paterson employed a long brass pin, but habitually ensured that the suspects were stripped naked, rubbing the witches all over, then inserting the pin somewhere and challenging the suspect to guess where it had been inserted. Paterson was active in Elgin, Forres and Inverness. In the parish of Wardlaw, Inverness-shire, Paterson abused and pricked fifteen suspects (including one man). Several of these died in prison before coming to trial.

We are told the extraordinary truth about Paterson by one seventeenth-century commentator: 'This villain gaind a great deale off mony, haveing two servants; at last was discovered to be a woman disguised in mans cloathes. Such cruelty and rigure was sustained by a vile varlet imposture'.[20]

John Paterson was born Christian Caddell (or Caldwell) in north Fife, and seems to have decided to pursue a career as a witch-finder in the Lowlands under the name of John Dick or Dickson. In this guise she travelled into the Highlands and examined a 60-year-old named John Hay, a messenger in Tain, who had been accused of being a wizard by a woman. Without any authority, Dick pricked the man all over his body and even shaved his head in order to ascertain whether any witch marks were there. Hay was transported the considerable distance to the tolbooth in Edinburgh. But he was eventually freed, along with two accused women.[21] Hay's complaint put the authorities on the trail of Dickson, but the pursued woman had changed her name to Paterson and moved on, still pursuing the same business. Christian Caldwell was arrested and sentenced to transportation to Barbados in May 1663 and disappears from history. Women prickers had been known at an earlier date in England, when they had operated openly without any censure. Half a dozen women prickers were employed in one location in England in 1579.[22]

Some of the godly Covenanters were ardent seekers of arcane knowledge from sources which would have been condemned as witchcraft, if those sources themselves had not convinced society that they received divine revelation from God and not from Satan. The woman seer, Janet Douglas, was a divinely inspired seer in the 1670s, and notable 'fanatical' Protestants openly consulted with her.[23] Douglas was a native of the Hebrides who professed second sight and gained fame while still a child, seeking out objects made by witches. She travelled to Glasgow alone at the age of 11 and caused such a commotion that she had to be taken into protective custody. Her subsequent move to Edinburgh was similarly chaotic and sparked the authorities to investigate her talents. She survived the attention and allegedly escaped to the West Indies. Beside Douglas, there was a substantial cohort of women prophetesses who had an ardent male audience and who were at the forefront of resistance to the state's campaign against the legacy of the Covenanters.[24] Despite all this repeated evidence of fakery and controversy, the synod of Glasgow were still considering letting prickers try to find insensible spots on suspect witches as late as 1699.

Prophecy became a byproduct of belief among some of the elect and famous visionaries that became numerous in the ranks of the Covenanters, and among those renowned for their supernatural foresight were Alexander Peden and Donald Cargill, plus many others. It was not unheard of for ordained ministers in the mainstream of the Church of Scotland to be seers themselves, or to have had encounters with the supernatural. Even those outside these categories could be readily prone to the same sort of superstitions which they heartily derided their congregations for. The Reverend John Logan readily believed that a Highland woman went without food for seventeen years. The Reverend John Stewart credited the marvel of a tree which would never grow leaves after a man had been hanged on it. Another Highland priest averred the reality of signs, apparitions, strange sights which presaged wars and upheaval. The minister and writer, Robert Wodrow, credulously described a range of quasi miraculous and supernatural incidents associated with his fellow divines, all of which were under the cloak of reformed Christian piety.[25]

Some ministers were reputed to be active seers themselves and did nothing to disguise their supernatural abilities, usually accepted by themselves and their followers as being inspired by God and not by Satan. Several Protestant divines decided that this power to view future events was mediated by angels, despite the general Protestant disdain for this class of supernatural being. This substratum of priestly visionaries could possibly cite saintly precedence in towering antecedents like St Columba. Examples of ministers having this power extended into the eighteenth century, suggesting the urge to find deeper sources of spiritual knowledge was not merely a reaction to perceived persecution by the state.

Christian visionaries flourished in the seventeenth and into the eighteenth centuries, with ample evidence that these men, and women also, sincerely believed their visions were divinely inspired. Although some may have been persecuted, it was mainly on the basis of the beliefs of the sects they belonged to, rather than as possible witches. Lachlan Mackenzie and Ninian MacVicar are just two of the ministers who had access to otherworldly knowledge. The aura of some of the most successful Scottish ministers not only ensured full congregations, but left some kirks overflowing with people. Certain preachers had carefully cultivated reputations like Old Testament prophets and stories of their seerdom abounded. Some of these priests heard voices, both heavenly and otherwise, saw the future and even performed deeds which could be interpreted as miracles.

Not that all the priestly powers were redemptive or joyful. The Reverend John Welch, son-in-law of John Knox, once had an unhappy listener display displeasure at his preaching by throwing a loaf at him. This man, Philip Stainfield, was later convicted of murdering his father, and his death on the scaffold was believed to have been pre-empted by his sacrilegious treatment of the holy man years before.[26] When a Catholic mocked his religious speech at a dinner party held at Edinburgh Castle, Welch told those present to observe the 'profane mocker'. The man fell down below the table and immediately perished. Another time, when Welch criticised Episcopalian ministers, one of their number, Patrick Galloway, died and Welch got the credit (or blame) for his death. But his magic worked both ways. A story is told of how Welch, when in France, exhorted God to save the life of a fellow Scotsman who had apparently died. His friends believed that the young man had fallen into a deep coma and had doctors try every technique they could think of to rouse him. It was only when the minister intervened that the man finally woke up. If it was not actually raising a man from the dead, it was the next best thing.[27] John Welch had times when he was surrounded by the sort of beatific glory which is most associated with popish saints whom he would have ardently despised. Once the holy man was seen by someone walking in his garden, suffused by a heavenly, saintly light, and muttering words of spiritual ecstasy to unseen angelic beings around him.

Conspicuous figures in sixteenth-century Scotland had occasionally been accused of witchcraft or diablery for political purposes, and this was repeated in the following century. Archbishop James Sharpe of St Andrews gained eternal opprobrium for deserting the Presbyterian cause and becoming a bishop. Due to his part in persecuting Covenanting Presbyterian hardliners who refused to accept the Episcopalian imposition under the restoration of Charles II, in May 1679, nine religious hardliners ambushed Sharpe's coach on Magus Muir in Fife and murdered him. A rather crude and imprecise rumour credited Sharpe with entertaining 'the black muckle deil' in his study and that he had levitated and performed other dark feats.

Discovered on his body after his assassination was said to have been a parchment spell in Hebraic or Chaldean script, an accusation bandied about other discredited figures. Also discovered on the corpse, allegedly, was a pair of pistol balls, a piece of silk, some nail clippings, and a small tobacco box containing a live bumble bee, which his murderers believed to be his familiar. Accusations against high-profile clergymen, especially those of different sects, was nothing new in Scotland, naturally. In the sixteenth century, smears of supernatural activity had been levelled against the controversial Patrick Adamson, Bishop of St Andrews, who consulted three witches, according to rumour, and who attracted the opprobrium not just of Presbyterian rivals but also lay figures like the poet Robert Sempill.

Another of the most renowned second-sighted priests was the Reverend John Morrison, who ministered near Inverness from 1749 to his death in 1774. The Petty Seer, as he was called, could foretell events and could also see current actions happening at a remote distance from his own location. His prophecies were as widespread and believed in the Highlands, for many years, as the Brahan Seer's. Other clerics were reputed to have wandered into the camp of mankind's enemy. The minister of St Andrews, Reverend Robert Blair, came to the rescue of a young ministerial candidate who fell into a state of melancholy because he was struggling with his studies. Walking near the town one day he encountered a man dressed like a cleric who gave him an excellent sermon to present, but in turn made him sign a contract in blood. When the gullible man informed Blair, who at once realised the cleric was Satan, the student was overcome with terror. All the ministers of the Presbytery took him to an isolated kirk and prayed. While the whole church violently shook, the minister prayed and the youth's 'paper and covenant' fell down from the ceiling and he was free of his association with the Devil.[28]

The culture of visions and wonder was deeply embedded in Covenanter culture, whether it was ascribing external events such as the Great Fire of London to God's revenge on the English for denigrating pure Scottish religion, or summoning up miraculous portends which presaged disastrous events such as the Battle of Bothwell Brig in 1679, when militant Covenanters were dispersed by a government army.

The resonance of the supernatural side of the Covenanters during the period of their persecution stretch far into the nineteenth century. Hugh Miller spoke admiringly of the recondite atmosphere of Scotland in those days, when a sort of 'wild machinery of the supernatural was added to

1. Fresco showing possible image of Michael Scot tearing pages from a book. Is he destroying blasphemy or holy writ?

2. Ritual magician summoning a devil.

3. St Andrews. Scene of early witchcraft executions.

4. Enemy of witches (and of his sister Mary, Queen of Scots), James Stewart, Earl of Moray, regent of Scotland.

DAEMONOLO
GIE, IN FORME
of a Dialogue,

Diuided into three Bookes.

EDINBVRGH

Printed by Robert Walde-graue

Printer to the Kings Majeſtie. An. 1597.

Cum Privilegio Regio.

5. *Daemonologie*, the work of King James VI.

6. Botriphnie, Banffshire, home of the healer Andro Man.

Above: **7.** Elf Hillock, Botriphnie, where Andro Man first encountered the Elphen Queen.

Left: **8.** Memorial of William Shaw, Dunfermline Abbey. Master of Works to James VI and codifier of early freemasonry.

9. John Napier of Merchiston, scientist, mathematician, reputed magician.

10. The old tolbooth, Edinburgh, where many witches were confined.

11. A wizard's army. Scottish Highland mercenaries under Donald Duibheal Mackay in the Baltic.

12. Ritual of allegiance. Kissing the Devil's rear.

13. Sir George Mackenzie. Royalist, writer and eminent lawyer, and an opponent of witch hunting excesses.

14. Illustration from Richard Bovet's *Pandæmonium*.

15. The home of Major Weir, West Bow, Edinburgh, which remained unoccupied for decades after his death.

16. Dark transport. Major Weir's spectral coach careering through Edinburgh, long after his execution.

Above: **17.** Witches condemned at Newcastle, identified by a Scottish witch pricker.

Right: **18.** The unidentified witch-pricker takes recompense for his work at Newcastle.

Above: **19.** Edinburgh from Calton Hill, scene of the adventures of the Fairy Boy of Leith.

Left: **20.** Man or beast? The Laird o' Lag transformed into a monster in the public imagination.

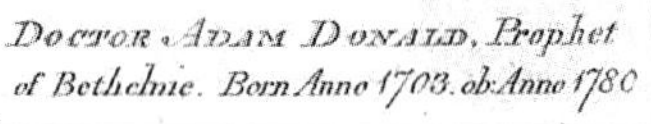

Right: **21.** Adam Donald, Prophet of Bethelnie.

Below: **22.** Humorous English view of the fearsome water kelpie.

Left: **23.** The Sabbat. Imaginary meeting or commonplace gathering?

Below: **24.** The other Major Weir. The 'jackanape' familiar of the dead Laird of Redgauntlet.

the commoner aspects of a living Christianity. The men in whom it was exhibited were seers of visions and dreamers of dreams ... they looked far into the world of spirits and had at times their strange glimpses of the distant and the future'.[29]

Among the wonders seen before Bothwell Brig was a shower of swords and bonnets which fell in Glasgow and a tumult of falling headgear and weapons descending near Lanark, as well as a phantom army marching in the sky. None of the visionaries, or those who remarked upon them, believed such things were satanically inspired.[30]

At a more everyday level, many devout Christians in Scotland practised using the Bible for prophetic purposes, selecting passages at random in order to gauge the future. The ritual was used not only by ill-educated peasants, but also by men of standing, such as Sir Archibald Johnston of Wariston, one of the signatories of the National Covenant in 1638. Other apparently God-fearing Kirk men indulged in other superstitious activities. In 1619, former Kirk elder and provost, Alexander Peblis, was censured for riddell-turning to look into the future. This method of divination, spinning a sieve of the point of shears, was useful for reading the future and also for locating lost goods.

Also actively acquainted with the byways of the Otherworld were those Covenanters persecuted in the 'Killing Time' of the late seventeenth century. As Wodrow and others documented, dozens of condemned Covenanters made wild prophesies connected to the ultimate triumph of their own righteousness while on the scaffold. So common was the occurrence that the authorities took to having drum rolls played to drown out the predictions. The extent to which persecution heightened religious fervour and incidentally gave rise to seership among extreme Protestants at this time is a fertile line of enquiry. Royalists were quick to link the heightened spirituality of Covenanters with witchcraft.

Another man whose reputation has survived to the present is Sir George Mackenzie of Rosehaugh (1636–1691). As an eminent legal official he had an important impact on the national attitude towards witchcraft, reflective of the changing national attitude towards the supernatural. Despite his well-articulated scepticism of individual instances of witchcraft and disparagement of the brutal methods of witch-prickers, Mackenzie did believe in the existence of witchcraft. Moreover, for a major part of Scotland he was a Royalist bogeyman, who gained an evil reputation and reputed black magical abilities through his ardent persecution of Covenanters and others who denied the authority of the Crown.[31] Mackenzie was Lord Advocate of Scotland from 1677 to 1686 and, during his tenure, generally discouraged witchcraft prosecutions.

But there is still a question of his complicity in prosecutions during an earlier period, 1661–3, when he was one of three Justice Deputes active in the Lothian circuit in burghs around Edinburgh, and there was an active witchcraft panic in the country.[32] Mackenzie is on record complaining of his poor recompense in his role of killing hundreds of people (some of them presumably witches), compared with the rewards given to soldiers who had killed just a few.[33] The Justice Deputes were encouraged towards severity by being promised a share of the 'fines and escheats' of those they found guilty.

Mackenzie's rise in his legal career occurred soon after the national trauma of an English invasion of Scotland and the absorption of the country into the Commonwealth. Despite their own depredations in the northern territory, some of the invaders were horrified by the barbarity of Scottish zeal in pursuing witches. In one case, in October 1652, English judges had ordered the minister, sheriff and tormentor to be found out, and to have an account on the ground of their cruelty. They had hung women up by their heels, whipped them, and tortured them with lit candles.[34] It could hardly have been an isolated incident. A great witch-hunt erupted in Scotland between 1658 and 1662, following on the end of the Commonwealth and English rule, plus an upsurge in hardline Calvinistic religious fervour.

Mackenzie's own attitude to witchcraft was nuanced, as might be expected from an intellectual and a lawyer. First of all, he did not deny the existence of witches as a class. 'I am not of their opinion, who deny that there are Witches', he wrote, 'though I think them not numerous; and though I believe that some are suffer'd by providence, to the end that the being of Spirits may not be deny'd.' He also admitted the possible powers of charming by witches, comparing those who deny it with those rivals who might persecute doctors or mathematicians on the basis that their superior knowledge looks like witchcraft, only because they cannot comprehend it.[35] Mackenzie (as well as others) did rail against the blatant abuses practised by some witch-prickers and gave some instances of the injustices suffered by some of those accused as witches, particularly women. He noted that those accused of witchcraft were 'poor ignorant creatures and oft-times women who understand not the crime they are accused of; and many mistake their own fears and apprehensions for witchcraft'. Then he cites two examples of that class of victim. One was an old male weaver who, when asked how he saw Satan, answered, 'like flies dancing about the candle'. The other was a woman who asked her persecutors innocently, 'if a woman might be a witch and not know it'.[36] His findings chime well with other examples. A man who came before the court in Edinburgh in 1652 claimed to have spoken with the Devil many times, who gave him a piece of silver, which he put into a crevice of his neighbour's wall, causing all his cattle and horses to die, and eventually her. He had been given a new name by Satan and had slept with Satan too in the form of a woman. Most people thought his tales unbelievable and he retracted his confession. As the anonymous author of *Diurnal of Occurrences* remarked:

> The truth is, he lived in so poor a condition, and was through his simplicity so unable to get a livellyhood, that he confessed, or rather said any thing that was put into his head, by some that first accused him upon the confession of some who have died for witches. By this you may guess upon what ground many hundreds have heretofore been burnt in this country for witches.[37]

The cases that Mackenzie detailed highlight the fact that Scottish prosecutors could and did insist on the death penalty for those who practised what many may have seen as charming, with no malevolent intent.

> Drummond was burnt as a Witch, albeit he had never committed any malefice, but had only cured such as were diseased, yet having in a long habit and tract of time, abused the people, and used Spells and Incantations, which had no relation at all to Devotion.

This, according to Mackenzie, may him fully culpable. The second case he mentions also highlighted subtle guilt, which was rightly punished. John Burgh was guilty of pretending to cure all diseases, by throwing into water an unequal number of pieces of money, and sprinkling the patients with the water, 'so that it may be justly said, that these died rather for being publick cheats…then for being Witches'.[38]

Alexander Drummond was executed in 1629. John Burgh or Brughe in the end was condemned in 1643. Like others, Brughe enjoyed a long career before his end, being active as a healer for thirty-six years. He was also said to have use a magical stone the size of a pigeon's egg to cure patients, which he advised sick patients to immerse in drinks. The ostentatious details of Brughe digging up bodies in order to perform rituals was doubtless invented by his prosecutors. (Another healer accused of exhuming bodies for the purposes of ritual practice was Patrick Lowrie of Ayrshire.) Brughe was made to confess that he encountered Satan, along with others, three times in the kirkyard of Glendevon:

> at quhilkis tymes ther was taine vp thrie several dead corps, ane of them being of ane seruand man named John Chrystiesone; the vther corps tane vp at the kirk of Muckhart: the flesch of the quhilk corps was put abone the byre and stable-dure headis' of certain enemies in order to destroy their cattle.[39]

As Lord Advocate, Mackenzie seems to have had some effect on dampening the appetite for prosecuting witches. He criticised the obvious cruel and amateurish practices of prickers and railed against the use of torture against suspects. He also frowned upon the fact that commissions to try witches were most often granted to gentlemen and lairds in the localities where the suspects lived, men who had insufficient knowledge of the intricacies of supernatural criminality. Nor did the defendants have anyone pleading for them. Mackenzie also disputed some of the common claims cited in trials about the marvels reported of witches; particularly that the Devil was able to change into animal form. He recalled visiting a wretched woman who, being accused of witchcraft, knew that she would have starved if she regained her freedom, for all would have turned against her, and there would not even be lodging for her, so the best option she could choose was confessing guilt and guaranteeing her own death.

Beyond his professional and intellectual interest in witchcraft, George Mackenzie was a representative of the Crown and he was instrumental in upholding law and order against what he saw as the disloyalty of the militant Cameronians and other Calvinists who failed to accept the authority of the Stuart monarchy over them. Actions against these recalcitrant religious groups involved military action, harassment, legal measures against their religious gatherings, and sometimes execution. Little wonder that Mackenzie and other conspicuous figures in power were stigmatised as oppressive monsters.

Following the fall of the Stuart monarchy, Mackenzie retired from Scotland and went first to Oxford, dying in London in May 1691. His supposedly agonising death was gleefully foretold by the visionary Scottish divine Donald Cargill, and was seen as God's just punishment for his sinful oppression. His remains were brought back to Scotland and he was laid to rest in Greyfriars Kirkyard in Edinburgh, the internment attended by 'a greater concourse of people than was ever seen on any similar occasion'. However, the reputation of the great man continued to be derailed by his supposed intolerance long after the significance of the religious controversies faded away from Scotland. Walter Scott portrayed him among a ghostly assortment of other persecutors of the people in 'Wandering Willie's Tale' (from *Redgauntlet* –1824), as 'The Bluidy Advocate MacKenzie, who, for his worldly wit and wisdom, had been to the rest as a god'. A curious legend also surrounded the Lord Advocate's physical remains. There is a story that, even before his coffin was laid to rest in Greyfriars, the coffin began to move, its occupant being post-mortem uncomfortable at being placed so near to a prison where many Covenanters were jailed. In the nineteenth century it was common for local schoolchildren to taunt each other into approaching the still-feared Mackenzie mausoleum to ridicule the restless lawyer with the chant:

> Bluidy Mackenzie, come oot if ye daur!
> Lift the sneck and draw the bar!

By rights, the remnant of ill-feeling which polluted the Lord Advocate's reputation should have faded well before the modern age, as Mackenzie was all but forgotten, but in the 1980s and 1990s a legend sprung up around his mausoleum in Greyfriars. According to rumour, there were reports that people had suffered bruises, scratches, and even bite marks near Mackenzie's grave, and one person was even knocked unconscious. The most extraordinary tale is that an itinerant broke into the mausoleum in 1998 in the hope of finding secreted treasure there. However the floor collapsed beneath him and he ended up in the less than pleasant surroundings of a plague pit. Whether this actually happened or not is uncertain. In 2003, two teenagers entered the mausoleum and broke into the coffin, then played with Mackenzie's skull. They were apparently given probation. A book written about supposed supernatural activity centred around the mausoleum terms the phenomenon 'the Mackenzie Poltergeist', and seems to blame the occurrences on the late Sir George Mackenzie, about whom it has no good thing to say.[40]

Chapter 5

Major Weir

Considering the landscape of historical characters associated with the supernatural in Scotland, Major Thomas Weir casts a grotesquely large shadow and also presents some problems. Much of his story is mired in legend, a process which enveloped him very soon after his death, and there is little evidence that he was, either in reality or by accusation, involved in witchcraft or magical practice. His story was initially popularised in Sinclair's *Invisible World Discovered*, published in 1685, fifteen years after Weir's execution.[1]

Weir was a military man, active in the 10,000 strong Covenanter army sent from Scotland to Ulster in 1642 in response to a Catholic uprising in which a thousand settler Protestants were slaughtered. He was commissioned in Colonel Robert Home's Regiment for nineteen months, but there is little record of him in this campaign, which was part of a convoluted war involving multiple military factions, none of which achieved decisive victory. He was also, equally obscurely, involved in the civil wars in his native country, serving in south-west Scotland. Retiring from the military, the middle-aged Weir migrated to Edinburgh and embedded himself with the establishment there and became captain of the city guard. In this capacity he was overseer of the imprisoned talisman of the Royalist cause, James Graham, Marquis of Montrose.

Weir's staunch ultra-Protestantism and adherence to the tenets of the National Covenant made him one of the most conspicuous members of that sect in the Capital. He was one of the 'Bowhead Saints', a reference to a coterie of strict Calvinists in that neighbourhood of Edinburgh. Although Weir was a solemn and sanctified presence at any suitable religious gathering, those inclined to admire the major sometimes called him 'Angelical Thomas'.

The earliest account of Thomas Weir is contained in a manuscript written by the Reverend James Fraser, who first encountered him in 1660. Fraser writes that he was born in Clydesdale in 1607, and other sources confirm that the family was firmly middle class. Originally called the De Veres, the Weirs were of Norman origin and had a respectable prominence in Lanarkshire and other parts of west Scotland. Thomas's branch came from Kirkton, near Lanark, and were connected with various noble families in the district, and likely well enough respected, though his father was implicated in some minor scandal or social dispute locally.[2] There is no mention in any early source of Thomas Weir's early life, nor what career he pursued before soldiering. West and south-west Scotland particularly were breeding grounds for Presbyterian fervour through the seventeenth century, so it is hardly surprising that he became a man of conspicuously pious behaviour. Thomas's sister, Jean, (sometimes misnamed Grizzel), stated that their mother had been a witch, who had the shape of a horse shoe on her brow, as she had herself when she frowned. When she appeared like this, it gave her the power to know whatever secrets her family members might have at that time. Beyond her testimony, there is little beyond this to indicate that the Weir family background was inclined towards the supernatural.

After his retirement from the burgh guard, Thomas Weir presented a bleak image to most who encountered him. Fraser gives a forbidding and unflattering description: 'his garb was still a cleck [cloak] and somequhat dark, & never went without his staffe. He was a tall black man; & ordinarly looked down to the ground a grim Countenance and a bigg nose'.[3] There was no place in Weir's world-view to even acknowledge regular Presbyterians. When he passed a regular minister of the Kirk in the street, Weir would pull down his hat to obscure his view of the ungodly wretch.

Weir's position among the religious elect was ruined when both he and his sister confessed to various crimes of aberrant behaviour, and both were tried and executed in April 1670. The Major was drawn to the place of execution on a sled, being too infirm to walk because of his age. One contemporary notice of the deaths of the Weirs was John Lamont of Fife. He noted that Thomas was condemned for incest with his sister, plus bestiality. Although there is mention of his supernatural behaviour, he was not charged with witchcraft. He went to his death on 11 April, with the same icy indifference he had shown when incarcerated. When requested to ask for God's mercy on the scaffold, he replied, 'Let me alone. I will not. I have lived as a beast and I must die as a beast'. But he was pressed to comply, and after reluctantly requesting mercy, he supposedly muttered, 'And now what better am I?' before being strangled.

His sister died the following day, and presented a contrast to her brother's extreme apathy, according to one contemporary diarist:

> On the scafold shie cast away hir mantell, hir gown tayle, and was purposed…to caft of all hir clothes before all the multitude; bot Baylie Oliphant, to whom the businese was intrusted, stoped the same, and commanded the execwtioner to doe his office. Bot whille he was abowt to throw hir ovir the leather, shie smote the execwtioner on the cheike; and hir hands not being tyed when shie was throwen ovir, slie labored to recover hir selfe, and put in hir head betwixt two of the steps of the leather…[4]

Most of the charges against her came from her own confession. When she was keeping school at Dalkeith, a woman came to Jean and asked her to intercede with, or perhaps battle with, the Queen of Fairies on her behalf. The next day another woman came to her and gave her a root or piece of tree which would give her all she desired. Another woman enjoined this first woman to spread a cloth at her door and perform a ritual with her which was designed to resolve all their troubles. She encountered the Queen of Fairies, who gave her the ability to spin a remarkable amount of yarn. This collusion with the two other women hints at Jean's involvement with an active group of other witches, but the record does not elaborate on their activity beyond this. Thomas Weir's scant magical activities, if there were any, seem to have been conducted alone. There is little mention in Jean's confession regarding any malefice or magical working.[5] As with her brother Thomas, there is little biographical information about Jean Weir, though one source states that she was married.[6] It is interesting that the justiciary record hints there was relatively little legal interest in her relations regarding witchcraft, albeit she was willing to say more about this, unlike her brother.

The English author, George Hickes, penned an account of Weir, published in 1678.[7] In a work primarily devoted to James Mitchell, a fanatic preacher and an acquaintance of Weir, who was executed in January 1678 for the attempted murder of Archbishop James Sharpe, Hickes portrays Weir as a callous persecutor of cavaliers, hounding them even on the brink of their executions. It was notoriously known that Weir distinguished himself with vindictiveness against the imprisoned Montrose before his execution on 21 May 1650. A barrage of personal verbal abuse was accompanied by a spiteful programme of keeping him awake and filling his prison cell with smoke. Montrose kept his composure and was widely admired for his dignified manner of death. The contrast to Weir, who sullenly met the same fate twenty years later, was marked.

To Hickes, Weir was a relentless religious bigot and hypocrite who had a prodigious memory for biblical text, which outdid even legitimate preachers. In Hickes's account, Major Weir in his old age became troubled by conscience and confessed his sins to members of his own sect. But they refused his plea to bring him to wider justice because of the scandal it would cause. The root of his mental trouble had become evident a year before his confession, when he had fallen ill in his home and the sickness made him speak to everyone who visited him like an angel.[8] Later, after confession, he became indifferent to his fate. This collapse in will was possibly the last effects of some mental illness. He veered between lethargy and firm assurance that he was damned. The only human connection he could summon up was used to torture himself with guilt about being the cause of a country girl being whipped. She had seen him commit an act of bestiality with his own horse and reported him to a minister, who did not believe her and had had her punished by being whipped through the streets of Lanark by the hangman. The woman was a witness at his execution, at the Gallow Lee between Edinburgh and Leith.[9]

After some months the ministers who first examined the major confided in Sir Andrew Ramsay, Lord Provost of Edinburgh, who thought Weir's senses were disordered and sent him medical support. After some ministers were sent to examine Weir, both he and his sister were taken to prison. Thomas Weir was charged with incest with his sister, a maid servant, and also with his own step-daughter, Margaret Bourden (although some sources state he was never married). This abuse began while his wife was still alive and continued after her death. When Margaret became pregnant, Weir married her off to an Englishman.[10] Among the witnesses to this relationship was Thomas and Jean's sister, Margaret. Weir was also accused of adultery with married women, including an affair with Bessie Wemyss which endured twenty-two years. Further, Thomas had committed bestiality with mares and cows.[11] The picture of the major's personal and family history is patchy. Like the little we know about his upbringing, his wife (possibly a widow surnamed Mein) and the sister who testified against him are similarly unfamiliar. Towards the end of his life he seems to have lived alone, though his sister Jean possibly lived nearby.

Jean Weir was charged with incest and witchcraft and consulting with witches and devils. It was alleged she kept a familiar spirit. While Thomas readily confessed the sins of the flesh, he was more circumspect about contact with supernatural agencies, stating at first that he had seen the Devil in the dark. He went on to admit that he had slept with Satan in the form of a beautiful woman.[12] The most sensational aspects of confession came from Jean rather than Thomas. She stated that she and her brother had travelled to Musselburgh on 7 September 1648 in a coach and six horses that were all ablaze, and the Devil told the major that the Scots army had been defeated at Preston. Jean did not believe it when she was informed that her brother was dead. She then insisted that he was now in company with a horde of devils. She blamed him for abusing her sexually from the age of 16 until she was 56, at which time he despised her for being old.[13] The trial record seems to infer, contrary to other accounts, that Thomas Weir first had sex with his sister when she was 10, and continued while she was growing up and into adulthood.

The proceedings against brother and sister caused a sensation far beyond Edinburgh. The official record notes that the proceedings were detailed at greater length than usual 'because the manner of their lives and deaths made a noise even in forreign nations as well as at home, they being looked upon by all as the greatest Hypocrites and most flagitious persons that had been for many years discovered in any nation'.[14] The moral decay that sexual crimes entailed may have made it a gateway in some cases to direct traffic with Satan. In 1628, a Berwickshire weaver named John McReadie was tried for having committed incest with both his mother and sister. Additionally, he was called 'ane ordinar practiser of sorcerie, witchecraft, charming and uthers devilish practises'.[15]

Soon after Weir's condemnation there was an upsurge of legend centred around him, providing an abundance of material for people who prefer history to be people with titillatingly picturesque and bizarre human aberrations. Even the earliest record of Weir's life, written by James Fraser, contains elements which read like folklore. Weir, it was said, had some precognitive fear of the word 'burn', so he was terrified when he met a man with that name and would not even step over the stream named Liberton Burn, fearing a foreshadow of the conflagration that awaited him.[16] A merchant's wife who had some contact with Weir before his death once saw three women cavorting in his window, then a loathsome giantess outside his house, 'moving her body with a vehement cachinnation and unmeasurable laughter'.[17]

Much of the myth of the major centred around his staff, that later legend insisted had a life of its own. His sister believed this potent magical weapon was the source of his power and often hid it away from him. George Hickes wrote:

> When they were seized, [Jean] desired the Guards to keep [Thomas] from laying hold on a certain Staff, which, she said, if he chanc'd to get into his hand, he would certainly drive they all out of doors, notwithstanding all the resistance they could make. The Magical Staff was all of one piece, with a crooked head of Thorn-wood, she said he received it of the Devil, and did many wonderful things with it; particularly that he used to lean upon it in his Hypocritical prayers, and after they were committed, she still desired it might be kept from him; because if her were Master of it again, he would certainly grow obdurate, and retract the Confessions which he had so publickly made.[18]

According to the Reverend James Fraser of Wardlaw, the black staff was cast into the fire with its owner and 'gave rare turnings, and was long a burning, as even himself'.[19] Edinburgh legend later had the staff perambulating night-time Edinburgh at its master's command.

Another post-mortem tradition of Major Weir involved the reputation of his house. His dark, ghostly figure haunted the property and no-one could be persuaded to live there for fifty years, though part of the building was used as a magazine for lint and a brazier's shop. Eventually a domestic tenant was found, 'a poor man of dissipated spirits' and ex-soldier named William Patullo, who was happy to find a property for his family at the ridiculously low rent which the landlord was asking. But he and his family only lasted a single night there. Lying in bed, Patullo saw the disconcerting spectral vision of a calf staring at him, which then vanished.[20] The disreputable structure was pulled down in 1878. That demolition may have finally laid the spirit of Major Weir in Edinburgh to rest, but the writer Andrew Lang informed William Roughead that the forms of Thomas Weir and his sister were seen in the neighbourhood of their Ayrshire home as late as 1909.[21]

Whether these were the old and corrupt forms that inhabited Edinburgh or their more forlorn youthful shades is not recorded.

For those who were opposed to the Covenanter creed, the major's downfall provided a wealth of ammunition against his co-religionists. Yet he still had supporters. A rumour spread that extremist Protestants had substituted someone resembling Weir to justice, and it was this unfortunate who was executed, while the real Weir, an anti-hero but still one of their own, escaped incognito to Holland and resided there among exiled Scots of like mind. Thomas and Jean's beliefs were not dimmed by death. At the place of execution, Jean Weir exhorted the crowd to adhere to the National Covenant.[22] In death Thomas Weir became, along with that other notable Edinburgh worthy, Deacon William Brodie (1741–1788), city councillor by day and burglar by night, a totem for the concept of duality within the psyche of Scotland.

Both figures fed into the classic Scottish works, *The Confessions of A Justified Sinner* by James Hogg (1824) and *The Strange Case of Dr Jekyll and Mr Hyde* by Robert Louis Stevenson (1886). Long before he began writing historical novels, Walter Scott pondered in 1798, 'I think I would choose Major Weir, if not for my hero, at least for an agent, and a leading one, in my production'.[23] Scott masterfully reassigned the name of Major Weir to the grotesquely sentient monkey, a 'great, ill-favoured jackanape' and 'cankered beast' which is the pet/familiar of the ghostly laird in 'Wandering Willie's Tale', the superb self-contained tale within *Redgauntlet* (1824).

Weir was a 'fine flower of dark and vehement religion' to Stevenson, who grew up with tales from his father of the fiery coach still careering through the capital's streets, drawn by six black horses with fiery eyes.[24] Robert Chambers described the dark carnival in more detail:

> His house … was sometimes observed at midnight to be full of lights, and heard to emit strange sounds, as of dancing, howling, and, what is strangest of all, spinning. Some people occasionally saw the major issue from the low close at midnight, mounted on a black horse without a head, and gallop oft' in a whirlwind of flame. Nay, sometimes the whole of the inhabitants of the Bow would be roused from their sleep at an early hour in the morning by the sound as of a coach and six, first rattling up the Lawnmarket, and then thundering down the Bow, stopping at the head of the terrible close for

a few minutes, and then rattling and thundering back again –
being neither more nor less than Satan come in one of his best
equipages to take home the major and his sister, after they had
spent a night's leave of absence in their terrestrial dwelling.[25]

Many writers have similarly pointed out the omnipresence of Satan in the first few generations of Protestant Scots after the Reformation. This oppressive mental and spiritual condition has been succinctly summarised by one recent historian. The 'emphasis on the innate susceptibility of humans to demonic wiles was central to how Reformed ministers throughout the seventeenth century conceptualized Satan'.[26] Michelle Brock has pointed out that some ministers went so far as to claim that humans were irredeemably linked with Satan and may even have a perverse, innate love for him. 'Many Scots espoused a remarkable obsession with personal depravity in connections with the actions of Satan.'[27] Given the insistent emphasis on damnation, it is laudable that so few ministers of religion themselves succumbed to darkness. One who did was George Sempill, a former preacher of Kilallen near Paisley, accused of being a 'bissie practizer and consulter in points of witchcraft' which was considered by the Privy Council in 1639.[28] Sempill was rumoured to have a book by Michael Scot in his possession. Worse still was Gideon Penman, minister at Crichton, who had been deposed from the ministry in 1675 following money troubles and accusations of adultery with a servant. Three years after that he was incarcerated in Edinburgh, accused of being a warlock. Among a group of eight or ten Lothian witches brought to the courts in September 1678, two or three swore that the cleric was an ally of Satan's, who was present at their meetings, 'and that when the devill called for him, he asked, wheir is Mr. Gideon my chaplain? and that ordinarly Mr. Gideon was in the reer in all their dances, and beat up thesse that ware flow'.[29] Penman however was not punished, but released and drifted into obscurity.

Satan lingered for a long time in Scottish life. In the Scottish iteration of the Great Awakening, a renewal of Christian fervour which swept through the western world from the late seventeenth century until the middle of the eighteenth, there were evident dark shadows. In outdoor events held at night, the preacher, George Whitfield, exhorted spellbound listeners on their damnable state and inspired visions and wonders in the mind of some, who imagined they were wrestling with demons or Satan himself. If the meetings were reminiscent of the conventicles of persecuted Covenanters held on the hills and moors not many generations before, to some there were also similarities with the dark sabbats of witches and warlocks. A group of worried ministers decried the huge meetings held at Cambuslang and elsewhere in 1742 as being from Satan. The suggestion was also made by others. The pent up emotions and hysteria displayed by some of the participants had much of the same ingredients as the behaviour seen during the period of witch hunts. Only now, the impetus for persecuting witches had been drained and would soon be outlawed by the law.[30]

In secular terms, Weir is one of the prime historical characters who might be cited as an example of the formerly fashionable concept of Scottish Antisyzygy, the warring duality of opposites within a single being. This idea has fallen from favour as being an overly simple designation which had connotations of savage/civilised equating to Celt/Saxon that seems overly simple in the modern world.

Chapter 6

Twilight People

Marginal Lives and the Modern Age

This chapter considers the currents of supernatural activity which persisted into the threshold of the modern era and, further back, those lifestyles which might have been analogous to magical activity. Some groups were always suspected of witchcraft and other sins. Gypsies, travellers, and tramps were repeatedly legislated against and persecuted. More affluent inquirers into the occult, however, could indulge in astrology, alchemy and academic study of magic without much fear of repercussions. Respected tradesmen and others could explore the recondite rituals of freemasonry, first codified by James VI's courtier William Shaw. The Scottish Enlightenment, which energised the intellectuals of the nation and dispelled antique thinking, did not immediately percolate to all parts of the country.

On the brink of the modern age, in the eighteenth century, there was a rare case of possession associated with possible witchcraft. In January 1720, Patrick Sandilands, the young, third son of James, 7th Lord Torphichen, was reportedly bewitched. After repeatedly falling into profound trances, he could not even be revived by horse whipping. His renal secretions were black as ink. Candles would go out when he was in a room and his whole body was sometimes thrown around by an unseen force. He was also able to tell his sisters of events that were happening at a distance. At other times, he would appear tormented by an unseen presence. When being watched by his tutor in bed one night, two strange flashes illuminated the night outside the window, a short time apart. The boy told the tutor that, between flashes, he had been transported to Torryburn, 20 miles away. The boy knew when his abductions would occur; it had happened before, he said. He was closely watched, and once his body rose in the air and he had to be lowered down.

Lord Torphichen put the blame on a supposed witch from Calder, and she in turn implicated two women and a man as accomplices. The ignorant woman readily admitted wicked practices, including giving her own child to Satan to make a roast of. She was believed by Torphichen, the minister and most people locally. A few decades earlier, they would have been condemned, but the only action against them was being questioned by the minister. Luckily, the extraordinary events around the boy quickly subsided and he re-entered normal life. He grew up to command a ship in the East India trade but was lost at sea.[1] Something strange may have transmitted in the family line. One former Lord Torphichen was notoriously reckoned a warlock. When a ferry sank in the Tweed and some lives were lost, it was said that the black crow seen sitting on the boat was actually Lord Torphichen.[2] While Torphichen's suspicions in this case were not fatal, he was instrumental as a member of the Privy Council who decided on the fate of brothers George and Lachlan Rattray of Inverness, who were executed for witchcraft in 1706.

The tale has superficial similarities with the tale of the Fairy Boy of Leith. The story of this nameless boy was first related in 1684,[3] in Richard Bovet's *Pandaemonium, or The Devil's Cloyster* (1684). An Englishman named Captain George Burton came to Leith on business and was introduced to a 10-year-old lad, who claimed that every Thursday night he consorted with a multitude of fairies beneath a hill between Leith and Edinburgh (likely Calton Hill). Here he played for them on his drum and also journeyed with them to France and Holland. Their underground realm was described as marvellous and huge. The boy, who had second sight also, told fortunes of people. He said that Burton would have two handsome wives and foretold a woman with him would have two bastards before she wed, which so enraged her she stormed off. The boy was watched on a Thursday night but managed to slip outside a house and vanished forever. Such young male human targets are perhaps related to the cases of older male mortal intermediaries with the fairies. Very few of these quasi-humans seem to have been women. We should also note that the vicinity of Calton Hill, anciently Craigengalt (or Crag Gayt), was a chosen site for the execution of witches. It was a semi-urban seat of the fairies similar to Tomnahurich in Inverness and many other smaller Otherworld portals throughout Scotland. There are also other examples of young boys being captivated (or captured) by the fairies, to the consternation of their mortal families. A notable later version was the boy of Borgue in Galloway, Johnny Williamson, who went missing for extended periods. His family resorted to begging a Catholic priest for a remedy, which worked, but drew upon them the fury of the local minister, for whom papists were far worse than fairies.[4] Was there a tradition of younger males specifically being enticed into magical initiation by the fairies at one time? Older males who entered their realm seem often to have been treated more roughly.

The modern age also saw blurred boundaries between early practitioners of poetry, medicine, folk healers, and magic workers. Legitimate medical practitioners were divided into surgeons, physicians, apothecaries, and even barbers, who were often antagonistic towards each other. Many country people had no recourse to these professionals. Even those who classified themselves as folk healers and used spells and potions to cure people, denied they had their skills from Satan or were doing anything wrong. Church authorities hardened their attitude against charmers in the seventeenth century but were hard-pressed to eliminate them completely. Many areas could not logistically cope with them. Dalkeith Presbytery noted in 1630 that there were numbers of charmers and consulters in their bounds, and in that time and place 'witches without practice' – those who healed without diabolism – were only forced to promise to desist.[5] Later, in different places, authorities did more than merely admonish offenders.

Even at a relatively late date, some legitimate medical practitioners used elements of folk medicine and magic in their treatment. One example is Robert Trotter (*c*.1736–1815), who worked in the Glenkens area of Galloway, and was known as the 'Muir Doctor'. He sometimes sent his patients to a healing well and sent children who had had whooping cough to be pulled through the hopper of a local mill, a widely believed superstitious cure. His otherworldly aura was with him to the end, for as he lay on his deathbed a loud rap sounded on the table, prompting him to observe, 'That's a call for me. My time here will not be long'. Unexplained rapping was noted as a death omen for the Trotters through the nineteenth century.[6]

Occupying a less scrupulous medical niche was Adam Donald of Aberdeenshire (1703–80), whose nickname was the Prophet of Bethelnie. Exposed as a fraud after his death by his daughter, he carved a remarkable career for himself and overcame his disadvantages to earn a comfortable living by doling out remedies for medical issues. He was regarded by his parents as a changeling because his mother found him one day in his cot looking strangely different from the infant she had given birth to; he grew up large, ungainly, ill-suited to learning and somehow unable for normal work. Despite this, he gathered a collection of foreign books (which he could not read) and cultivated the image of being in communication with unworldly powers.

As well as being consulted for missing items, Donald treated lingering illnesses in humans and animals, increasing his renown by charging at most a modest shilling for all his services, though sixpence was his usual rate if no medicines were prescribed. People readily came to see him, it was said, from as far as 30 miles away and possibly more.[7]

While folk healing may have dwindled into a minority practice fairly recently, other practitioners of recondite skills which had been recognised for centuries fell victim to cultural change, such as the traditional travelling storytellers in Gaelic culture. While bards and druids provide a shadowy record before written history, kings and great leaders always had recourse to poets and *seannachies* who guarded and glorified the genealogical traditions. There was also a class of storytellers and poets, both in the Highlands and in Ireland, who were itinerant by nature, and therefore beholden to few, who demanded food and drink and payment for their artistic services. Refusal (or any slights to their dignity or rights) could result in magical retribution. Bards would satirise those who offended them, sometimes resulting in the offender coming out in boils or, in extreme cases, being killed.

As early as the sixth century, Irish society was troubled by the economic burden of maintaining these roaming bards and their extensive revenues. Their successors were also a problem in Scotland into the early modern age. The *Cliar Sheanchain*, were roving poets who made a living off well-heeled households. Their reputation and the ingrained code of Highland hospitality meant that they could not be turned away when they sought admission to a house. One of the only effective means of refuting these poetic locusts was to answer their satire in even more biting fashion or otherwise combat them in verse. Notably, several women poets were reputed to have given as good as they got against the verbal barbs of the poets, though tradition did not give these females the authority to expel them from households once they had installed themselves within.[8]

Traces of *Cliar Sheanchain* in official records are meagre, though traditions of them which lingered into the mid-twentieth century stated that they latterly numbered no more than a dozen or a score of men. Some laws lumped in wandering bards along with beggars and *sorners* (those who scrounged food and lodging) in 1407 and an act of 1567 prohibited any Irish or Highland beggars or bards to enter the Lowlands on pain of forfeiture or imprisonment. The problem did not disperse, and an act in

1579 tried to define and legislate against all manner of able-bodied but deceitful beggars. These included minstrels, taletellers, gypsies, jugglers, tricksters, and those 'feinzies thame selffis to have knawlege of prophecie, charmeing, or utheris abusit sciences, quhairby they persuaid the people that they can tell thair weardis, deathis, and fortunes, and sic uther fantasticall Imaginationes'. *Sorners* were again mentioned in legislation in 1449 and unlawful wanderers were mentioned also in 1457, when authorities in the burghs were urged to take actions against 'sorrnares, bardes, maisterfull beggars, or fenzeit fulys'.[9]

Wandering bards are mentioned in the Statutes of Iona in 1609, which were enacted by powerful Highland magnates who carefully excluded bards attached to their own clans.[10] Details of the activities of these bards, propagating and disseminating oral legends over a huge cultural area, is irrecoverable, and traces of the endeavours of those *sorners* and wandering taletellers who tramped through the Lowlands for centuries can also only be guessed at. As well as ballads and songs and tales, we may assume that these rovers spread superstitions, medical lore, and perhaps sometimes transmitted magical practices between different places.

Vagrancy was a catch-all which covered a multitude of marginal, sometimes magical lifestyles. Gypsies too were rumoured to have magical powers in Scotland, as elsewhere. The gypsy leader, Johnny Faa, cast his glamour over the Countess of Cassillis, in legend at least, and made her besotted with him, according to one ballad. In Orkney in 1612, Gypsies were accused of 'the geveing of thameselfis furth for sorcerie, giveraris of weirdis, declareris of fortownis, and that they can help or hinder the proffeit of the milk of bestiall'. Magnus Linay and his wife were accused of learning base magical practices from that race.[11]

Several men such as Donald McIlmichall, John Stewart, and Patrick Lowrie, fell into the vagabond category, which included 'conjuring' or healing to make ends meet, along with begging or other activities. Alexander Hamilton, brought to trial in 1630, was described as a vagrant and made himself unpopular in East Lothian not just on this account but because of sinister threats to those who refused his requests for food and drink. When he came to the house of Elizabeth Lawson, Lady Ormestoun, she summarily dismissed him with the remark, 'Away, custroun carle, ye will get nothing heir'. In revenge, Hamilton consulted with Satan and received from him a blue thread which he placed at the door of the property. This had the effect of causing Lady Ormestoun and her daughter to fall seriously ill and die. Keith Thomas has pointed out that cursing others was often the last recourse for the habitually poor and powerless class, including beggars and tramps.[12] Guilt of those who refused begging requests could turn into anger, suspicion and accusations.

Hamilton first met Satan in 1624 in a place named the 'Hugstoun Hilis' near Haddington. He agreed to be his servant and asked for money from Satan, which was refused, but he did so shortly afterwards. Alexander was given a magical baton to summon the Devil when he pleased. When Thomas Home in Clerkington fell ill, Hamilton was consulted and diagnosed that he had been bewitched by a beggar wife who had laid an enchanted thread at his door. Hamilton consulted the Devil and was given instructions for a potion to heal the man.[13] Hamilton's mode of living also inspired another charge against him. George Broun, Laird of Colestoun, had banished Hamilton from his lands because he was an idle beggar and vagabond, so Hamilton again solicited Satan to gain revenge. However, the Devil rejected the request to harm the laird because there was a prior request from a witch who had a pending grievance against the same individual.

However healers gained their powers and however popular their services were, it seems that they were frequently at the edges of society, and not always because they were suspected of witchcraft. Details of their complex lives are not always forthcoming. Their known activities and connections are often clouded by details given voluntarily in confession or suggested by them. Patrick Lowrie of Haylie, Ayrshire, was strangled and burnt on Castle Hill, Edinburgh, in July 1605. He was aged around 48 and was a reputed warlock, healer and a vagrant. A local byname for him was 'Pat the Witch'. He had been notoriously known as a magic worker for around twenty-three years. His character was marked by disputes with his wife and others in his community.[14] He also had a reputation as 'an expert leech'. Back in 1595, he had encountered a woman named Katherine Bras lying sorrowfully in her yard. She had argued with her husband and he had become cold and hard towards her. Lowrie offered to restore his affections for forty shillings, which Bras did not have. She told the tale to the Kirk session years later.

Details of his alleged healing are sparse, but melodramatic. He had, twenty years since, cured the horse of the infamous Margaret McGuffock, the 'Witch of Barneweill'. Lowrie cured a woman who had been struck blind by his sorcery and also healed a child afflicted by an incurable disease. This bairn, the daughter of Elizabeth Crawford in Glasgow, had been ill for eight or nine years. His method was to take a cloth off the child's face and *saining* it, crossing her face with his hand. He then kept the cloth for eight days and placed it on the child's face again. The girl slept for two days without moving and then Patrick Lowrie woke her. She had the vision in her eye restored so that she could see perfectly with it after five days.

Patrick Lowrie was also accused of consorting with others at places such as the common waste at Sandhills in Kyle, near the burgh of Irvine, where he met with other evildoers on Whitsunday in 1604. The same group met also in kirkyards, where they 'raisit and took vp sindrie dead persones furth of their graves, and dismemberit the said dead corpis, for the practising of witchcraft and sorcerie'.[15] On a more petty, but still alarming level, Lowrie was accused of turning milk to blood at Beltane time. Other charges against him included acting together with another witch and spoiling Bessie Saweris's corn and also making her sick.

Lowrie's associates were the women witches Jonet Hunter (who was executed before him), Margaret Duncane, and Katherene McTeir. He also had unusual Otherworld contacts. On Hallows Eve, 1604, together with others, such as the witch Jonet Hunter, he met Satan on Loudon Hill. Unusually, the Devil appeared in the shape of a woman named Helen McBrune and this being gave him a hair belt (reminiscent of the hair bedecked stick owned by Ritchie Graham), which had a clawed clasp on it.[16]

Lowrie was investigated by the Kirk session of Dundonald parish between June and July 1604. He complained locally that John Wallace of Craigie and William Cunninghame of Caprington were unfairly pursuing a prosecution against him. He seems to have requested a trial before impartial people. There was some suggestion that local secular authorities were after his goods. Another local man of importance, David Myll, testified on his behalf that Patrick had been cursed by his father, who swore he would come to a bad end, and he had made repentance. But he was still condemned to death.

Another man who was in a marginal position in society was featured in George Sinclair's compendium *Satan's Invisible World Discovered*.[17] His real name was Alexander Hunter and he had been given the byname Hattaraick by Satan. For some time he earned a modest living, peddling charms and curing people and animals, though his main occupation was as a herdsman. Then, one summer day, Satan appeared to him on a green hill side in the shape of a grave 'mediciner', and addressed him: 'Sandy, you have too long followed my trade without acknowledging me for your master. You must now take on with me and be my servant, and I will make you more perfect in your calling'.[18]

Hunter consented and he became renowned for his abilities and became a notorious *jockie*, a term for a wandering beggar synonymous with *sorner*. He made his way, begging meals and meat in return for charms. His predictions were given credit by most, and he used intimidation against those who went against him, including predicting the death of one man who owed him money. On one occasion he came to Samuelston and was accosted by one of the sons of the property who assaulted him. Hattaraick mumbled a curse against him and soon afterwards the young man had some kind of dark, possibly supernatural encounter, on the road home one night. He did not disclose the details of the event, but the man's sister summoned Hunter and he admitted cursing her brother, who had been in ill health ever since. He promised to cure him and took away one of his sarks which he needed for the purpose. When he came to claim his recompense for the healing after the man recovered, he told his sister that the man would be going away soon but would never come home. Taking advantage of this knowledge, the woman persuaded her brother to place all his finances in her hands, instead of with another brother, and so benefitted greatly when he died abroad. Needless to say, she escaped blame while Hattaraick was strangled and burned for being a witch. An alternative version of events is that given by the man who accused him, William Davidson. He said that he was consulted by Susanna Sinclair, Lady Samuelston, about the best method to destroy her brother, John Sinclair of Hermiston. When Davidson refused, she turned to Hattaraick and a warlock named Patrick Learmonth instead, who laid some curse around the gentleman's house and also helped the lady to destroy her ailing husband.[19]

The traces of Hunter's actual activities have been obscured by his elusive identity. There is a 1629 record from Haddington which refers to him as 'Alexander Sinclair alias Hunter', and in a list of accusations the scribe has written, 'You called yourself Seaton, for this was your usual habit, to change your name and surname as it suited you'.[20] Sandie Hamilton may have been another name he used. Apart from his wilful use of aliases, there may be some confusion by early commentators about the real identity of Hattaraick, with one modern writer at least suggesting that George Sinclair confused a man named Alexander Hunter or Sinclair with his contemporary, Alexander Hamilton. An entry in the minutes of Haddington Presbytery on

7 November appears to think that Hattaraick was really Alexander Sinclair's accuser, William Davison.[21]

Alexander Sinclair was identified as a warlock by Bessie Litill, an accused witch from Longniddry, who first encountered him when he sent someone to ask for a loan of money (which seems an odd act on first acquaintance). When she refused, Sinclair identified that she had a piece of money secreted in her clothing. Sinclair (in the guise of Seaton) was a healer, but quite a troublesome one. When he turned up at the house of a man named Heres, declaring his medical skill and saying that he could heal him by taking away one of the man's shirts and using it for a ritual, the sick man denounced him as a witch. Heres' wife offered Sinclair some food and drink, possibly to mollify him, but he refused and demanded money, correctly identifying the value of the currency that she and her husband had hidden away. Before he left, he said that her husband would die within the week, which proved true. Much of his reputation was built around an aura designed to convince people he could cause harm unless they gave him food or money. It was said that he carried around with him a bee in a tin which he fed with three drops of his blood every day. Each year Sinclair would go to Norham in Northumberland, renew his contract with Satan, and would be given a new bumble bee, evidently his spirit animal.

Like the warlock Alexander Hamilton, the instances of Sinclair's healing abilities were hardly accompanied by benevolence. When he came begging to one household and was offered grey bread, he demanded superior white bread, then went off in a rage when it was not given. The housewife fell in a dead faint. Her neighbours dragged the warlock back and he bade them administer some whisky he knew was in the house. The lady recovered but her greyhound and an ox belonging to her immediately dropped dead. A year later, he turned up at her door and expressed surprise that she was still alive because there had been five evils laid upon her. He prophesied that she would go to Ireland and then return. She later told authorities that she had indeed gone to live in Ireland for many years before returning to Scotland.

William Davidson of Saltoun, Sinclair's accuser, had himself been accused of being a witch and healer by Margaret Muirhead, a supposed witch who implicated several people and generated a cycle of accusations locally in 1628. He admitted acts of sorcery and healing but denied that he healed some by transferring their illness to others. He had fled Saltoun when accused, but didn't get far because of his poverty. He was also over 60. When questioned, he said he had been taught charming by Bessie Gray, and had been practising for thirty-two years. He confessed to the usual round of features that his accusers expected: renouncing his baptism, and meeting the Devil (whom he consulted about curing, and also destroying his enemies). In return for being Satan's servant, he was told he would want for nothing, which was blatantly untrue. Among other acts, he healed Andrew Wilkieson with foxglove leaves, though he denied transferring the illness onto his nephew. He also used south-running water to affect cures and, more unusually, placing salted hake and raw meat under two men's heads. He was also charged with malicious acts. One was refusing to heal a woman he had made ill and another was giving poison to a woman to cause her grandchild to die, possibly to end its misery. These charges he denied, and he was found not guilty of these acts. Like some other charmers, he admitted healing in the belief that he was doing no wrong and thought others would agree. But he was strangled and burned anyway.[22] Davison named at least seven suspects, three of whom were male.

Another male accused who was also described as being a vagrant was William Scottie, brought to trial in Orkney in 1643. Among his acts of witchcraft, he stroked a cow which immediately fell dead and also was seen going around the houses of two people widdershins, implying an intent to harm them.[23]

It is possible that some healers did not always need to practice their arts in conjunction with other occupations, though these were perhaps few and far between. Many healers who had a portmanteau of earning activities occupied low-levels jobs, and only some resorted to petty criminality. Bartie Patersoune of Newbattle, Midlothian, was 61 years old when he was brought to trial in December 1607. His occupation is described as tasker, which means that he mostly earned money by piece-work, particularly reaping crops. Patersoune may have fallen prey to official attention when several of those he treated died, which was a common occupational hazard for a healer.

The first mentioned charges against him was purveying poisons under the guise of medicines. These noxious drinks had caused the deaths of Johnne Myller and Elizabeth Robiesoun. But the indictment then details the positive curing of James Broun, who was treated by giving him medicinal drinks, and rubbing him with salves made of green herbs. At home, the patient was made to kneel by his bedside a set number of times and ask 'his helth at all leving wichtis, aboue and vnder the earth, in the name of Jesus'. He then had to take some wheat, salt and rowan wood to wear continually for the sake of his health. A cure for the ailments of women involved grinding almonds with egg whites and smearing it on their faces. All of which the prosecutors damned as 'manifest Sorcerie and Witchcraft'. A witness was found to testify that Bartie had transformed into a cat and howled at him all night.

Like other healers, Patersoune made use of water in his rituals, specifically water from the Dow Loch. He cured his own child with loch water by carefully washing it thrice. He threw the child's sark into the loch, declaring that if any appeared out of the loch the child would mend, but if nothing appeared, it would die. The healer also carried the efficacious water to people and animals that were sick. Two spells used when administering the water were noted. The first, to be said by the patient twenty-seven times, was as follows: 'I life this watter, in the name of the Father, Sone, and Haly Gaist, to do guid for their helth for quhom it is liftit'. The second incantation was used for charming beasts: 'I charm thé for arrow-schote, for dor-schot [door shot], for wondo-schot [womb shot?], for ey-schot, for tung schot, for lever-schot, for lung-schote, for hert-schot, all the maist, in the name of the Father, the Sone and Haly Gaist. Amen'.[24]

There is much else in Bartie Patersoune's repertoire of healing which suggests some fusion of religious and folk beliefs. Arrow shot, mentioned in the first invocation, is more commonly called elf-shot, referring to the deadly stone weapons which malicious fairies directed at both beasts and men. One of Bartie's charms used to staunch blood also invoked the Trinity: 'Lord as thow deid on the ruid, with all thy strength stenche thow this blood. Father, sone & halie gaist, Thow stem & stenche this bluide in haiste'.[25]

The mechanism by which Bartie and his fellow charmers retained remnants of Catholic practice seems more likely to have been inherited through secular sources, and probably from those in the same line of business who were nominally Protestants. It seems more a case of the ritual being adhered to because of their conservative habits rather than any abiding devotion to the Church of Rome. Though the Kirk rooted out papistry in all its guises, there was never detected a specifically Catholic-supernatural conspiracy which was a primary force behind devilry in Scotland. But we could also mention the case of the charmer Moreis Scobie (from Balhaldie, Dunblane), heard by the Presbytery of Stirling in 1610. Among his clients was 'ane bairne of the laird of Lundeis callit Collein campbell'. He learned a charm for healing directly from Sir Andro Hudsone, a priest in Glendevon, and presumably a Catholic:

> The Lord is blessed that heirin in baith merrie in harit
>   and hand,
> The Lord is blessed that herin is he salbe they warrand;
> God of his gudenes that he can call and he sendis
>   hestallie
> The fusone of middilyird God send it hame to the;
> The Lord he can, the Lord he zid syne hestallie,
> Quha hes bein heir, this ny[t] he sayes, quha hes bein
>   heir hier this day?
> The Elriche King hes being heir this ny[t], and rest fra
>   me away,
> The pouar of woman and mankynd, and bay[t] sone
>   gratn throw me
> The fusone of mirrie Middilzrid he hes tane fra me
>   away,
> Grant me the gist sone againe that I granted to the
> Or ellis thow sall have hell to thy dwelling and
>   domisday at zo[r] dur,
> The father, the sone, and the holy gaist and him I have
>   with thee.[26]

Whether the priest was Catholic or not, this rhyme is obviously some distance away from liturgical writing. *Elrich* (or *eldritch*), meaning weird or unearthly, has distinctly unchristian connotations, though we can't be sure who this night-time visitant was. Scobie himself was excommunicated for non-attendance at the Presbytery in August 1610.

Returning to Bartie Patersoune, included in his judicial record was an illustration of the healer's Sator Square, an enigmatic acrostic device used widely in Europe in medieval times for invocations and ritual:

S A T O R
A R E P O
T E N E T
O P E R A
R O T A S

The palindromic square was used as a protective device against bad luck and illness, and its use by a Scottish healer signifies a fairly complex range of beliefs among native practitioners. Bartie wrote out the square and had patients hold it up to their breast while repeating a Latin spell which would lead to their healing. The justiciary record contains occult illustrations which had been in the possession of the healer. There does not appear to be any proven instances of malice by Bartie Patersoune. In one incident where he was consulted by a man who believed that he had been cursed by an accused woman witch, he advised the man to tell the woman to give him back his health.

While there were many women working with natural powers and tools in folk medicine, the higher reaches of the medical profession was barred to them for centuries. Men who had healing renown, both in legend and real healers, often feature in folk tales. Typical perhaps of the tales of the cunning man in Highland tradition are the stories of how particular legendary figures gained their healing abilities. The acquisition of incredible healing powers was often accidental or through peculiar good fortune. Typical of the tradition is the Sutherland drover, Farquhar, who was one day accosted in England by a doctor who asked him where he acquired his hazel staff. Informing the man that he cut it in Glengollig, the doctor promised Farquhar gold if he both brought him a similar staff and the seventh serpent which crawled from a hole at the base of the tree. He captured the white snake, bottled it, and hurried back to the doctor in England to collect his reward. The doctor asked him to help in boiling the serpent, which Farquhar agreed to. However, the drover touched steam from the brew and stuck his finger in his mouth, and instantly, 'he knew everything, and the eyes of his mind were opened'. He kept quiet about this, but the doctor himself tasted the brew and divined all its virtue had vanished. He threw the pot at the drover, but Farquar flourished with his gift of universal knowledge and became a doctor himself. He travelled the land curing people and became known as Farquhar the physician. When he heard that the king had a serious malady of the knee he went to palace, but could not gain admission. So he stalked up and down outside and chanted, 'The black beetle to the white'. The second day he did the same thing and the king asked who he was, then called him in. Farquhar repeated his strange phrase and it was discovered that the king's corrupt, regular physicians had inserted a black beetle into his leg, which gnawed at flesh and bone, prolonging his malady and their own expensive false treatment.

The king hung all the doctors, and Farquar gained the hand of the king's daughter. Yet he did not flourish in the end because an ill-wisher poisoned him.[27] The serpent of knowledge motif is told about many omniscient heroes, in Gaelic literature and elsewhere, and the knowledge given, by fate rather than merit, is overwhelmingly supernatural in nature rather than mundanely scientific. The hero of the tale can be identified with 'Ferchard Leche' (leech signifying doctor), who had a grant of land in Sutherland from King Robert II in the fourteenth century.

The most prominent medical family in the Highlands was the MacBeths (sometimes styled Beaton). The MacBeths originated in Ireland and had a great store of knowledge based on classical medial authorities. On top of this rather ancient, text-based medical knowledge, which was becoming redundant by the Early Modern age, the MacBeths and their peers were reputed to have access to a store of traditional Gaelic healing lore, mainly based on herbal knowledge. Their effectiveness in the healing profession, over several centuries, won them renown on the western seaboard of Scotland. The Islay poet, Gille-Coluim MacBride, called them 'the kindred of Mac-beathadh, accurate in their practice, carvers of bones and arteries'.[28] Even after the heyday of the medical family had vanished, their reputation was remembered. One visitor to Skye in 1823 wrote that he had been told about the marvellous Farquhar Bethune who could cure any disease, his knowledge being based on a book printed in red (which was still known about), a volume which contained things 'both secret and sacred', a magical grimoire.[29]

There was an uncertain overlapping in the seventeenth and eighteenth centuries and likely earlier between formally trained medical practitioners and folk healers, and also quack doctors and people who claimed to have healing talents, some of them having quasi-magical abilities. (We are also reminded that the ghostly spirit guide of the sixteenth century witch, Alison Pearson, was a human doctor before he took up abode with the fairies.) A Highland writer in the 1630s complained of the prevalence of 'a few common chyrurgeons, and traversing sharltons out of Ireland'. One such was a Dr John Sholes who had treated some noble families.[30] It would be enlightening to know how many Irish 'charlatans' were in Scotland and what they were practising. In Lowland Scotland, there was distinction between physicians and surgeons and a broader, lower class which was inhabited by informally qualified people, including magical healers and plain quacks. Even beyond the Victorian era, there was a network of 'bone-setters', men whose supposed skill was in treating breaks, fractures, sprains, dislocations and other ailments, favoured mostly by agricultural and manual workers who had a distrust of legitimate doctors, or who could not afford their services. Although there were no incantations, spells or supernatural practices involved, most of these 'bone-setters' claimed to have inherited their untaught powers from a male predecessor via 'heir-skep' or 'heirship'.[31] One of the last of this profession was Donald McConachie, a farmer from Knockando in Morayshire, who died at the age of 82, around 1911. His own father was a bone-setter, and so was his renowned cousin, James McConachie, whom he assisted. Donald would treat as many as twenty or thirty patients on a Saturday and, like magical healers of old, he travelled widely to treat people, in his case ranging as far south as Glasgow, and also to Badenoch and east Aberdeenshire.[32]

The cliched supernatural powers ascribed to seventh sons of seventh sons was believed in many different societies around the world. A healer named George Beir was questioned by the Presbytery in Haddington, East Lothian, in 1646 and gave details of his history and his claimed ability to cure scrofula, the king's evil:

> yt he never learnt his skill from any bot only yt he was the 7 sonne and was desired be … Mr Ja Knox at Kelso understanding yt he was the 7 sonne, to say qn he caine to anie [sick person] laying his hand on the sore pt, 'I touche thee, Lord cuir thee' … yt he never used the cure before the sd Mr Ja Knox bade him, that ever since as he had occasion, he hes used the cuire, yt he applyes nothing bot clean clothes and binds 2 black silk threads about the patients neck.[33]

Beir was reprimanded and told not to practice any more. His explanation, a mixture of a misfortune of birth and persuasion by another party, together with a lack of papist or supernatural mumbo-jumbo in his healing ritual, meant that he escaped prosecution. Other factors in his favour were that he charged no money for his services and that his alleged ability was restricted to this single medical condition. His admission that some people were cured and some not after seeing him was probably a canny one too. It would be good to know more about the role of the healing talent-spotter Knox in the affair.

In Highland belief, there were also some diseases which could only be healed by certain kindreds. *Glacach nan Dòmhnallach*, MacDonald's

Disease, a consumptive disorder, had to be cured by people of that surname. The cure was administered by a certain spoken charm and by touch. No money was accepted for its administration.[34] Suspicion of medical matters, combined with superstition and other factors, could magnify scientific knowledge into magic. The Red Book of Appin was a legendary manuscript originally owned by the Stewarts of Invernahyle. In reputation at least, the Red Book has become a famous grimoire, containing a wealth of arcane knowledge. But, as the book has long since disappeared, its exact contents are unknown. The fact that it disappeared added to his allure and has allowed much speculation about its contents and authority. A claim that the Red Book conferred upon its owners insight into any questions that inquirers would be making to it beforehand has little substance.[35] Some authorities believe that it was a veterinary work detailing remedies for cattle disease and first gained its uncanny reputation because the family who owned it possessed an enviable herd. Yet various folk tales crowded around this volume, especially after its whereabouts became unknown. It was said to have come into the family's ownership when a young Stewart was invited to meet a mysterious stranger at the Crooked Pool near Loch Awe and sign his name in a red book. After consulting sixteen ministers, the lad attended the rendezvous, but protected himself within a magic circle. The satanic stranger furiously turned himself successively into a hound, a raging bull, then a flight of crows in order to break the boy's protection. But to no avail, since the boy signed the book and was allowed to take it away as a prize.[36]

Although the Red Book vanished, probably during the nineteenth century, accounts of its mystical properties proliferated in West Highland tradition. Around 1860, a man recounted asking the guardian of the book for its loan as a boy when his family's herd mysteriously lost its *toradh*, or substance, a circumstance usually ascribed to witches or ill-wishers. Although the Red Book may have been expected to have belonged to an individual or family with a sinister reputation, the Appin Stewarts seem little different from other Gaelic landowners. The family, who owned a large part of Appin from the fifteenth century until the end of the eighteenth, was mainly headed by either belligerent warriors or noted agricultural improvers.[37] However, it seems that they were less mundane than met the eye. The Reverend Robert Kirk, in his *Secret Commonwealth*, composed around 1692, wrote, 'There is a Family of the name of Stuart in Appin of Lorn which has a sovereign Charm against the Fairies, which they communicate onely to their Offspring. The charm they write on a piece of paper, the words are intermingled with crosses. It is hung about the neck of persons affected. They call this charm the Gospell'.[38] It seems from this that the Stewarts had a gamut of magical powers which they used to enhance their standing in the area.

Other kindreds in the Highlands gained a reputation for otherworldly powers by virtue of hereditary occupations. The MacMacMhuirich of South Uist were hereditary bards in the Western Isles and claimed descent from an exiled Irish bard. They achieved status initially through service to the Lords of the Isles as lawyers, doctors and poets. Their prominence in these professions and proficiency in maintaining the ancient traditions of Clanranald gave them the reputation of having magical abilities. One folk tale from South Uist, where the kindred were remembered as followers of the black arts, relates how Dark Lachlan, son of Donald MacMhuirich, combatted two witches who had transformed into ravens and attacked their ship, which was on a voyage to Skye to ask for Macleod of Dunvegan's daughter in marriage. The witches were maids to the young woman, who were enraged that their services would no longer be required. Lachlan's companion Alasdair, Laird of Boisdale, shot one of the birds, which flew off. Later, on Skye, Lachlan graciously cured the wound of the injured girl by rubbing the muzzle of his gun three times round the wound.[39]

The north seems to have been rich with manuscripts held by various individuals and families, containing a variety of lore and knowledge. Magical books also appear in the folklore record of the region, associated with notorious alleged wizards, such as Lord Reay of Sutherland (see next chapter). Further north still, a sinister Book of the Black Art was prevalent in Orkney legend. This volume was printed in white ink on black paper and contained spells and charms which gave its possessor immense power. If a mortal died with the book in their possession, it was immediately claimed back by the Devil. Powerful as it was, its ownership might become a burden, but the only way to rid oneself of it was to sell it for a lesser sum than one had paid for it or by giving it to someone as a gift. The book, however, often had other ideas about its ownership. A man from Sandwick, sick of its corrupting power, once tried to throw it overboard into the sea, but when he got home found it lying safely on his kitchen table. A Sanday girl mistakenly accepted the book from a local, female witch, and desperately tried to destroy it. Throwing the book off Grunavi Head had no effect – it was back in her bedroom before she got home. Both these unfortunates are said to have been relieved of the curse by a local clergyman. Several copies of the book existed. The Reverend Charles Clouston (d. 1884) destroyed the Sandwick copy by buying it and burying it in his garden. The Reverend Matthew Armour (d. 1903) obtained the Sanday copy. It was rumoured in Shetland that one copy of the book was sinisterly prefaced with the words, 'Cursed is he that persueth me'.[40] A volume called the Book of Black Earth was another grimoire alleged to have existed in the Highlands. It was said to have belonged to Alexander Stewart, the Wolf of Badenoch (1343–1394), the unruly Earl of Buchan and son of King Robert II. The assertion that he was a notorious consorter of witches and warlocks is of unknown provenance.[41] Another mystery tome was the Red Book of Balloch, which may have disappeared many years ago (if it ever existed) from the charter room of Taymouth Castle. This book was shaped like a barrel and was bound with twelve iron hoops or clasps. In this volume were the original predictions of the seventeenth century seer called the Lady of Lawers, one of the Breadalbane Campbells.[42]

A magical book was also reputedly owned by Factor McLaren, a nineteenth-century resident of Tiree, who had a reputation as a wizard. His book gave him any knowledge he wanted, though he had to wear a protective steel band around his head when he consulted it., Several tales of him, recalled in oral tradition, remember his aptitude in magical arts, though he was a qualified doctor (and factor). One story had him demanding the sacrifice of a horse in payment for magically freeing a grounded boat.[43]

Chapter 7

Men of the Black School

The Wizard Lairds

In Scotland, some men of the lower landowning class of lairds gained the reputation of engaging in enduring commerce with the Devil. Whether or not this was true, it reflected the attitude which those lower down the social ranks viewed their landlords. Most of these figures came from the seventeenth century, though two early notorious wizards, Lord Soulis and Hugh de Gifford, were earlier. De Gifford died before the end of the twelfth century, and traditions about him are of dubious antiquity. Lord Soulis is remembered in folktales which picture him as an unpopular baron in Liddesdale who so alienated the local population that they boiled him in oil after failing to get the king to deal with him. In reality, he had a less dramatic fate, rebelling against King Robert Bruce in 1320, then being imprisoned in Dumbarton Castle, where he died.

One of the most enduring traditions was that of the disreputable laird studying nefarious magic in a Black School, located in Padua in Italy. Foreign scholars resorted to universities in Padua, Toledo, Seville and Salamanca, which were viewed as cradles of magic by their countrymen. Perhaps it was the sparsity of Scots who went abroad in the early period which led to them being regarded this way. In the fourteenth century, there were never more than five or six men each year who went from Scotland to Europe for study. The university of Padua in 1331 had a statute which mentioned the Scottish 'nation' there, in conjunction with the English, although there is no record of any Scot enrolled at that time.[1]

In one folk tale, various Scottish lairds have been classed as fortunate escapees from the powers of Satan while studying the dark arts.[2] According to one variant, Satan was conducting a seminar one day in Padua when he announced that he would claim the soul of the last student who left the room that day. In the panic, a Scotsman unfortunately found himself in last place at the exit, but he had the wits to exclaim, 'Deil tak the hindmost!' The Devil pounced upon his shadow in lieu of the desired human soul. From that day, the laird never cast a shadow behind him. The tale is an example of an migratory legend, a story that can be found in many countries, albeit with minor variations. (Migratory Legend ML3000, in Reidar Christiansen's *The Migratory Legends* – 1958). While analysis of the tale in Scotland by Mark Hanford states that it was most popular in the Highlands, we should extend that to include the North East, and indeed areas beyond, like Angus.[3] The story was also used for native transactions with Satan. Into the nineteenth century, Scottish schoolboys referenced the tradition by taunting each other's parentage by saying, 'Your father had no shadow!'[4]

One Scottish version of the story overloads the story with three Scottish lairds studying the Black Arts at the same time: Cameron of Lochiel, McDonald of Keppoch, and Mackenzie of Brahan.[5] Other heroes of the tale are Donald Duibheal Mackay, Black John of Garafed, Sir Robert Gordon, or James Carnegie of Pittarrow, who became Earl of Southesk. Cameron of Lochiel also features in a story whereby he saves the soul of a woman who had swapped her soul in exchange for the mending of a sugar bowl, compelling the Devil to take the woman's shadow instead.

Unlike in Iceland, where similar tale-types proliferated, and the figures involved were nearly always priests, the Scottish versions focus on the dubious abilities of notorious secular local figures. The lairds who were the subjects of these traditions had mixed reputations, combining awed admiration, grudging respect for uncanny powers, and outright hostility as individuals who had evil influences over their communities. Some as wizard lairds may have been damned for earthly habits rather than diabolic behaviour. Local people remembered Sir James Carnegie of Pittarrow (*c.*1582–1669), who later became second Earl of Southesk, as an expert swordsman, but also a 'griping oppressor of the poor'. A nineteenth-century tale told of his time at Padua:

> The devil himself was the instructor, and he annually claimed … the person of a pupil at dismissing the class. To give all a fair chance of escape, he ranged them up in a line within the school, when, on a given signal, all rushed to the door... On one of these occasions, Sir James Carnegie was the last; but having invoked the devil to take his shadow instead of himself … the devil was caught by the ruse, and was content to

seize the shadow... It was afterwards remarked that Sir James never had a shadow, and that he usually walked in the shade, to hide this defect.[6]

People on the Angus-Kincardineshire border taunted his memory with a rhyme which ran, 'The Laird o' Pittarro, his heart was sae narrow, He wadna let the kaes [rooks] pike his corn-stack'. The *kaes* referenced human enemies who secretly damaged his property. Carnegie was nicknamed the Black Earl, both for his dark complexion and his character. When he died in March 1669, Satan arrived to collect his overdue soul in a fiery coach drawn by six coal black horses. The vehicle thundered off and vanished down the Starney Bucket Well in the Deil's Den, near the family burial ground on the Kinnaird estate.[7] This coach was seen at certain times, driving through storms, emitting a strange blue light. Use of satanic coaches to transport aristocratic ne'er-do-wells to the netherworld was not uncommon. The Duke of Queensbury's final coach ride detoured as far as Mount Vesuvius, a notorious portal to hell.[8]

The Carnegie traditions were first detailed in 1654 by John Lamont of Newton in Fife, who admits that Sir James never owned Pittarrow, though his father did.[9] The family historian, on the other hand, considered that the tradition must be attributed to one of the earl's younger brothers, Sir John or Sir Alexander Carnegie, successive lairds of Pittarrow. It is also possible that the legend was attached to the previous estate owners, the Wishart family.[10] Oral tradition and written folklore are sometimes slanderous of famous individuals. A prime example of reputation sacrificed for the sake of good entertainment is George Buchanan. Although no wizard laird in life, he suffered a humiliating post-mortem legacy. In life, Buchanan was an influential Latinist, historian, and much feared tutor of King James VI. In death, Buchanan became 'the king's fool', subject of many Lowland chapbooks, and even finding his way into Highland tradition.[11]

Returning to the lairds, moving north from Pittarrow, we can note the Aberdeenshire landowner, Alexander Skene of Skene, another victim of Satanic shadow theft. One tradition has him recklessly crossing the frozen loch at Skene in his carriage, threatening the driver not to halt the reckless speed. The driver looked outside and saw two spectral black dogs perched on the wheels. The carriage made it safely across, but sunk on the far shore, and the marks of the wheels were indelibly imprinted in the earth. Another tale has him magically freezing two unfortunate robbers who accosted him.

Echoing a tale about Michael Scot, a raven and a dove were seen fighting about his mansion when he was on his deathbed, and he only succumbed to peaceful death when he was assured that the dove, symbol of his entry to heaven, had beaten its opponent.[12]

In the black school tale associated with Sir Robert Gordon (1647–1704), the laird summoned Satan while a student at Padua when he was 17, ardent to access forbidden knowledge. In exchange for almost limitless knowledge, Gordon eventually surrendered his soul but deferred payment for twenty-five-years. He returned to Gordonstoun and busied himself improving his estate and working on inventions, including an ingenious sea pump. His misunderstood scientific acumen gave rise to his uncanny reputation. Local rumour stated that he once boiled a salamander for seven years in the hope that it would yield him occult secrets. In 1704, Gordon's mortal allotted term was ending and he sat with the minister of Duffus, awaiting the Devil. Near midnight, Satan arrived, but the laird had fiddled with the clock in order to delay his fate. When the right hour approached, he fled and hoped to find sanctuary in a nearby kirk, but he was overtaken and slain. His clerical friend spotted his corpse on the roadside being devoured by a hell hound.[13] An alternate version states that Satan pursued the old wizard for three whole days, through the town of Elgin and thereabouts, before he finally caught him. Sir Robert lived on in gleeful local verse, 'The wisest of warlocks, the Morayshire cheil, The despot of Duffus the friend o' the deil?[14]

Donald Duibheal Mackay, born in 1591, had a colourful career which made him a target in his native Sutherland for accusations of uncanniness. Created the first Lord Reay, he was an alleged bigamist, convicted adulterer, and a ferocious soldier who commanded a Swedish regiment of mainly Scots mercenaries, 'Mackay's Invincibles', in the Thirty Years War. He died in Denmark in 1649, bankrupt, though he had lent fortunes to several European monarchs, none of whom repaid him. Like Michael Scot, he was a reputedly powerful magician who employed devilish imps to work wonders.[15] Also like Scot, Lord Reay possessed a magic book that supported him in his devilishness. When he loaned this magic volume to a relative who was also a wizard, the man's servant unwisely opened it on the way back to Reay's home. A legion of little men leaped out of the pages and cried 'work, work!'. The terrified man quickly bade them to tie together ropes of heather in order to keep them occupied. When all the heather from the landscape was made into ropes, the frantic servant bade then go to the bay of Tongue and coil all the sand into ropes. When this task proved impossible, the army of imps disappeared into the sea with a great howl and Lord Reay was deprived of his infernal servants.

Despite having bested his Satan, Donald Duibheal sometimes encountered him in Scotland, willingly or no. The pair had a violent quarrel in the sea cavern called the Cave of Smoo, and the print of his horse's hooves are seen in the rock even to this day. There was also an iron ring nearby, where the wizard used to tether his unfortunate human victims, letting the action of the tide dispose of them. It is said that Donald also penetrated the depths of the cave further than any man had gone, despite a phantom voice calling him back. In the deepest place he found a cask which contained a tiny being which, when the cask was opened, assumed the dimensions of a fearful giant. He persuaded the giant to shrink and re-enter the cask, where it remained trapped, genie like, and he quickly left the cave.[16] The wondrous caverns of Smoo feature in other folk tales.

The tangible, dark legacy of Lord Reay and others of his ilk seems to have died with them, though there is a Sutherland legend that his book survived. The McLagan Manuscript, in the School of Scottish Studies in Edinburgh, mentions a Black Book that was apparently in the possession of a local man. When he was dying, he gave it to a friend in Ross-shire, and this man became famous for curing people who had been affected by witchcraft. The narrator in the document requested a look at the book, which was refused, but the owner said he would leave him it when he passed away as he knew he would not misuse it. He enquired for the book after the man died, but the family said it had been sold to a doctor, who had then passed it on to a museum.[17] Whether any of the reputed dark lairds deliberately dabbled with magical practices is obscured by the fact that so little is actually known about many of these characters, despite their notoriety in their own lifetimes.

The late seventeenth century in Scotland also produced deliberately manufactured legends based on maligned figures of power. Prime examples of this were those military or legislative enemies of the Covenanters, men such as John Graham, Viscount Dundee, and the judge, Sir George Mackenzie of Rosehaugh, as we have seen. In common with the state-sponsored name blackening which extended to public figures in the sixteenth century, these men had their reputations maligned by political enemies during and after their lifetimes. The seventeenth-century examples were sponsored by hardline members from the Presbyterian religion rather than affiliates of the government. As a result, the allegations against persecuting figures feared by the Covenanters fall into the category of barely believable supernatural rumours rather than credible accusations. Therefore, Royalist generals like Tam Dalyell were accused of playing dice with the Devil and other evil acts. The persecuting Viscount Dundee met his end at the Battle of Killiecrankie in 1689, via the magic of a well-aimed silver bullet. Dundee's butler once brought him a cup of wine, which turned into blood, and when he plunged his feet into cold water, it boiled and steamed immediately. Also tarred with accusations of wizardry was Sir Robert Grierson of Lag, noted for his persecution of Covenanters. He is said to have hung his prisoners from an iron hook. Allies of Dundee, like Coll Macdonald of Keppoch and Sir Ewen Cameron of Lochiel, managed to have contrasting auras, being folk heroes to some of their constituencies in the Highlands, while being satanic associates for some Whig-Covenanter opponents in the Lowlands. Grierson had a unique afterlife reputation in his home region. As ghoulish entertainments, a member of many households would dress up as the well-remembered laird, 'in shape of beast as hideous as the ingenuity of the performer intrusted with the part could make it'. The creature would be made to look as monstrous as possible and bore little resemblance to any human.[18] Lag's last illness (he died in 1733) was complicated by severe gout. Cold water from the River Nith, brought to sooth his aching feet, satanically turned to steam when it contacted his flesh. A mock elegy, containing the prince of darkness' lamentation for his erstwhile friend Grierson, appeared in print and ran to at least ten editions in the eighteenth century. Walter Scott used the Laird of Lag as his template for Sir Robert Redgauntlet who features in the supernatural 'Wandering Willie's Tale'.

Unnatural aptitude in misunderstood technology or sciences was often a spur to men being characterised as being in league with darkness, but one suspects that the process was accelerated when such individuals were unpopular in their districts through their non-magical characteristics and actions. Another distinguished Scot to be tarred with an unfairly uncanny reputation is John Napier (1550–1617), a mathematician, astronomer, physicist, and discoverer of logarithms. As well as these endeavours, he developed an interest in theology and the occult. Napier's father, Sir Archibald, also had a reputation of being a wizard and his mother was sister of Adam Bothwell, Bishop of Orkney, who also had the same status. Napier is said to have kept a black cock as his familiar. When some property went missing he told his servants to each go into a darkened room and stroke the neck of the bird, which would crow when the guilty one touched it. When all had done so he examined their hands and identified the thief because he was the one with clean hands. Napier had anointed the bird with soot to catch out the perpetrator.[19] A somewhat similar tale is connected with the later warlock, Gregor Willox.

One figure at the end of the eighteenth century attracted a complex legacy of legends, both complimentary and otherwise, which gives insight into how traditional reputations were formulated. Captain John Macpherson was an officer of the 82nd regiment in the eighteenth century and acted as a recruiting agent for the British army in his native area of Badenoch. Such a role did not endear him to large sections of the Highland population who retained sympathies with the deposed Jacobites. Macpherson was known as the Black Captain or the Black Officer, nicknamed for his black hair and also his reputation. Some accounts termed him *dorcha doirbh*, a 'dark savage man'. More well-disposed contemporaries termed him *Iain Dubh mac Alasdair* (Black-haired John son of Alexander). He was reputed to have abandoned his wife and children and there were secret rooms beneath his house, from which the sound of people being tortured were heard by passers-by at night. He was reportedly zealous and underhand in his efforts to find recruits, and would often threaten or bully young men into accepting the king's shilling. He became notorious for attending all the fairs and local markets in the region, sometimes getting potential recruits drunk and forcing them to agree to enlist.[20] This deviousness was indeed criticised during his lifetime and very soon afterwards. The poet, Donnchadh Gobha MacAoidh (Duncan MacKay) admitted:

> Black recruiting without blessing
> He never reckoned anything without trouble,
> Yet it has caused a trampling of his name
> That detractors love to relate about him.[21]

In retirement, Macpherson devoted himself to agriculture and hunting, and his crops and herd were the envy of neighbours, to the extent it was whispered that this was due to supernatural means. The unearthly sounds heard emanating from the cellars of his house at Balachroan gave rise to speculation that the captain had a compact with the Devil. Macpherson firstly asked Satan to make his crops yield a huge harvest, which the Devil readily agreed to, demanding that he should have the roots. The captain deliberately avoided planting root crops and sewed grain, and when he reaped the bumper harvest he gave the useless stalks to Satan. Satan furiously accused him of cheating, so he was mollified by the promise of having the top part of the crop. The fields were planted with carrots, turnips and other root vegetables, so the gullible demon was fooled again next season. Satan was tricked a third time when he was promised the part of the herd which sheltered in the corner of a stockade; Macpherson simply constructed a circular stockade.

But his opponent was to have the last laugh. While the facts suggest that the Black Captain ultimately perished by accident in the harsh conditions of the Cairngorm Mountains, tradition surrounded the incident with omens and supernatural occurrences. Several years before his demise he had insisted on going hunting in the wilds of the Forest of Gaick, despite his friends pulling out of the expedition. He darkly insisted that he had an appointment with someone in that deserted place. With a single companion, he lodged at a remote bothy overnight, and he was visited by a dark figure which caused the hunting dogs to bark ferociously. His companion heard the captain promise to meet the unknown figure in the same place in a year's time, bringing with him a party of men. Rumour magnified the encounter and it was later remembered that a strange fire on a barren peak nearby had been seen at the time when Macpherson occupied the bothy.

On 30 December 1799, the Black Captain set out for the same place with a deer hunting party of four other men. Several days later it transpired that the same bothy had been covered by an avalanche. There was widespread apprehension in Badenoch about what had happened. According to local historian Affleck Gray, some people resorted to consulting hidden powers. This was done by placing the youngest child of a household on top of a wooden domestic item called a *cogan*, and they were then asked a question. This was done in a household at Nuide after the storm, when it was asked whether the hunting party would return that night. No, was the answer. Would they come back the following night. No, again. When would they come back? Never, never, was the reply.[22]

A search was later made and the bodies of the men were found in the ruins of the bothy, which had been flattened by an avalanche. When the funeral party, with Macpherson's coffin in front, was making its way down the glen several days later, another storm blew up and the freak conditions did not abate until one of the mourners suggested putting the captain at the rear.[23] This was done, and the wild weather abated. Affleck advises that the legends around the catastrophe proliferated throughout the whole region. The freak event was variously blamed on Satan or the vengeance of God. It was an event which quickly found its way into local folklore. The news of the disaster also spread south at speed and was later written about by both Sir Walter Scott and James Hogg, amongst others. In the Highlands, it has been noted there is a difference in recorded traditions about the man and his demise depending on locality, with those in the central area of Badenoch and Strathspey focusing on his recruitment notoriety and those further afield encompassing more outlandish supernatural elements. Among his own class and peers, Macpherson was well respected, and several Gaelic eulogies were written following his death. It can be imagined that the earlier wizard lairds were also regarded in a dualistic way by their contemporaries, poor or well-heeled. But one commemoration of Macpherson at least, written by the contemporary bard Donnchadh Gobha MacAoidh (Duncan Gow Mackay), was less flattering in recalling his reputation:

> The Black Officer of Ballychroan it was,
> He turned his back on his wife and children;
> Had he fallen in the wars in France,
> The loss was not so lamentable.[24]

The uncanny reputation of Macpherson not only lingered in the central Highlands for generations, it also travelled with Gaelic speaking migrants to Canada. In Cape Breton there was a tale told about *Caiptean Dubh Bhaile Chròic*, 'the Black Captain from Baile Chròic'. This was recited in Gaelic by the storyteller Dan Angus Beaton as late as 1978, and the underlying traditions were carried to Canada by two Scots, one of whom reputedly survived the fateful avalanche. In this tale, Macpherson's reputation is magnified in its darkness. He asks another military man how to obtain success in a particular battle, but the man advises him to avoid the fight. The Black Captain then makes a deal with the Devil to win a succession of battles, and Satan also usefully sends a black dog to indicate every traitor in the captain's ranks, who are immediately killed. Satan attempted to collect the incorrigible Macpherson after an agreed time of twenty years, but he had built an impregnable fortress and manned it with 500 soldiers. The Devil turned up anyway at the appointed time, in the shape of a hellish goat. Despite the defences, the fortress was reduced to sand. Every man was killed, and all their bodies were found there, except for the captain's.[25]

The reasons for Macpherson's enduring ill-fate are intertwined with the dramatic disaster in Gaick, but also undoubtedly to his own character and history. Born in 1724, he had followed his chief, Cluny Macpherson, into the Jacobite army in opposition to the British state and had gone south to Derby before the retreat back into Scotland. This early Jacobite heroism earned him the praise of another native poet and younger contemporary, Calum Dubh nam Protaigean (Malcolm Macintyre):

> In despite of people of malice and of ill-will…
> Thou wert a Captain on the race of Gillies…
> Thou didst win the battle there was at Penrith:
> Thou didst lay low the English troop.[26]

Macpherson was not the only military man from the Highlands to have joined the British Army after the defeat of the Jacobites, whatever their previous affiliation, so it is unlikely this action alone earned him a poor reputation. His zeal in recruiting men to military campaigns from which a good man would not return may have been one factor which was held against him. There was also his tendency, during his later years as a gentleman farmer, to be litigious with his neighbours. He was in dispute with one man for over twenty years, and he was also taken to court by two men who had likely served as soldiers under him. Like most people perhaps, he was different things to different people. The historian and Liberal MP, Charles Fraser-Macintosh, summarised his different facets: 'I have many of his letters, showing him servile to superiors, agreeable to equals when he chose, tyrannic to his inferiors'.[27]

Chapter 8

The Highland Experience

One of the myths associated with the Highlands, that it was infested with all varieties of superstition and idolatrous belief, is a direct reflection of the view of the region as a backward, if not barbarous place. One example of this attitude can be cited. Bishop John Carswell (1520–1572), a Gael himself, castigated his own people in the introduction to his Gaelic translation of the Prayer Book in 1567:

> And great is the blindness and darkness of sin and ignorance and of understanding among composers and writers and supporters of the Gaelic, in that they prefer and practise the framing of vain, hurtful, lying, earthly stories about the Tuath de Dhanond, and about the sons of Milesius, and about the heroes and Fionn Mac Cumhail …with a view to obtaining for themselves passing worldly gain, rather than to write and to compose and to support the faithful words of God and the perfect way of truth .[1]

Following his death, Carswell's widow remarried and was again widowed. Margaret Campbell was involved in an extraordinary conspiracy which involved the murder of John Campbell of Cawdor in 1592, and a threat to assassinate the young Earl of Argyll, of whom he was guardian. The assassin sought supernatural help from her and other supposed witches, including her servant from the island of Lismore. Echoing the heady mixture of politics, religion, murder and supernatural sometimes evident around the court of James VI, the intrigue centred around the chief of the Campbells was equally dramatic. The witches in the region were both co-operative and drawn from both sexes. Margaret had been taught by and learned charms from 'Auld Mackellar of Cruachan', whom himself had been instructed by the prioress of Iona. The assassin, Campbell of Arkinglas, dispensed with the witches' services and turned instead to the Reverend Patrick MacQueen, stated as being a better enchanter than any of them. He was powerful enough to summon seven devils to do his bidding and could build an entire castle between sunrise and sunset. It is in Margaret's confession that we first hear of the vernacular term 'second sight', ascribed to her servant, who she stated firmly was not a witch.[2] This trial in Argyll had many of the attributes of supernatural-political intrigue that we have noted in earlier Lowland examples, albeit here the scheming occurred in the upper echelons of the Clan Campbell. Beyond this, witchcraft in the heartlands of the Highlands did not generate the amount of prosecutions evident elsewhere in Scotland. So, whether that means there was less witchcraft there, or if it took a different form there has to be looked at, in conjunction with those other aspects of the supernatural which seemed prevalent in the region.

The connection between witchcraft and the omnipresent Highland phenomenon known as second sight was always intangible, and seldom mentioned in records. A notable latter-day case was that of Archibald Roddie, accused of being a charmer in 1723. A client who used him to heal his horses said he only did so because he was skilled, not because he had magical abilities. Another, who sought his help to recover stolen items, said he did not know that Roddie was a charmer 'and only thought he had the second sight'.[3] An English traveller named Thomas Kirk who went to the Sutherland town of Dornoch was given some information about the relationship between second sight and other forms of occult belief and practice:

> They foresee sad accidents that befall men whom they never saw, and can describe them, but with great deal of terror to themselves, for they would gladly be quit of this faculty. The gentleman told us that they believed their ancestors had been witches, and got that boon of the devil: that such and such of their posterity should have that particular favour from him, to be tormented with a foresight of horrible spectacles, &c.[4]

What seems to be clear about second sight, *taish* in Gaelic, is that it could touch all sorts of people, almost indiscriminately. It could be heritable, but might equally strike an unfortunate individual out of the blue and remain with them for life. It could be part of the toolkit of a magical practitioner, but was more likely to be a psychic disability suffered by a hapless everyman or woman. Vivid representations of future or current events, glimpses of far distant occurrences, came randomly and were almost always unwelcome. The extra sight seldom represented happy things, nor bland and reassuring images.

The Highlands, we can see, were not untouched by witchcraft, even at the highest level. The regional folklore is replete with formidable, mostly female figures who may or may not have been inherited from primordial legend and myth. They were, on the whole, accorded huge power and were not hugely enamoured of ordinary people. Witch prosecutions were scattered through the decades and can't always be correlated with the strength of Presbyterian infrastructure and mindset in particular areas. The last Scottish witch, as no one is allowed to forget, was put to death at Dornoch in Sutherland in 1727. Less well-known is the fact that the last witchcraft executions sanctioned by the Privy Council were in Inverness in 1706, when brothers George and Lachlan Rattray were convicted and eventually banished. But the numbers tend to speak for themselves when it comes to numbers of witchcraft prosecutions in the north and north-west of Scotland. Thomas Brochard has calculated that the Northern Highlands accounted for just eight per cent of Scottish named accused witches in the years 1560–1640.[5] The same author also points out that most of the Highland cases occurred near that region's east coast or in areas relatively close to the Lowlands.[6] There may have been around 230 prosecutions in the Highlands and Islands (though this would include the mainly non-Gaelic county of Caithness).[7]

Christina Larner also observed that Tain in Easter Ross had a history of witchcraft prosecutions that stretched from 1590 to 1699.[8] She also inferred that the localised control of clan leaders dealt with wrong-doing, supernatural and otherwise, before it became a major problem to communities. It has often been observed that there is a complete absence of witchcraft prosecutions in the Outer Hebrides and in Skye. But the folklore record seems to suggest that malicious magical workers were recognised in the glens and islands and dealt with by the people who lived there, sometimes fatally. In the records of witchcraft documents, there is little discernible difference between cases in the Lowlands and those in the Gaelic speaking areas, though the concept of demonic pacts was a less common feature in the Highlands.[9] There are many possibly ingredients for the lack of ferocious or sustained witch panics in this region. The Protestant faith did not have the same infrastructure of ministers in the north and the mountainous landscape meant the enforcement of religious discipline was lax.

The fact that there was no native word strictly denoting a witch is a significant fact. An earlier word from medieval Irish, *amaid*, had a variety of meanings: foolish woman, woman with supernatural powers, hag, witch. The replacement term *buidseach*, witch, derives from English, and may have come into being sometime between the late sixteenth and mid-seventeenth centuries when the concept of malignant witchcraft directly aligned with harm, and the powers of the Devil came into focus throughout the British Isles. While *buidseach* denotes a male witch, the female equivalent is *banabhuidseach*, which is more common, reflecting as in the Lowlands the more common association of witchcraft with women. The word *fiosache* equates with the English term seer and comes from a root connotating 'knowledge or information'.[10]

The suggestion that there was generally no Highland Gaelic equivalent of the fearsome community witch who terrified Lowland towns and villages has some validity. Even in folklore there is little mention of that stereotype, the satanic bugbear of every central belt Kirk session. This was someone, usually female, who was a canker of fear in the neighbourhood, polluting everything in the vicinity, sometimes for decades, and whose crimes ranged from the exceptionally petty to the grandiose heights of satanic conspiracy. The Highlands did have some tales concerning these types of witches, but there were grander tales too of witches who could freeze the rivers and peaks and demolish whole forests out of sheer malice. This type, a more elemental, and essentially non-human 'witch' is very rarely found in the Lowlands.

Another contentious area is the general attitude to people in the Highlands about non-human entities, particularly fairies of all sorts, the class of beings which were keenly equated with demons in the Lowlands, by the Kirk if not the people. Did Highlanders have a more dangerous relationship with the *sithean*, or fairies, than others in Scotland? The contention that these beings were perceived to be more treacherously hostile to humans in the Highlands than they were in the Lowlands has been made by the scholar Ronald Hutton, who had stated that the misfortunes suffered by people respectively in both regions were therefore commonly attributed to the fairies or to witches. This is debatable; people in the Lowlands believed just as much in fairies as those in the Highlands. The difference was that their (Kirk) elders and betters hammered home the facts that fairies were intrinsically diabolic.

Reading into the comparative and cumulative folklore record not just for Ireland but also for the equally Gaelic Isle of Man in the early modern period, we can see the same lack of all-powerful community witch correlated by an alarmingly active and malicious fairy realm interacting with humanity.[11]

There may be some difference generally in the portrayal of wizards as 'Men of Power' in the Gàidhealtachd. Some folktales involving male witches in the Highlands have a tendency to emphasise their mystery and magical strength as well as their selfishness. Typical was the North Uist wizard 'Macpherson of Power' (*Mac Mhuirich nam buadh*). While becalmed on an ocean journey one day, the skipper asked Macpherson to raise a wind, in an incident remembered in 'Big Macmhuirich's Supplication' (*Achanaich Mhic Mhuirich Mhòir*). The wizard chanted a spell but the captain was unhappy with the result and declared, 'Weak and trifling you have asked it, when I myself am at the helm'. After a further incantation the captain was still unimpressed. So the wizard declared:

> If there be a wind in cold hell,
> Devil; send it after us,
> In waves and surges;
> And if one go ashore, let it be I;
> And if two, I and my dog.

In the subsequent sudden storm, the boat capsized and all on board lost their lives, except (of course) the wizard and his hound.[12] A modern oral tale set in the sixth century has the (pagan) wizard accompanying St Columba from Iona to Lismore. In this version, it is MacMhuirich who begs for a wind to be raised and he perishes and the saint survive when the ship overturns.[13]

The sinister nature and persistence of wizardry are also evidenced in the folklore record. A Tiree headstone placed above the remains of a meddler in the black arts would not remain still in place until it was secured to the spot by a chain. More alarmingly, an old Ross-shire wizard who died in his son's house and who was laid out in preparation for the wake would not rest. One of the children in the house unwisely looked through a chink in the door of the closet at midnight and observed to his mother, 'Mother, mother! My grandfather is rising!' The undead magician tried to get through the door, but it was locked, so tried to bury underneath to escape, to the terror of the household, and was only stilled and allowed to be buried by the crowing of the cock at dawn.[14]

So if we accept that witchcraft and fairies were a feature of Highland life no less than Lowland life, what about the prime progenitor of all mankind's ills, Satan himself. He was certainly alive and well and as feared in upland areas as elsewhere. The Highland euphemisms for the Devil were more euphonious possibly than his nicknames further south. If mentioned at all, he was sometimes termed *an donas*, 'the Bad One', or *an riabhach mór* 'the big grizzled one'. John Gregorson Campbell supplies an array of bynames which show that Satan was never far from people's thoughts. In the North Highlands, the Devil was *Bidean, Dithean, Bradaidh*. More generally, he enjoyed an array of nicknames:

> The worthless one (*am fear nach fhiach*)
> The one whom I will not mention (*am fear nach abair mi*)
> Yon one (*am fear ud*)
> The one big one (*an aon fhear mór*)
> The one from the abyss (*an t-aibhisteir*)
> The mean mischievous one (*an rosad*)
> The big sorrow (*an dòlas mór*)
> The son of cursing (*mac-mollachd*)
> The big grizzled one (*an riabhach mór*)
> The bad one (*an donas*)
> The bad spirit (*ain-spiorad, droch-spiorad*)
> Black Donald (*Dòmhnall Dubh*).[15]

While we are keeping score, we should mention here the panoply of Lowland nicknames for Satan also. Variations on a theme are Auld Clootie, Auld Hornie, Auld Nick, Auld Sym, Auld Carle, Auld Chiel, Auld Harry, Auld Sandy, or the Auld Ane. Other names include the Halyman, Goodman, Whaupneb, and the Earl of Hell.[16] Compare this with Ireland, a country that was notably free of witchcraft persecution, various reasons for which have been given, including a supposed reluctance on the part of the native Catholic population to betray their fellow countrypeople to an English judicial system which was controlled by the Protestant English.[17]

While the outside world took little interest in the mysteries of the Scottish Gaelic world until the dawn of the Age of Enlightenment, and it was largely shunned by Lowland Scots, the existence of the unseen world was integrated into the daily fabric of life in the north. While it may be a gross generalisation to say that evil and unexpected events were blamed on fairies in the Gaelic world, and witches in the Scots-speaking world, there is some truth in it. There's also accuracy in the observation that people who had occult powers in the Highlands were often uncomfortable with the 'gift' and may not have had any choice about possessing these powers. This was believed to be the case with those burdened with the second sight (the ability to see future events or those happening elsewhere) and the evil-eye (the power to bring misfortune to living beings and inanimate objects through looking at them). The prevalence of belief in the evil-eye was long-lasting and a marker of wider superstitious credence in Highland society. There was a huge body of belief around *cronachadh*, the evil-eye, including a body of charms and rituals designed to prevent or counteract it. The Gael's common armoury of curses again the evil of *sithean*, human evildoers, and all, may have left them feeling less powerless than witch-ridden communities in the Lowlands.

Some have believed that the evil-eye was a mainly male gift, or affliction. This is contradicted by a study of the subject which quotes two ministers in saying it mainly affected females.[18] It was always supposed that this power was not exercised out of malice, but the possessor of it could cause harm merely by casting his eyes upon certain things. Some of those who had it had to be exceptionally careful of everything in their surroundings. An example is given of one man who believed he had the evil-eye. The man had to avert his eye as the milk was being carried from his byre, in case he soured it, and had to shut his eyes while passing his own lambs. He dared not look his neighbour in the face for fear that something bad should befall him.[19] People who had deep set eyes were often suspected of having the evil-eye.[20] In some districts the condition was believed to be hereditary. Even expressing admiration for a particular beast could contrarily cause illness or death in that animal. People who had eyes of two different colours were also branded as having the evil-eye. The indiscriminate nature of the malady engendered fear, so that some pedlars only went abroad at night, fearful of being looked upon by strangers, and some mothers took care not to stare at their children. If a child was afflicted by an illness which was suspected as having been caused by the evil-eye, the local wise person was sent for and a sixpence was placed in a bowl of water and then upturned. If the coin stuck to the bottom of the bowl, this was a sign that the evil-eye was to blame.[21] There was some belief that the evil-eye might be sponsored by discontent, an unhappy mind, or by envy, covetousness or other mean feelings, but equally it was also thought best by some not to enquire too closely as to its cause (perhaps for fear of infection or transference of the malady?). There seems to have been countless ways to avert or lessen the effects of the evil-eye, which demonstrates its widespread nature. One method of warding off the curse was to use *burn airgid*, water which had silver coins immersed in it. Another ritual, used to stop the evil-eye harming and animal, was to 'wet your eye', *fliuch do shuil*.[22] Evil-eye was noted worldwide but in the rest of Britain its occurrence was less concentrated. Unlike in the Highlands, however, the use of the evil-eye in England and Lowland Scotland was mostly regarded as a deliberately malicious power that a witch had full control over.[23] The evil-eye condition in Ireland was seemingly split between those who unwittingly inherited it and those who had it and chose to do harm with it.[24]

Second sight (in Gaelic *an dà shealladh* or *taibhsearachd*) was, for some commentators, a mainly male aberration. It may be easy to dismiss this as chauvinism, albeit that this opinion was held by some acute observers of this and allied wonders. The Episcopalian minister, Robert Kirk, author of *The Secret Commonwealth*, stated that men mostly had the facility, and that it was a hereditary trait mostly passed from father to son, 'females being but seldom so qualified' and 'their predictions are not so certane'.[25] But there were evidently many women who did have this power too. Kirk seems to contradict himself somewhat with the observation that 'many Highlanders, yet far more Islanders were qualified with this sight. That Men, Women, and Children indistinctlie were subject to it'.[26] There is also the widespread Scottish tradition that occult powers can be purposely passed on between family members, but only from female to male and vice versa. A wise man named Peter Towie, from Aberdeenshire, claimed to have been gifted his powers by his wife before she died. A similar tradition of transfer to the opposite sex was believed in Ross-shire until modern times.[27]

The reason for the supposed prevalence of the power in the Highlands, and possibly particularly in the Hebrides, is uncertain, and though there were certainly instances of the ability noted from different countries, these were isolated examples and did not seem to be embedded in native culture to the same extent.[28]

The relationship between the subject of second sight and belief and interaction with fairies, and also whether second sight indicated, to religious observers and others, an association with witchcraft, is not always clear. Many of those credited with having second sight in written and oral accounts were not, in any other way, different from other community members, and nor were they stigmatised for unlawful occult practices. The Episcopalian minister, Robert Kirk, blurred the boundaries of second sight and fairydom in the late seventeenth century, though few modern writers have followed his conception of the Otherworld connections. But Kirk's delicate interlinking of these worlds is seen as being aligned with traditional Gaelic beliefs by some others, with the ability to see fairies being postulated as a specialised variety of second sight.[29] In the south, there was an effort to link all fairy interaction revealed by community members with diabolism and witchcraft, but there seems to have been little recorded mention of second sight in Lowland witchcraft records, so we do not know the extent to which it was evident, nor how it was seen when it did appear.

The further question of whether those who had the facility of second sight could actually control it to any extent is not wholly clear, though there are examples of those who claimed the ability in order to control others. Martin Martin relates the story of a man named Roderick the Imposter in St Kilda at the end of the seventeenth century. This man had been 'endued with that rare Faculty of enjoying the Second Sight, which makes it the more probable that he was haunted by a familiar Spirit'. Roderick, in the mould of a cult leader, had imposed a set of religious beliefs upon some people in that remote island, insisting that he had received them from St John the Baptist. He had encountered this saint at 18 when he had transgressed the Sabbath and went fishing. St John was seen as a Lowland man, with a cloak and hat. The saint instructed Roderick in a number of religious duties, including observances of fasts and keeping a small mound on the island sacred to him. He also received a special instruction from the Virgin Mary which helped women prevent miscarriage. Taking advantage of his charisma and power over the community, he debauched some of the young island women. It was this aspect of his behaviour rather than the religious/magical aspect which made the St Kildans turn against him. He was removed from the island and exiled on Skye.[30] What part second sight actually played in Roderick's cult infrastructure is difficult to say. In one instance, he terrified a man by predicting that he would die in battle, though the man actually ended up being drowned. He also said that he was in contact with some dead islanders. Roderick may have generally been employing a hotchpotch of traditional folk beliefs and garbled Catholic rites to have his sway over the locals.

Apart from the idiosyncratic example of Roderick, there were clearly other individuals that had some control over second sight in a meaningful way. One aspect of this was their ability to transfer to power to see visions by physical contact with another person. Robert Kirk suggested a definite ritual for a curious enquirer to temporarily acquire visionary status. He puts his foot on the seer's foot and the seer puts his hand on the enquirer's head. Then the enquirer looks over the seer's right shoulder.

> Then will he see a multitude of Wight's like furious hardie men flocking to him hastily from all quarters, as thick as atomes in the air, which are no nonentities or phantasms, creatures, proceeding from ane affrighted apprehensione confused or crazed sense; but Realities, appearing to a stable man in his awaking sense...[31]

The tumultuous array of fairy spirits are terrifyingly visible, but whether other things may be seen is not stated. This ritual of transmission was not unique to Scotland. A Staffordshire man named John Scott asked an astrologer named William Hodges to show him the person he would marry. Hodges took him into a field and brought his magic crystal and had the man put his foot on his and look into his crystal, where Scott saw the woman he would eventually wed.[32]

The purposeful seeking of supernatural visions through ritual was clearly reserved for a few men and women and not those who were simply passive victims of unsought second sight. Various means were employed by these few to summon meaningful visions from the ether, which may provide insight into the type of behaviour which witches of both sexes may have employed also. The words *frith* and *frithir* in Gaelic are associated with seership and augury. The root word *frith* has connotations with rage, angry glances, divination and incantation. The seer (*frithir*) who wished to answer an enquiry, which could be as commonplace as a request for the location of a person or item, had to make ready by fasting and then, on the first Monday of the quarter, just before dawn, he had to go with uncovered head and feet and closed eyes to the doorstep and place a hand on each door jamb. There he would open his eyes and make his divination based on what he saw there.[33]

The most famous seer in Highland history, and a rival in overall Scottish fame to True Thomas, was the Brahan Seer, often identified with Coinneach Odhar. Coinneach, like Thomas, is not an easy figure to dislodge from the uncertain enigma of folklore. Like Michael Scot, various places have claimed the seer as a native. The most publicised place of his birth is Baile na Cille, in Uig parish, Lewis, and it was here that he gained the power of prophecy as a child. Another place in Lewis which claims him (in an early written account) is Ness.

There are divergent traditions about the era in which he lived also. The earlier claim identifies him as one of a group of seven men and twenty-five women named in a commission of justiciary permitting the Sheriff of Cromarty and others to search for an arrest of those named who were accused of:

> exercising the diabolical, iniquitous, and odious crimes of the art of magic, incantation, murder, homicide, and other horrible crimes and sins, committed within the boundaries of the earldom of Ross and the Lordship of Ardmanach [The Black Isle] and other parts within the Sheriffs district of Inverness.[34]

The last named is wrongly identified by the Scots speaking clerk in Edinburgh who drew up the document as Keanoch Ower, termed 'the leading or principal enchantress'. Another commission, dated three months later, mentions 'Kenneth alias Kennoch Owir, principal or leader of the art of magic'.[35] One of the women named appears to have been associated with the case of Lady Munro of Foulis, who was charged and acquitted of attempting to murder her stepson by magical means. While some of those in this very early witchcraft record suffered death, there is no record that this Coinneach Odhar did. Among those named in the commissions are Mariota McAlester, called Loskoir Longert, the latter being an alias meaning either 'burn the ladle' or, more dramatically, 'burn the castle'. A male accomplice, who was executed (along with another man, William MacGillivrey) in November or December 1577 is Thomas alias Cassindonisch, probably *Cas-an-donais*, 'Devil's Foot'.[36] Other witches elsewhere in Scotland adopted, or were given, aliases, usually by Satan himself. Otherwise, if the members of the gang were involved in criminal/occult enterprise, the adoption of false names would throw the law off their trail. It may have been an act of bravado that made Kenneth keep his original name, albeit with a descriptive appellation.

Keanoch or Kenneth and others had escaped after the first commission and was not one of the ten executed in the first round-up. Who was this elusive Kenneth? His appellation *Odhar* means sallow or dun, which may signify that he was suffering from some illness. A man named Kennocht Owyr featured in legal proceedings in 1576. Margret Waus, wife of a burgess in Inverness, alleged that James Fraser had colluded with her own servant to defraud her of furs and skins. The servant had been hired for a ten-year period in November 1568, and part of the agreement between them was that any skins he brought into Inverness were hers. The servant was Kennocht Owyr or Owir, and he had allegedly met and illicitly traded with James Fraser in half a dozen fairs and markets in the region. Fraser denied any illegality though he admitted buying skins from a trader who was in this Kennocht's company.[37] This occult outlaw fits in well with a type of marginalised character we have encountered elsewhere, a jack-of-all-trades, few of them legitimate, who was also a traveller and an elusive character. Those witches condemned in 1577–78 were put to death at Chanonry Point, at Fortrose in the Black Isle. This was also the reputed site of the seer's demise in later tradition. The rather flimsy details, suggesting an active group of malevolent criminals, seems at odds also with the Brahan Seer's later reputation as a rather blank or neutral soothsayer who found fame with a uniquely doom-laden set of prophecies relating to multiple places in the Highlands.

Later tradition associated the Brahan Seer with the earldom of Seaforth, a title which did not get awarded to the Mackenzie family until 1623. This legend, popularised since the nineteenth century, states that the seer worked and lived mostly near Brahan Castle, home of the Seaforths, and he is also associated with nearby Strathpeffer. and here he allegedly died. His legendary end was brought about by revealing to the countess that her husband was well and happy, albeit he was in the arms of another woman in France. The noblewoman then ordered the unhappy seer to be burned alive, which caused him to curse the whole Mackenzie line. Like some others detailed in this book (notably Willox Macgregor), the Brahan Seer employed a magical talisman, a stone which he used to see visions. He variously obtained this as a gift from the ghost of a Norse princess or else retrieved it from a raven's nest.[38]

As a man, rather than a prophetic cypher, Coinneach defies investigation. Did he proffer more general predictions for a paying clientele as well as the rather grandiose prophecies affixed to a wider range of landmarks around the north and north west? If so, little evidence of this survives. His legend, for lack of human detail, rivals that of True Thomas, whose heyday was many centuries before him. There is a faint hint of him being unpopular, or perhaps feared, during his lifetime. One folk tale about how the seer acquired his magical stone states that it was found in his waistcoat one day and saved his life. His employer's wife despised him and had left poisoned food beside him while he slept in a remote place while out cutting peat. He would have eaten the food, but the magic stone, which had appeared out of nowhere, gave him the power to divine her intention, and also provided a gateway for seeing the motives of others.[39] It has been suggested that a Mackenzie of Easter Ross carried the legend of Coinneach Odhar to Lewis where it took root in the seventeenth century, to the extent that he was regarded as a native there and that legend overtook the original story.[40] This may well be true. It is tempting also to imagine two such men, whose identities somehow became confused over time. To theorise that the later man, if he existed, consciously took on the name and attributes of the original elusive seer is imagining too much.

The interest in Scottish, mainly Highland, seers which came to fascinate a part of the English intelligentsia from the late seventeenth century almost amounted to a mania. It was based, to some extent, on age-old superstitions of belief common in many parts of the world, that the far north, whether it be Scotland, Lappland or Siberia, were habitually the abodes of magic superstition and, by extension, prevalent pagan evil.

There was difference of opinion about whether the facility was a natural and unchosen 'gift', or whether it could be acquired or learnt. Martin Martin speaks about a novice seer, implying some sort of tutelage. There are abundant mentions of second-sight being passed down in families. There is also mention of the power being a commodity which could be bought and sold. A late seventeenth-century letter contains an anecdote about a seer being willing to pass on the mechanics of his ability to an enquirer for a pound or two of tobacco.[41]

One of the most outlandish latter day seers was the deaf mystic Duncan Campbell, who found some fame as an adult in England. His biography, which may have been authored by Daniel Defoe (or more likely a contemporary), spuriously has him being born in Sweden, son of a shipwrecked Shetland father. The work shows unusually prescient sympathy for the pagan and shamanistic Sámi people, abhorring their persecution.[42] Despite his foreign birth (his mother was allegedly from Lapland) and the fact that his father Archibald actively fought for the Jacobites on his return to Scotland, Duncan carved a successful career as a society mystic for some decades until his death in 1730. His acceptance into aristocratic circles was a combination of exotic background and the novelty of his background and the enticing air of mystery he was offering.

Campbell appeared in London in 1694, when he was 14, but he was not noticed in periodicals until 1709, when his deaf-and-dumb condition was noted alongside his remarkable predictions that had captured the attention of the fashionable and thrill-seeking in the Capital, including Queen Anne. He communicated by touch and relayed his psychic prognostications by writing. Doubters quickly tried to demonstrate that he was a fraud, drawing on suspicions of his showmanship and oddly exotic background. (His Scottish father may also have been a fabrication.[43]) Deafness, and to a lesser extent other disabilities, was associated with second-sight and other supernormal powers. Among these was William Edmondstone the Laird of Duntreath, near Paisley, famed for his predictions in the seventeenth century. In 1651, the Presbytery of Haddington noted a rash of cases of people consulting mute people to find lost items. There were numerous cases of disciplinary action against people who consulted mute people in East Lothian in the seventeenth century.[44] In Ayr in 1684, the session rebuked several people who consulted a mute man with the reputation of finding lost items.

The reason for the decline (though not the extinction) of second-sight in the Highlands is a process which has been going on since the eighteenth century and, though there is no definitive reason behind the decline, it certainly parallels the shrinkage in traditional Gaelic beliefs and artistic activity, such as oral storytelling and certain types of poetry.[45]

One of the most popular divination methods in the Highlands (though used elsewhere in the world) was by means of a sheep's shoulder blade. In the eighteenth century, John Ramsay of Ochtertyre said that the scapula, or shoulder-blade, of a one-year-old black sheep was preferred, and the operation of divination had to be done under strict conditions: 'The moon must not change between the death of the creature and the making this use of its shoulder-blade'. The operation was highly dangerous; even in the current age the writer John MacInnes was told that, during the divination act, the diviner had to 'go very near the Devil's tooth'.[46] Kirk also states that a seer could impose his visions upon another person and cites the example of a man named Stewart who was dismissive of second-sight until a seer gave him access to the ability. The shock of the visions made him lose the power to walk and speak, and made his breathing dramatically increase.[47]

An interesting associated aspect of second sight is the *co-choisiche*, co-walker. This is nearly similar to the doppelganger, or fetch, a phantasm of a living person. But, instead of being a mere mirror image which can be seen be anyone, the co-walker is imbued with its own, often sinister or anarchic personality and it can appear to strangers and even hound the person who it looks like. MacInnes states that the Irish do not share with the Scottish Gaels the terminology relating to the 'two sights' or the 'co-walker', nor the concept relating to the latter.[48] The co-walker was reckoned by Robert Kirk to be a fairy shadow of an identical mortal person. They were frequently seen shortly before the deaths of the humans they resembled.

The fame of the far north as a supernatural region is often put down to the interest of the natural philosopher and chemist Robert Boyle with George Mackenzie, Lord Tarbat, in 1678. After the meeting, Tarbat sent the Englishman even more details of the strange phenomenon of second-sight, and this kick-started the southern interest in the subject.

From Scotland and England, the legend of Scottish second-sight and Highland otherworldliness spread throughout Europe and was a significant component in the Romantic revival. Translations of works by Martin Martin, Samuel Johnson and Walter Scott popularised Scotland as the home of second-sight and associated uncanniness in the late eighteenth and early nineteenth centuries.[49] But this interest abroad dwindled in parallel with the declining instances of second-sight in the Highlands, plus the increasing velocity of the Industrial Revolution. In a sense it was a pity that it was not a more substantial substratum in Gaelic society by the time that the Society for Psychical Research and like-minded bodies came fully into prominence in the late Victorian era. Their more rigorous processes and examination may have given greater results than were ever dreamed about by Robert Boyle and his associates.

Chapter 9

The Last Magicians

Gregor Willox and Other Cunning Men

Towards the modern age, the incidences of those known to have supernatural power in the community dwindled significantly, reflecting a change in belief, superstition, but also practice. The record of the warlocks and wizards who inhabited Scotland during the eighteenth and nineteenth centuries is as fragmentary and incoherent as the legends which describe the wizard lairds whose heyday was a century earlier. Like the tales of those lairds, the traditions of latter-day figures are a bounty for folklorists but frustrating for historians who might hope to unearth the human figures behind local traditions. Typical of these men, and representative of such figures from the heartland of Scottish tradition in the North-East, was Colin Massie, the Warlock of Glendye. Massie is said to have flourished in the late seventeenth and early eighteenth centuries in Kincardineshire, and the fullest account of his exploits was written by local writer Joseph Grant.[1] Massie, a stranger to the district, lived with his mother and ill-witted brother, and was apparently feared by the neighbourhood. But no details of his powers or activities as a warlock survive. Grant's story involves the warlock's revenge on a local laird who shot and killed Colin's mother, a witch, while she was in the form of a hare. The warlock captured the laird and held him under a spell, determined to kill him, but he succumbed to the pleasing of a young maiden and released the man unharmed. The whole tale, with its glib happy ending, is highly unsatisfactory, and the high-flown standard English spoken by the apparently bestial warlock is disappointing. Subsequent histories of the district do little to cast light on the elusive Colin Massie, though it is thought he was remembered vaguely in the parish of Birse. Along with his presumed magical talents, Colin regularly attended local witches' sabbats, where he enjoyed the role of official piper.[2]

Another supposed warlock was John Farquharson of Carue, tacksman in Parks of Coldstone, Blelack, Deeside. Gordon, Laird of Blelack, decided to evict the fairies inhabiting the Seely Howe, a hollow in Carne Hillock on Carue Farm. Before leaving for the Jacobite wars he told Farquharson to make them quit but the fairies refused to vacate until they were assigned another home. Eventually they were sent to the Hill of Fare, 17 miles away, near Banchory, but they hated it there and issued a curse on Gordon:

> Dool, dool to Blelack
> And dool to Blelack's heir
> For driving us from the Seely Howe
> To the cauld Hill o' Fare.

Farquharson was also cursed:

> While corn and girss grows to the air
> John Farquharson and his seed shall thrive nae mair.

Farquharson is supposed to have suffered bad luck from that day and left his native country, never to return. Gordon died without lawful issue and the estate passed to his nephew, Charles Rose, whose own son was reputedly half-witted and died a pauper in 1869.[3] A local author added that John Farquharson was previously a longtime friend of the fairies; they visited him often in his home and he was designated with the title of 'Fairy Doctor'. They would even serenade him, and one surviving refrain from a song of theirs ran, 'Johnny, I lo'e ye, Johnny, I lo'e ye, Nine times in ae nicht will I come and see thee'. Following the flitting of the fairies, Farquharson did not in fact suffer as the common tradition insists. He removed to Moray and lived peacefully on a farm near Forres until his death.[4] While we should never be so cynical that we disregard the merits of a good folk tale, we might wish for more details about the actual magical activities of men like Farquharson. The displacement of the fairies significantly parallels with local human eviction and disruption caused by loyalty to the house of Stuart.

A fair number of supposed warlocks or wise men were documented in relatively recent times in various parts of Scotland. Allowing for the bias of those who described them, none of the magical workers survive the process of scrutiny with impressive credentials. It is hard to determine whether these cunning men represent the degraded tail end of a legitimate tradition or whether such warlocks were always dubious in their powers and only revealed as such by modern observers who exposed them in print. Modern assessments of such men are hampered by incomplete sources. Most writers who described wise men during the nineteenth century were either hostile of their subjects (sometimes humorously) or treated the subject with colourful quaintness.

Born in the 1750s and dying in 1833, the archetype of the late charlatan-trickster type of male wizard was Gregor Willox Macgregor of Banffshire. His father, Robert Willox Macgregor, was deer forester at Strathavon on the Duke of Gordon's estate for two decades, starting in 1762. His role was to prevent poaching and deliver venison to Gordon and his sub-tenants but he was unpopular in the locality because of his manipulation of people and his self-serving nature. In a letter to the duke's factor he remarked on the favour the nobleman paid him by calling at his house and Willox noted that the visit would have galled his enemies. He also earned opponents for stanchly repelling deer poachers and trespassers on the Gordon lands. It may be in his time that the name Willox was recast as 'Wild Ox' in the locality.[5]

But Willox got into trouble when a deer carcass was found on his property; he claimed it was out of season and the meat was only fit for dogs. Venison he sent to Gordon Castle was rotten, and the cook there furiously complained. Another complaint involved cattle straying into his property. Willox tried to demand payment from the owners who wanted the animals' returned. In 1793, two tacksmen wrote to the duke complaining of Macgregor because of his oppression and 'besides he acts the conjurer and frights the ignorant in this way and makes a great deal of money by water he gives them of a white stone which he says cures all diseases'.[6] Robert Macgregor was forced to leave his position the following year.

Gregor Willox Macgregor followed his father in both official and magical careers. He was born illegitimate, which spurred him on to achieve distinction His claims of being from a family renowned for magical ability are unproven. It's tempting to link him to Duncan Greggor who got in trouble with the Kirk session of Elgin in 1734. Gregor's child was refused baptism on the basis that he was a reputed charmer. He admitted the ability to cure fevers with a ritual involving immersing lead in water and invoking the Trinity. If cured, the metal bobbed on the surface of the water like the heart of a fowl. He confessed to also curing by means of herbs, but nothing diabolical. He was referred to the Presbytery and was rebuked and the case dismissed.[7]

The lineage of the Strathavon Macgregors seem to have derived from the Macgregors of Rolo. We know there was a John Willox who tenanted the farm of Easter Raigmore between 1718 and 1735, who seems to be the ancestor of the magician.[8] Another ancestor also had a disreputable reputation:

> The first of this notorious race of wizards of Strathavon, before setting up as a wizard, had a small property in Strathdearn, on the south side of the River Findhorn, below the site of the present Free Church. His name was James or Gregor Willox Macgregor. He left the district in consequence of having shot at a neighbouring proprietor. As the story goes, he obtained his power as a wizard by getting possession of the magic bit of bridle of a water horse which frequented a small loch at the Pass of Slochmuick.[9]

The kelpie's bridle was the principal family heirloom, which most stories said had been won by a Macgregor ancestor in combat with the mythical water horse. Willox magnified its importance by stating that a family member had won from a water kelpie. An elaborate story that Willox was fond of relating detailed how his 'grand uncle Macgregor' encountered the aquatic being at Loch an Dorb, in the shape of a fearsome black horse. He snatched the bridle from it, at which the enraged being changed into a man and pursued him home, though Macgregor was able to elude him.[10] Looking through a hole in this bridle gave the possessor the power to see supernatural creatures, the power of a seer. According to Sir Thomas Dick Lauder, who viewed this brass object, it had no resemblance to any kind of bridle he had seen.

The other object Macgregor utilised was a magic stone, usually described as a crystal of pure white, or like a glass bulls' eye. The folklorist Walter Gregor called it the Willox Ball and said it formed half of a glass sphere. 'It was concealed for untold ages in the heart of a brick', he says, 'and was cut from its place of concealment by a fairy and given generations ago to an ancestor of the present owner as payment for a kind service'.[11] Whatever form it took, there were many healing stones in Scotland that were used for curing ills, either in humans or in cattle. Using portable stones as a tool in magical healing occur occasionally in witchcraft records. There is a record of a healer named John Brugh, of Dollar in Clackmannanshire, using 'ane enchanted stane as of the bigness of a dow' in 1643. A healer from Fyvie, Gavin Sinclair, also used a stone in healing. So did the Elgin charmer John Rind and his wife Elspet Smith, who used a shall reddish stone which was immersed in water (and sometimes whey), the liquid then used to cure animals and humans.[12]

A further tale Willox told was that his grandfather overpowered a hapless mermaid and carried her home, keeping her in the rafters of his cottage. His jealous wife began an affair with a young man in revenge. When Macgregor felt pity upon the creature and released her back into the ocean, she told him of the treachery and gifted him the magical stone as an heirloom for his family. Another story he told was that his grandfather had acquired the mystical orb in Italy.[13]

Gregor's main services were curing ailments in both humans and animals, plus curing barrenness, and also finding items which had either been lost or stolen. In common with some predecessor magical workers, Macgregor employed scant ritual, except perhaps a phrase or two of Latin and the invocation of the Father, Son and Holy Ghost. There are claims that he was a Catholic himself, but the evidence is insufficient. As well as being used to transform ordinary water into curative liquid, the stone was sometimes immersed in a bowl of water, and Gregor was able to read the surface of the water to gain information he desired, usually the identity of property theft.[14] By his time, the magical practices of Willox were looked on with a certain indulgence by enlightened religious authorities. The Reverend John Grant of Kirkmichael, writing around 1793, submitted a sarcastic description of an unnamed character who was surely the infamous Gregor Willox (or his father):

> It is the good fortune … of this country to be provided with an anti-conjurer that defeats both them [witches] and their fable patron in their combined efforts… If the spouse is jealous of her husband, the anti-conjurer is consulted to restore the affections of his bewitched heart. If a near connexion lies confined to the bed of sickness, it is in vain to expect relief without the balsamick medicine of the anti-conjurer. If a person happens to be deprived of his senses, the deranged cells of the brain must be adjusted by the magic charms of the anti-conjurer. If a farmer loses his cattle, the houses must be purified with water sprinkled by him. In searching for the latent mischief,

this gentleman never fails ... the power of his occult science, he still attracts a little of their gold from the pockets where it lodges; and in this way makes a shift to acquire a subsistence for himself and family.[15]

The nobility as well as the ministry was notably immune to Gregor's supernatural grandiosity. Gregor retained his family's attachment to the noble house of Gordon, even when he ceased to be formally employed by them. The magician offered his service to the Marquis of Huntly in 1794, vowing that he could bolster the peer's efforts to recruit men into the army. He also tried to offer the marquis an amulet which would protect the wearer from gunfire and arms. But when Huntly threatened to test the efficacy of the amulet by having his men fire at Macgregor, he quickly fled. This particular amulet seems to have been another part of his magical armoury, and he also had a sword which was employed in some magical rituals.

Many ordinary people had greater faith in him. Supplicants travelled to see him from as far south as Angus and as far north as Ross, some journeying two days to see him. He also periodically took tours around the northern counties of Inverness, Ross and Caithness to sell his magical cures. Despite this, it was claimed that local people disbelieved his powers, although he still generated significant fame or notoriety. He possessed an undoubted impulse for him to prove himself to be someone of standing, perhaps inspired by his own illegitimacy and also possibly by his awareness of other kindred who were more successful in the world. Affleck Gray states that he was distantly related to the royal court physician Sir Patrick Macgregor (1777–1828).[16]

In appearance, the wizard was of small, or medium height, but had a significant presence and piercing, deep-set grey eyes. Willox also wore a startling scarlet cloak with gold buttons, and his appearance in any locality was sometimes enough to guarantee that stolen goods were quickly restored to their owners before he could employ his magic to find them. He once came to the aid of Alexander Hay, town clerk of Nairn, who was worried by large scale theft of linen from the town's bleaching green, and when he made himself known in town, all the linen was quickly restored.[17]

The majority of Macgregor's supplicants were male, some of whom only shamefully used his services, with many claiming that their womenfolk at home forced them into seeking him out and stating that they did not believe in his powers.[18] There are many anecdotal stories of Gregor's efficacy in combatting malicious witchcraft. A man named Georgie Gall of Glenlivet encountered a strange foal one day, which seemed to be uncanny. Consulting Willox, next time he saw it he shot it with a crooked sixpence. It was soon known that an old woman with an evil reputation who lived nearby was confined to bed with a mysterious chest wound.[19]

The English traveller, Reverend James Hall passed through the area in the early nineteenth century and heard some stories about Gregor, but apparently did not meet him. He was sceptical of the cures effected by Willox and suggested those people who had beneficial results from his magic were the wonderful effects of imagination or wishful thinking. Hall provides two stories of Willox's magical operations. A Speyside man, who had been married for nine years without children, consulted Willox, to help his wife conceive. Gregor charged him a guinea and dipped his stone in half a gallon of water, saying the Lord's prayer three times in Latin, along with other Latin prayers, then gave the man a bottle of the water and instructed him to give his wife three glasses of the water each night. His wife's condition changed and she had a child every other year afterwards. In the second tale a farmer's wife who had been sick for many years came to believe her friends when they assured her it was because of bewitchment. Gregor Willox was sent for and duly arrived at the farm.

> When Willox came in his scarlet coat, breeches, &c. he perambulated the house, gardens, barns, &c. frequently standing and holding out his nose, as if to smell where the witchcraft was lodged. At length he pretended he had discovered it; and, running hastily, put his hand into a hole of the wall of the house, and pulled out a fowls stomach, broiled and cut into certain bits, which he said had been put there by a certain person, in concert with the devil. The poor woman, it seems, got a little better; and, so credulous was the farmer, as well as his neighbours, as to believe that Willox cured her.[20]

Another story applauds Willox's psychological acuity in finding out the perpetrator of a crime, a skill he may have honed over many years. He was summoned by the landlord of an inn at Spittal of Glenshee, who had been plagued by an outbreak of petty theft. Willox gathered all of the inn's employees in a barn around a pot which contained a live cock. The pot was lidded and the magician ordered all present to go around the vessel and touch it, declaring that the guilty party would be identified by the crowing of the fowl. All did so, but no crowing occurred. Gregor muttered something about trying another test. He told everyone to hold up his hands, then shouted at one man that he was the thief. The man immediately confessed. Willox, it was said, had carefully noted that the man had been the only one whose hand had not actually touched the pot, which had left soot marks on all others.[21] Sir Thomas Dick Lauder gave three tales of Willox which shed some light on his methodology. In the first, he aided a clergyman to locate the source of his herd's death which some ascribed to witchcraft. Willox privately admitted he would solve the matter through common sense and located a poisonous plant in a hollow which the cattle had been eating. In the second story, the magician aided a similarly mysterious plague in the cattle belonging to the owner of Castle Grant which was due to a malicious poisoning. Less creditably, he diagnosed the cause of a man's dislike of his wife, blaming witchcraft, and showing the man black and red floating images in his magic crystal, signifying the black and red-headed witches responsible. The man pulled his hand aside and saw beneath a black-headed and red-headed pin which were reflected in the magical stone. The outraged man angrily remonstrated with Willox, but the great wizard himself voiced outrage and said that he had only acted in a friendly manner towards his victim. But he took the precaution of threatening him with a knife, in case the man tried to back up his complaint with violence.[22]

Like many who profited from sorcery, Gregor Willox Macgregor did not prosper in the long-term, and he died in relative poverty. One of his faults is that he aspired to be a *duine uasal*, a gentleman, despite having been born illegitimate. It was said that Gregor 'talked like a printed book', and his wife, Mary Rose, came to despise his pretensions, the fancy clothes and the deer hounds which he kept. She advised women friends to beware marrying a man without means to maintain his assumed dignity, who like her Gregor, would make it an excuse to live in idleness. Macgregor found himself occasionally written about in newspapers and also attracted the interest of Sir Thomas Dick Lauder and other curious writers during his lifetime, but his reputation, or rather the belief in his powers, had ebbed towards the end of his life.

Lauder and his companions visited Macgregor in his old age at his cottage at Gaulrig in Strathavon (where Macgregors had lived since 1648). All of his former finery was gone, and he was bent, clad in homespun grey and grizzled looking. Despite the writer's expectations of seeing a vulgar and cunning countenance, the wizard showed himself dignified, if dulled by age. But he soon enlivened and shot a 'transient gleam of electric fire' at his visitors who all felt 'as if it had penetrated into the inmost recesses of our very souls'.[23] The impression was more due to Lauder's romantic hopes rather than any residual spiritual magnetism which Willox retained. The visitor noted that Willox's cottage stood above a small ravine which had the reputation of being haunted by fairies and indeed contained an artificial looking mound supposed to be their home. Whether Macgregor had been influenced by these surroundings or had invented the traditions is unknown.

Following his death, various family members remained in the district and the magical heirlooms were still sought out and used to magical purposes until the end of the nineteenth century. Several competing stones in Strathspey are still claimed as being the actual magical stone of Willox. Willox's sister seems to have dabbled in his healing pursuits in the decades after his lifetime. The *Morayshire Advertiser* in June 1862 reported that a woman in Kellas, who believed that her illness was due to bewitchment, sent for Willox's sister, who lived around 40 miles away. A fire was kindled in the kail yard and a male cat was tied by its hind legs and held over the fire until it burned to death.[24] This *taghairm* ritual was widely known in the Highlands, and this may have been one of the last times it was enacted. As for the magical bridle, it was said to have been used by Meg Willox, either the sister or daughter of the wizard, to threaten her neighbour. When this woman's cow died, a deputation from the nearest town visited Meg and took the bridle from her. What happened to it subsequently is unknown. Willox's last recorded family member was Christina Macgregor, who died around 80 years old in 1905.[25]

Although the most prominent in his class, there were other flourishing male witchcraft practitioners in the eighteenth and nineteenth centuries, even if their magical practices are only remembered in the anecdotal notices of local and folkloric writers who seldom thought of describing their practices in detail. There was the Morven practitioner *Dòmhnall Mollach*, 'Hairy Donald' (Donald Livingstone of Bunamhuilinn) who was famed for his ability to both heal and hurt cattle. A sceptical minister who demanded proof of his power witness a charmed cow fall over some rocks after Donald bewitched it.[26] Donald was an 18-year-old survivor of the Jacobite army at Culloden in 1746 and lived to the age of 88, a folk hero because of his strength and daring deeds.[27] While we have more biographical details about these magical practitioners, in most cases, than those from the sixteenth and seventeenth centuries, it still gives us less information than desirable if we try to make a comparison. Men like Willox Macgregor were more interested in payment than helping their clients, which is possibly symptomatic of a decline in the ethics and repute of charmers and cunning men.

In rural areas, concerns for the welfare of livestock meant that charmers were still operational in remote communities until modern times. Tales of the magical acumen of *skeely men* (and women) were repeated far and wide in the countryside. Walter Gregor tells of such an expert called in by a farmer worried by the deaths of several cows. The man said that a cow which was currently sick would also die and then blamed the misfortune on a neighbour who would come into the house with a little black jar and ask for milk, which must be denied. The farmer did not believe this neighbour was to blame, but sure enough she entered carrying the jar. There then followed a strange magical contest, where the woman (obviously a witch) tried to edge closer and closer to the man while he sat on a bench. He only escaped by jumping bodily away from her. 'Had the woman laid her hand on him, all his skill was gone.'[28]

Another latter day warlock was Alexander Henderson, of Meikle Wartle, Aberdeenshire. Born towards the end of the eighteenth century, he died aged 90 plus in December 1888. His father was the tenant of Skares Farm, which gave him the delightful nickname Auld Skarey, and his son was known to some as Young Skarey. The father evidently had to supplement his income by being a travelling fish merchant and made a side income of sorts by peddling charms. Alexander was apprenticed to a *soutar*, or cobbler, in Aberdeen then left the area and joined a travelling theatre company. He returned home in 1821 and resumed his old trade and also adopted his father's secondary lifestyle as a magical worker. Details of his career as a warlock are sketchy, since he did not come to the attention of writers until decades later. His earnings were as precarious as his father's and he lived in restricted means in a one bedroom cottage. Visitors were impressed by his keen wit and his ability to quote extensive passages of the Bible. But those who sought information on magical matters were often disappointed. He was once quoted as saying, 'There's nae sic a thing as witchcraft, tho some fowk believe't'. Despite this reticence, Henderson was well known for his ability to take charms off humans and animals, locate lost goods, and lay ghosts.[29]

Henderson's father was long remembered in oral tradition. The Angus-based traveller, Betsy Whyte (1919–1988), related an anecdote of 'Old Scary', a semi-whimsical figure who kept a coffin under his bed, explaining that he would not have to travel far after his death.[30] Scary was still remembered in Aberdeenshire, according to Whyte. A longer tale has Scary encountering a girl struggling to keep up with the men in gathering in the harvest with her scythe. She explained that she was exhausted and would lose her job if she couldn't work. The old magician said she didn't know how to sharpen her scythe properly. He sharpened the tool with a stone and gave it back to her, after which the scythe went cutting the crop by itself, so frenziedly that the girl had to tell the men to stand back, otherwise it would have chopped off their legs. The warlock warned her not to sharpen the scythe again that season and told her not to let any other touch it.[31] In this tradition, Scary is a benevolent figure employing his powers without payment, who only put his spell on the scythe out of pity for the girl, who was being laughed at by the men. Whyte observed that such figures had a special place in rural society, half the time laughed at, but also treated circumspectly, just in case offence was caused and they put some curse on you. In earlier times, they would hardly have been subjects of mirth.

For every few men (and women) like Gregor Willox Macgregor, there were occasional low key characters, into the nineteenth century, at the tail end of a magical tradition. The difficulty of determining whether there were many individuals into the Victorian age who consciously practised magic or witchcraft is hampered by the fragmentary anecdotal evidence. Typical is the anecdotal remembrance of one such character, from Bridge of Savock, Aberdeenshire, known as 'Auld Sautie or Sawtie' (incidentally one of the bynames given to Satan). He had a reputation of uncanniness and, when any came to consult him, he hid somewhere within earshot while the enquirer spoke with his wife. He then made a great show of arriving from some far part of the farm, and accosted the seeker with apparent uncanny knowledge about his enquiry: 'Aye, ye have come about your brindled coo. It's been ailing since Feesday', or the like'. This was enough to convince more gullible clients of his supernatural abilities.[32] Sawtie, whose real name was Forman, was also able to exploit the fears in the community. When a farmer asked him to diagnose why his cattle were ill, Sautie identified the culprit who had betwitched them and advised the man the herd would not thrive until he drew blood from the witch, 'draw bleed o' im abeen the breath'. The man immediately took the knife which his servant was using to prepare bannocks, went to the neighbouring farm and knocked down the farmer, who had been ploughing, then cut a cross in his forehead aboved his eyebrows. His cattle recovered their health.[33] Drawing a witch's blood was a certain method of dispelling their power.

Chapter 10

Final Embers

The Goodman's Croft and the Horseman's Word

Look at most large-scale maps of modern Scotland and you might see the Devil's name peeping out from odd corners of a two-dimensional landscape, tucked away in peculiar places of lowland arable farms, or delineated by strangely jagged inverted fractures in the coastline. Some of these places are symbolically linked with the power of darkness because of geographical peculiarity, the remembrance of an uncanny event, or some local tradition.

Other places were determinedly not named after Satan, but were dedicated to him, or some other supernatural being. For centuries ordinary crofters, tenant farmers and even rich landowners were in collusion with the same unseen guiding spirits behind witchcraft and unlawful magic. For a century and more the reformed Kirk tried to outlaw the practice of landholders setting part of their land aside, deliberately uncultivated, as an ongoing appeasement to Satan. These portions of land were particularly noted in the North-East of Scotland, where they went by various names which pointedly omitted the formal title of the Devil. The Good Man's (or Gude Man's) Croft was a feature on farms large and small. Other names for it included the Gi'en (Given) Land (or Rig), emphasising the purposeful, votive nature of the land's usage. Other variations included the Guidman's Craft, Goodman's Fauld, Ground or Taft, or Clootie's Croft, and the Black Faulie. A variant from Banff was the Hellie Man's Rig, Hellie Man being a pseudonym for Satan. The compact between presumably otherwise God-fearing farmers and Hell deserves some consideration.

Sir Walter Scott regarded the Gudeman's Crofts as survivals of ancient sites dedicated to pagan deities, where ordinary mortals were banned from trespassing. Some modern authorities link them with pagan sanctuaries, *friðgeard*, around natural objects noted in medieval English records.[1] But there is no proof that these oddments of land were always set aside in this way, and some evidence that previously normal land was selected and set aside into the modern age. A hard-bitten country man in centuries gone by would not have had access to such high-flown analogies, but would had subscribed to the common knowledge, that if he did not sacrifice some of his valuable arable soil to forces better not named, some evil would perhaps befall his cattle. Protection of herds was mentioned in some censorious records about the crofts. While it might be easy to explain the crofts as a grudging superstitious insurance policy which only involved corners of fields, this is not borne out by analysis.

In some cases, substantial plots of very decent land were involved. Nor can we assume that it was just the case of male farmers turning a passive, blind eye to older, darker beliefs. Farmers could and did try a variety of things to protect their beasts, some of them superstitious, when disease was prevalent. In 1669, five men in Towie and Strathdon, Aberdeenshire, were found guilty of 'practiseing unwarrantabl cures of their cattell' and were ordained to make public repentance before their congregations.[2] While the great majority of tenants and landowners were men, some were not. Janet Wishart, accused of witchcraft in Aberdeen in 1596, was accused by one witness at her trial of going to the head of the Gudeman's Croft on her farm, called the Round About, at twilight and removing her clothes below her waist to perform a ritual which involved throwing stones onto the ground in a particular fashion.[3] No other such cases involving this particular ritual seem to have been recorded.

Religious authorities were vocal about the blatantly un-Christian dedications of land. In 1594, the Kirk condemned the horrible superstition in Garioch (Aberdeenshire) and diverse parts of the country dedicating parcels of land to the Devil under the name of the Goodman and called for a law to enforce the labour on all such lands, or else they should pass into the hands of the king.[4] A law did not transpire, so local ministers began to crack down on this rural idolatry. In 1602 and 1603 the Kirk session of Elgin castigated men at Clachmarres for dedicating a plot to the Devil for the sake of keeping their cattle healthy.[5]

Earlier we encountered Andro Man, who was actively creating these segments of land on farms around Banff and Aberdeenshire. Man cannot have been the sole practitioner, and since he was apportioning new crofts, belief in them was obviously a powerful presence in the minds of many farmers. The Hynd Knight is a supernatural being different from Satan. The Halyman was perhaps more Holy Man than Helly/Hellish Man, whatever the Kirk believed. The minister of Monquhitter, giving a description of the crofts, designated them as Old Man's Folds in the *Statistical Account*. Lewis Spence links the Hynd Knight to the Hynde Etin (*etin*, giant) of ballad and folklore tradition, pointing towards a local spirit linked to cattle which had to be appeased.[6] *Hynd* as a noun could mean farm servant, but as an adjective in Scots means 'gentle, courteous', which might be linked with the native habit of giving dubious beings such as fairies kindly pseudonyms to avoid saying their given names and incurring wrath. A more recondite and intriguing possible meaning of *hynd* implies being out of the earth or 'away from this life'.[7] Land dedicated to the *hynd knycht* was advised by local Kirk authorities in Lothian and Dunblane around 1586, showing it was not only a North-Eastern phenomenon. Diane Purkiss gives the Hynd Knight a female identity.[8] This recalls the land dedicated to St Brigit in Kildare, Ireland, described by Giraldus Cambrensis. The saint had a sacred fire, protected by a hedge, which no man dare cross. There were also fields called Brigid's Pastures which no one dared plough.[9]

The Hynd Knight has also been compared with the Highland *gruagach*, which was offered milk and other libations, especially at cup-marked rocks. But the hairy, unkempt *grugach* seems a being apart from the Hynd Knight, though there is a single record of milk being offered to the spirit of a Gudeman's Croft, at Delnadamph, Aberdeenshire. Here, and possibly other nearby similar places, the crofts were ill-omened but not fatal. A farmer who broached into the land lost the best tooth in his head; a farmwife her stocking; a horse would lose its shoe and a cow its hoof.

Throughout the seventeenth century there were ongoing efforts to quell the superstition, almost all in Aberdeenshire, Banff and surrounding shires. In 1602 and the following year, the Presbytery of Elgin censured different tenant farmers for setting land aside in the name of the Gudeman. Strathbogie district was notorious for Goodman's Crofts and, among other actions, the Presbytery there ordered land in Rothiemay that was dedicated to the Goodman in 1631 to be manured. Sixty years later, in the same place, John Clark was delated for dedicating a piece of his land as 'Helly Man's Lye'.[10] At Slains and in the Presbytery of Fordyce, superstitiously set aside plots were discovered and ordered to be ploughed over. There was one plot found in the parish of Oyne and others around Turriff. In March 1650, Norman Leslie and James Tuicks were accused of keeping Gudeman's Crofts on their tacks. They had sworn to leave the land unplanted in order to guarantee that their cattle thrived. They had performed a ceremony, swearing this, which involved throwing stones over a dyke (like Janet Wishart). The authorities ordered the land to be laboured. Tuicks confessed that he had desperately created a new croft on his land as a means to reverse disease among his cattle. The ritual of throwing stones or clumps of soil was noted at Nether Buckie in 1650, where 'men used to cast faills and deavets on it'.[11]

Even prominent landowners set a blind eye to setting land aside, until the matter came to the attention of religious authorities. In August 1651, Sir William Gordon of Lesmore was visited by the Kirk elders of Rhynie and sorrowfully admitted that part of his land was deliberately not used for agriculture, 'but that he had a mynd, be the assistance of God, to cause labour the same'. Several months later, in the same region but at the other end of the social scale, William Seivwright and George Stronach were accused of sorcery because they had set aside land for the 'old goodman', though they promised to manure the plot. They were held in censure until the land was returned to normal use.[12]

In 1793, the minister of King Edward parish reported that, until recently, there was a farm there which had a small spot of land deliberately set aside and uncultivated. It had been called the Given Ground, but had since been given over to growing corn.[13] At Killiesmont in Keith around 1790, the farmer James Scott destroyed the sanctity of the enclosure, known there as the Gudeman's Craft and also the Gi'en Land, and paid the price. One of his oxen used to draw the ploughshare through it dropped dead. It was killed by a fairy dart, evidence that the land was not perhaps protected by Satan but more elven tenants. This rig stood on an impressive, elevated site well suited to ritual. It was 200 by 12 yards in extent, obviously an anciently venerated place, as a flat round rock on the site was marked by nine cup holes. Several decades later Robert Watt, tenant of Fieldhead Farm, trenched the blighted piece, not risking his oxen to plough it. He was anxiously watched over by three women as he did so, who were watching to see that he did not succumb to the fatal strike of a fairy arrow as he performed the sacrilegious destruction. Despite the cup-marked rock being removed around 1860, the bad atmosphere lingered and a local man told Lewis Spence in the 1940s that his uncle, who farmed there, would not bury animals on the site lest it provoke more deaths among his stock.[14] The sanctity of the site was reported by Walter Gregor in 1884. He further described the stone's cup marks being in three rows of three; and the stone itself, when struck, made a hollow, rumbling sound. There was a tradition that a golden treasure wrapped in a bull's hide was buried beneath the rock.[15] Few other ancient monuments are known to be Goodman's Crofts. One exception was on Kirkton of Bourtrie Farm, Aberdeenshire, where an ancient ring of standing stones was designated by the name until the stones were removed by an improving proprietor in the early nineteenth century.[16] A strict classification of crofts into either long venerated sites, visible from a distance, and small, private plots found on nearly every estate is probably too simplistic.[17]

Economic pressure as well as changing beliefs may have explained why these odd patchworks of land eventually shrugged off their peculiar associations. An Aberdeenshire farmer converted the croft on his land to agricultural use with the observation that the Devil had use of it for long enough and now it was his turn. Yet the feeling of this land's otherness lingered. There was a custom performed when tenant farmers were forced to quit their farms and steadings. This 'lowsin a gaun plough' entailed the departing farmer loading as much ploughed soil from the farm he was leaving and depositing it on a neighbouring farm, ritually depriving the old land of its luck and its fertility. A farmer in either the late eighteenth or early nineteenth century in Aberdeenshire performed this rite and purposely deposited the earth on the Gudeman's Croft on neighbouring West Affleck Farm.[18] The same impulse, to curse a property when leaving it, can be seen in the actions of the Kirk session of Oyne in 1737 when they summoned Robert Bainzie, accused of performing the sacrifice of an animal just before he quit a property, to bring bad luck for an incoming tenant.[19] The same thing appears in the evidence of James Reid, of Musselburgh, East Lothian, executed in 1603. Among other acts of destruction, Reid possessed nine stones given to him by Satan, which he placed on the land of David Libberstone for the destruction of his crops.[20] The faded superstitious practices associated with these rag tag scraps of land could hardly of course be called survivals of any kind of ancient cult practice. They were muscle memory actions, conditioned by an ill-remembered collective belief system and a cautious insurance to guard against ill fortune.

Most surviving Gudeman's Crofts eventually succumbed to cultivation, but some seem to have survived and were even created in the Victorian era. Sir James Young Simpson reported that, when one of his relatives had purchased a farm within twenty miles of Edinburgh in the mid-nineteenth century, one of his first acts was cordoning off a triangular piece of land and building a wall to mark it off as an offering to resident spirits.[21] The American folklorist Kenneth Goldstein spent some time in Strichen, Aberdeenshire, in the 1950s and was told by some farmers that they maintained Gudeman's Crofts on their land.[22] Whatever the truth of that, the powerful aura of the crofts was long remembered. One plot at the Howe o Smi'ston in Strathbogie was recalled in the late nineteenth century:

> In spite of the express orders and injunctions of the Kirk, no one for long had the courage to cultivate it. At last the attempt was made, but the ploughshare had scarcely entered the soil when the best ox in the team dropped dead with elfshot, nor was it until several years elapsed, and the minister himself attended to 'sain' the animals and owners, that the land was brought under the plough.[23]

The tenacity of the practice, and its longevity in the North-East, is remarkable. But there were fainter, earlier examples elsewhere. In 1586, the Presbytery of Edinburgh tasked its members to 'inquyre the names of certane croftis or pertis of ground superstitiouslie reportit to be consecrate to the Dewill, under the name of the Goodman's Craft'.[24] In Fife, two portions of land were set aside in the same manner, at Kilconquhar and Kennoway. The land at Kilconquhar was called the Dome or Doom Park and was supposedly a burial place for those who had forfeited the right to Christian burial. In the same county, near Dunfermline, there were four entire acres of land styled Cluttis Croft mentioned in the early seventeenth century (the place also occurs in sixteenth century records). Whether any of these places were Gudeman's Crofts, in the same way as understood in the North-East, is unclear. The size of this last place is comparable with the croft on the farm of Boginspro, near Huntly in Aberdeenshire, which was a huge field uncultivated until the start of the nineteenth century.[25]

Berwickshire retained traditions of the crofts in Victorian times even if there were few surviving examples. A popular rhyme there which warned against meddling with this sacrosanct territory began with this verse:

> If you put a spade in the Goodman's craft,
> Mahoun will shoot you wi' his shaft,
> The craft lies bonnie by Langston Lees,
> And weel is liked by bairns and bees.

The same author noted another rhyme which seems separate from the one above:

> The moss is soft on Clootie's craft,
> And bonny's the sod o' the Goodman's taft.
> And if you bide there till the sun is set,
> The Goodman will catch you in his net.[26]

James Napier remembered a piece of land dedicated to the Gudeman in the west of Scotland as late as 1825. The farmer who left it barren did not know the reason why, but afterwards he gave it to a poor labourer, who cultivated some of it and the whole plot thrived.[27] In Galloway, there were traces of the same dedication to a deity, but the tradition was less well recorded. An untilled field in Dullarg, Parton parish, would curse the man who planted on it with death. Peter McCutcheon planted a crop there and died before harvest, though it was afterwards harmlessly farmed. A farm in Tongland (formerly Tungland) in Kirkcudbrightshire, had a dark reputation which was remembered at the end of the nineteenth century:

> On the farm of Balannan, Tungland, there are two fields adjoining each other, the one called The Drum, and the other The Croft, which have never been cultivated. The belief is that if cultivated, the death either of proprietor or tenant will be the consequence. Both fields were reserved during the last lease. They are not now reserved, but they still lie untilled.[28]

Also in Galloway, the practice of laying aside land for a supernatural being had been noted by John Mctaggart as a custom which had only recently become extinct, and he notes that the general term for these odd bits of land was *aplochs*, from the Gaelic *ablach*, a word signifying 'remnants', though it seems to have a primary meaning of 'crippled, mangled', probably in reference to an animal carcase.[29] A claim that the *apolochs* were dedicated to witches seems uncertain.[30]

Other places not specifically named after the Goodman had injunctions against human interference. A farmer in Caithness who trespassed onto fairy-controlled land soon suffered murrain in his herd. The starkly named Field of the Dead in Unst, Shetland, was also uncultivated and nobody was allowed to put a spade to it or they would die. A woman who dug up part suffered the death of her best cow. Undeterred, she planted a crop there, and her husband died. She then left the field alone.[31]

There may be faint traces of similar practices in parts of England, where the plots were sometimes known as Jack's Land or Any Man's Land, though it's unclear whether the land was dedicated or at least set aside in the same way as in Scotland.[32] A tradition was said to have existed as far south as Devon, where the spots were known as Gallitrap or Gallow's Traps. The Gallitrap in Lew Trenchard was dangerous because anyone entering the field would be unable to find their way out until the parson and the magistrate were sent for; the first to take the spell off him, the second to see him hanged.[33] In Ireland, there is also a similar tradition of land in Clare, Ireland, where part of a cornfield was left deliberately untilled.[34] A more compelling similarity is the Icelandic *Álagablettir*, which were areas of grass (not necessarily fields) which were not allowed to be cultivated.[35] The Icelandic sites, abodes of supernatural beings, do not seem to have been continuously created or maintained in the active sense that the Scottish places were. They were more like fairy knowes and other landscape features in Scotland which were forbidden to mortals because of otherworldly ownership.

The other late manifestation of widespread social belief in the powers of darkness was even more male centred than the practices around the Goodman's Crofts. The extremely informal societies related to several specific crafts which emerged perhaps in the eighteenth and nineteenth centuries did not amount to magical societies or occult groups any more than freemasons or hellfire clubs did. But these groups – centred around the Miller's Word and the Horseman's Word – were a manifestation of occupational groups which sought both to exclude outsiders and to bolster the rights and mystique of certain skilled work. And there was an undoubted occult element in their customs and rites. The rites and mystique of the millers is related to the Mason's Word, both derived from the exclusivity of medieval crafts. Both the millers and the freemasons evolved peculiarly pseudo-occult traditions in Scotland. But while the former was retained among the profession, the masons' rites evolved into freemasonry under the aegis of the upper class, particularly via King James VI's Master of Works, William Shaw.[36] But the aura of exclusivity and trade secrets is far more ancient. As early as 1629, the Scottish freemasons were rumoured to have links to supernatural or occult powers, according to the Perth poet Henry Gall, who wrote, 'We have the Mason Word, and second sight, Things for to come we can foretell aright'.[37] The English author John Evelyn (1620–1706) wrote of the disquiet that the Mason's Word, used by brethren to identify each other, caused among Scottish ministers. On one occasion they demanded it be revealed to them, suspecting some diablery, but it was not given.

Since prehistory some professions and crafts were considered as being something more than ordinary. The archaeologist V. Gordon Childe described an anciently occupied cave at Stanhope in Durham where there was evidence of both metal working and ritual practices. The occupants were perhaps regarded with awe by others outside their community, and apparently lived apart from others.[38] Smiths retained their aura of otherworldliness through the centuries, due to the transformative wonders they could perform with metal.[39] In 1691, a man named William Anderson of Hall of Forest, Dumfriesshire, was found guilty by the Kirk session of taking his child to the local blacksmith so it could be charmed with the forge hammer. Long after this, children suspected of being changelings – infants of fairy origin swapped for mortal babies – were taken to smiths and had a frightening ritual performed. The suspect child was placed on the anvil and threatened with a blow from the smith's hammer. If it was a fairy, the belief was that the fake child would jump up from the anvil and run and the real mortal child would be found safe at home. To cure a child with falling sickness Thomas Smyth, in Coldwells, Ellon, a famous charmer, would lay the naked infant on *study* (anvil), which he struck three times while saying, 'Ather pair (get worse) or mend in the name of the Father, the Son and the Holy Ghost, in God's name'.[40] Rickets were also cured by bathing a child in the smith's water trough.[41] The eighteenth-century traveller John Brand reported that people in Orkney who wished for magical charms resorted to a blacksmith, but only one whose father and grandfather had also been a smith.[42] In the Highlands, as late as the 1930s in some areas, blacksmiths administered bloodletting to cure certain maladies.[43] Popular tradition also consider the profession *unseelie*. In the ballad entitled 'The Twa Magicians' a 'coal black smith' tries to force his sexual attentions on a maiden by using magic. It may be stretching comparisons too far, but we should recall the Irish god Gobniu, who was a master of metalcraft but who also had healing attributes.[44]

Some other professions gained a reputation not through the level of their skills but by virtue of their significance in pre-industrial societies. Millers, in Scotland and other countries, were a profession regarded as a necessary evil by country people who had to use their services. The system of *thirlage* in Scotland, a form of feudal restriction which lasted until the end of the eighteenth century, entailed many tenant farmers being tied to using one particular mill, which led to resentment and some abuses. Not only were they often viewed as conspiring with landowners, but they were also habitually mistrusted for dishonesty. They were suspected of possessing strange powers too. One nineteenth-century observer noted that 'the mullert wis consider a great man an' na very canny. It wis believed that a the mullerts wis workers o' black airt an' could reist anybody's horse when they likit'.[45] A miller from Fogo, Berwickshire, in 1669 had people visit him every day to reveal the location of lost items. This supernatural skill was imparted to him by a female entity which visited him each night.[46] When the tenants of Artamford tired of their *thirlage* to the mill of Whitehill, they plotted to ask James Fraser the miller to grind an impossible amount of corn on a given day, knowing that if he failed, their obligation to the mill would be ended. The miller consulted with his friend, the miller of Bruxie, who magically gathered the power and speed of his own mill as well as others and transferred them to the mill of Whitehills, fulfilling the impossible workload. The miller of Lagan was renowned for supernatural power. At one time he fought a battle with a witch who had stricken his neighbour with illness. The witch, in the shape of a hound, entered the mill and fought with the miller. Such was the equity of their power, that the man could only get her to restore some of the strength of the stricken man. The mill was destroyed in their battle and the witch was so bruised that she died soon afterwards. The miller suffered from headaches for the rest of his life.[47]

There was also something semi-magical about actual mills. We have already noted how one doctor advised parents to put sick children with whooping cough through the hopper of a mill. Perth Kirk session and Presbytery warned superstitious people not to take sick offspring to the mill and put them in the flapper and perform some ceremony as this was 'a lesson of Satan'.[48]

Millers kept the secret of their craft by entering sometimes into a strictly regulated, secret guild that had occult elements in its induction and membership rituals. Their oaths derived, allegedly, from diabolic ceremonies and the Miller's Word gave them supernatural power, if properly applied, to do astounding things, such as stopping a mill in motion, making it go faster and also setting the mill machinery going without apparent aid of human assistance. This latter skill of wizardry was reported in the early seventeenth century and also of two millers in the late nineteenth century near Skene, Aberdeenshire.[49] Entering upon the craft, aspirants had to swear not to enter a church for three years and, during that time, read the Bible thrice backwards.[50]

Secret craft meetings took place by night, in places outsiders dreaded. The Word which gave them their power was much feared and envied and sometimes millers shared their mills with the 'Kiln carle'. This was a savage domiciliary spirit that was best avoided, but brave children sometimes approached its lair and tainted it with the following rhyme before running away:

> Kiln carle teethless,
> Cum oot and mak me eesless.

Mills were also, by repute, the habitation of fairies and some were reputed to have been constructed with the assistance of water kelpies.

Millers' godless reputation was sometimes enhanced because they worked their mills on the sabbath. Several individuals within the profession were accused of witchcraft and their occupation may have been a factor in their prosecutions. Michael Areskine of Newbattle Mill, Midlothian, was executed in 1630. Another miller, Donald Moir Macfarquhar, was convicted by the authorities in Inverness on four counts of witchcraft in December 1603 and sentenced to be burned. In November 1602, a miller named William Brander was brought before the Kirk session of Elgin for grinding corn on the sabbath, and ordered to desist, under the pain of being fined £20. He was also accused of charming the late William Richartson by witchcraft. He denied the latter charge, saying that 'he myndit no sick thing nother culd he do sick thing'.[51] The suspected Fife warlock John Corse admitted in 1657 that he was initiated into witchcraft once day when he met two mysterious men at Balbirnie Mill and he was asked to enter his name in a book.[52] We have already encountered the Paisley miller, John Stewart, who sought out the Devil to revenge himself upon an enemy in 1677.

The Horseman's Word, which was strongly modelled on the Miller's Word, is interesting because it only arose in the nineteenth century when horses were displacing draught oxen on Scottish farms as the principal animal labour. Its broad membership included blacksmiths, farm labourers, and any man who worked with horses. Where it began is unclear, but it was strongest in east Scotland (not solely the North-East).

Its precise geographical roots may not be possible to tell, but it may be significant that there was an influx of trained horsemen into the North-East to handle the two-horse plough which local workers were initially unable to deal with. The fact that a secretive cult with occult overtones arose at such a late date is instructive when looking at Scottish society, and particularly Scottish male rural society. While the millers strictly guarded access to their craft and its secrets, the Horseman's Word was not so narrowly regulated.

Soon after any farm loon came to work with horses, he might be inducted into the mysteries of the society, which again involved quasi-pagan induction rights and mystical secrets for the control of animals derived from a deal with the Devil. Even the invitation to join was conveyed in arcane mystery. A prospective member was, it is said, sent a single horse hair in an envelope. The initiation ceremony, varied from place to place, was conducted by a mock 'minister', and was reminiscent of witchcraft rites and mimicked the sacrament, with the newcomer having to bring a pot of jam (or some money), a loaf, sometimes a candle, plus a bottle of whisky. The words used were full of mystery and the kind of ceremonial question and response associated with entry into freemasonry, though darker. The novice was run through a long script of portentous semi-mystical questions and answers designed to overawe him. At the end the blindfolded young man shook a horned hand of what was supposed to be the Devil (sometimes a stick covered with animal skin) and allowed access to the Word and the arcane mysteries of the trade. In some areas the criteria for admission was to be between the ages of 16 and 30. It was said sometimes that the ceremony was overseen by a panel of four men, seated behind a mock altar of a bushel, upside down, pressed into a sack of corn.[53] The ceremony would often take place around Martinmas in November and early on the rite would be performed in isolated barns or farm bothies, adding to the mystique, though latterly it was sometimes conducted in hotel rooms.[54] Such was the power and reputation of the ceremony, and sometimes physical and mental abuse, that at least one unfortunate farm loon was reputed to have been driven mad and was confined for life in an asylum in Banff.[55] The fact that there was no structure and rules to the order meant that it was extremely difficult to pin down, though rumours abounded about its significance. In some places there were different meetings for juveniles and mature men, and there was some suggestion that a more occult-aligned inner order focused more on ritual of a dark kind.[56]

It has been argued (with little truth) that the Horseman's Word had its roots in pre-Christian society. It had common motifs linking it with secretive societies, like the freemasons. The inducted member was not only given the Word and various tricks of the trade – which included the power to control women as well as horses – and a variety of handshakes and signs by which he could be identified as an initiate.[57]. Those who refused to join were ostracised. Once inside, the member was instructed never to reveal society secrets to a madman, a woman, nor anyone else unsuitable. If he revealed the secrets given to him, he would have his flesh torn asunder by wild horses, his heart stabbed by a knife, and his body buried on the seashore.[58]

Many initiates into the brotherhood claimed their society was as old as the first horseman, Cain, and astute modern insight is quite right in claiming that much of the ritual 'feels old'. In the era of agricultural improvement, and uncertainty, the men first called on to master horses were 'dispossessed landed peasantry', with a full stock of legend and folk beliefs who brought these together into a self-protecting, albeit loose union to protect their rights and beliefs.[59] The skill of an adept horseman, as seen by an outsider, would certainly be viewed as recondite, if not downright occult. The society may have promised initiates powers that were really just inherent skills learned by following best psychological practice when it came to dealing with horses. In some areas, the Horseman's Word promised aspiring members the power not only to *reist* or halt a horse in its tracks but also to do the same to any man. The same power, as we have seen, was ascribed to millers. Associated powers included the boastful ability to operate a plough in a field without the need for man or horse, and to make a horse immediately come to the possessor of the Word. It is noteworthy that the wizard Laird of Skene was credited with *reisting* a mortal enemy who had offended him in the seventeenth century.[60] That this alleged power was believed to be prevalent before the beginning of the Horseman's Word Society is confirmed by the record of 1756, when a man named Peter Pairmy was accused by a local Kirk session in Orwel, Kinross-shire, of *reisting* a wheel plough, having used a word and touching the plough with a rod, bidding it stop until he loosed it. He was publicly rebuked and placed 'under scandal'.[61] Witchcraft records sometimes mentioned allegations of ploughs similarly being magically stilled, an obviously fearful thing for any subsistence farmer.

There were similar groups of semi-mystic horse workers in England in the nineteenth century, though it is a matter of contention about whether their groups, nearly identical to the Horseman's Word, wholly derived from Scotland. There was a minor movement of farm workers to eastern England from Scotland in the period and this may have bolstered or spread similar groups.[62] The fact that there was at least one analogous society, the Toadmen, which flourished in East Anglia among those working with horses, shows the powerful feeling of fellowship and intrinsic mystique in the equine community.[63] Exactly like the men of the Horseman's Word, ploughmen in this area used expert knowledge about the behaviour of horses to control and manipulate their behaviour, though some of their mysterious skill came from a mystical toad bone. The link between Scotland and East Anglia may have been forged by a migration of ploughmen from the former to the latter or else via the carter trade which employed men from Banff travelling south in the eighteenth century.

Even more so than their fellows in Scotland, the East Anglian enclave escaped the public attention of scholars and others until their society had all but faded away. Again, there were claims that the fraternity represented the vestiges of very ancient male rituals, stretching back to the Romans, though this seems impossible to verify. Albeit the society has vastly diminished in terms of membership, it still exists or did so until recently in small pockets in certain areas of Scotland.[64] It was also exported from Scotland and England to various places in North America and elsewhere and survived for some time. While the use of farm horses was a relatively late innovation in Scotland, the cult which developed around their use took on elements from the profession of millers and other trades. Blacksmiths, as described, were inheritors of the ancient occupational mystique we have already mentioned, using the elements to turn unwieldly ore into mental implements. Their skills wreathed in awe and some suspicion worldwide. In 1660 in Germany, a smith named 'Wild George' Schaff was accused of telling his apprentice he could gain skill by use of a magic ring. To gain smithing power, the young man was advised to enter the smithy backwards on a specific night, while chanting the Devil's name.[65]

If the society of horsemen had impressively gaudy rituals in its initiation ceremony, and promised much in its alleged control of horses, there was little ongoing ritual involved in membership. No ceremonial events were enacted at conspicuous intervals of the year, no arcane bonding ceremonies were undertaken, and the mystical aura was confined to the exclusivity of belonging. Ronald Hutton has perceptively linked the condition for these semi-arcane societies to freemasonry, which was of course another

Scottish invention (in the late sixteenth century). The Miller's Word and Horseman's Word, interestingly, seemed to flourish in areas of Scotland where the freemasons struggled for membership, suggesting an entirely different demographic.[66] What the societies of the Miller's Word and the Horseman's Word had in common (unlike the freemasons in earlier or later times), was a genuine masculine aura of exclusivity, a subversive ethos that came from the same mental impulses which shaped the lives of countless cunning men down the ages. The ideologies of the society members may have been different to the spae men (sooth sayers) and wizards, but in their own way, they were equally as iconoclastic.

The aura and otherworldly mystique was woven into the fabric of such groups and did much to ensure their exclusivity. There was a story told of one man who rose to become the unofficial 'high priest' of the Horseman's Word in his own district, despite the fact that he was born without the power to speak. Before his birth his mother had angrily turned away a begging tinker woman from her door and the woman had cursed her, saying, 'You'll have a bairn, and though you'll have plenty to gie him he'll no' be able to ask for it'. The child was born dumb a few days later and was reckoned a strange, elfin child with an affinity for animals, especially horses. The only sound he could ever make was a whistle, but this brought restive horses under control and made them come to his hand. He also had the power to make any horse so unmanageable that none could tame them. The man made a good living buying and selling horses and was treated with great respect. After he died, the horses pulling his hearse became so disquiet that they had to be dispensed with and a company of men carried him to his final resting place.[67]

Notes and References

Foreword

1. Miller, 1999, p.183.

Introduction

1. Dempster, 1888, p.227.
2. Henderson, 2016, pp.74–75.
3. Summers, 1946, p.18.
4. Schulte, 2009, pp.8–35.
5. Michel, 1862, p.2.
6. Tveit, 2020, p.31.
7. Rutkowski, 2013.
8. Maxwell, 1913, pp.29–30.
9. Murray, 1960, p.6, p.107; Murray, 1921, p.23; Russell, 1972, p.164.
10. Goodacre, 2012.
11. Goodacre, 2012, 203.
12. Hutton, 2017, p.217; Henderson, 2016, p.122, has called Goodacre's ideas 'eminently sensible'.
13. See, for example, Henderson, 2016, p.99.
14. Levack, 2008, p.41.
15. Larner, 1981, p.91; Simpson, 1996, p.7.
16. Henderson, 2016, p.78.
17. Schulte, 2009, p.52.
18. Scarre, 1987, p.21.
19. Larner, 1981, p.41; Levack, 2007, p.158.
20. Henderson, 1865, p.27.

21. Henderson, 2016, p.142.
22. Cramond, 1897, p.86, p.107.
23. Maxwell-Stuart, 2005, p.23.
24. Miller, 1999, p.194.
25. Henderson, 1865, p.70.
26. Stuart, 1846, p.xxxiii.
27. McPherson, 1929, p.163.
28. Dye, 2016, p.67.
29. Henderson, 2016, p.128.
30. Truckell, 1975, pp.52–54.
31. Cramond, 1897, p.298; Dye, p.126.
32. Henderson, 2016, p.145.
33. Anon., *Chron. Perth*, pp.94–95; Dye, 2016, pp.12–13.
34. McPherson, 1929, p.29.
35. Mackay, 1896, p.181.
36. Henderson, 1865, p.13.
37. Kidd, 1877, no pagination.
38. Thomas, 1953, pp.204–5.
39. Murray, 1919.
40. McPherson, 1929, pp.152–3.
41. Sinclair, 1871, p.46.
42. Robertson, 2013, p.26.
43. Stiùbhart, 2006, p.204.
44. Levack, 2004, p.105.
45. Murray, 1921, p.189.
46. Anderson, 1888, pp.253–4.
47. Willumsen, 2011, pp.61–74, p.71.
48. Henderson, 2016, p.79.
49. Paterson, 2012.
50. Scott, 1884, p.134.
51. Murray, 1921–1922, pp.46–64, p.50.
52. Hill, Alexandra, 2013, p.223.
53. Normand and Roberts, 2000, p.304, p.321.
54. Bain, 1894, p.486.
55. Wilson, 1875, p.336.
56. Fergusson, 1899, p.264.
57. Fergusson, 1899, pp.264–8.
58. Monteath, 1887, pp.61–65.

Chapter 1. Primal Men of Power: Michael Scot and Thomas of Erceldoune

1. Hill, 2013, p.223.
2. Brown, 1897, p.ix.
3. Thorndike, 1965, p.1.
4. Cohn, 2000, p.103.
5. Thorndike, 1965, p.38.
6. Kay, 1985.
7. Davies, 2009, p.37.
8. Brown, 1897, pp.211–214, pp.222–8.
9. Scot, 1892, p.34.
10. Wood, 1911, p.15.
11. Westwood, 1985, p.386.
12. Denham, 1891, p.348; Denham, 1895, p.118.
13. Preston, 1979, p.15.
14. Chambers, 1827, p.333.
15. Westwood, 1985, p.413.
16. Chambers, 1827, p.334.
17. Campbell, 1900, p.385.
18. Campbell, 1900, p.288; Philip, 1995, pp.384–7.
19. Campbell, 1889, 46–53.
20. Hanford, 1995, p.38; Mitchell and Dickie, 1839, p.290.
21. William Gardiner, *Miscellany of Literature, Science, History and Antiquities*, Cupar, 1842, p.67, cited by Hanford, 1995, p.91.
22. Bower, book 10, chapter 43, volume 5, 1990, p.429.
23. Westwood and Kingshill, 2009, p.84.
24. Murray, 1875, p.x.
25. Burnham, 1908; Murray, 1875.
26. Murray, 1875, pp.liii–lv.
27. Ibid., p.lv.
28. Albrecht, 1954, pp.80–91; Murray, 1875, pp.1–20.
29. Rose, 2003, pp.88–92.
30. Denham, 1895, p.119.
31. Lyle, 1968, pp.111–21, p.115.
32. Campbell, 1900, p.270.
33. Newton, 1910, p.35, p.161.
34. Chambers, 1870, p.221.

35. Murray, 1875, p.xvi.
36. Flood, 2016, p.118.
37. Murray, 1875, p.xviii.
38. Newton, 2010, p.147.
39. Cheape, 2016, p.157.

Chapter 2. Four Magicians and the King

1. Mackie, 1958, p.12.
2. Macdougall, 1982, pp.130–33, p.275.
3. Maxwell-Stuart, 2001, pp.57–60.
4. Anon., *Historie James the Sext*, 1804, p.48.
5. Balfour, 1824, p.345.
6. Maxwell-Stuart, 2001, pp.44–45, pp.52–57.
7. Wasser, 2013.
8. Maxwell-Stuart, 2001, pp.52–57.
9. Goodare, 2005b, pp.39–67.
10. Burton, 1852, pp.17–20; Jacob, 1931, pp.147–62.
11. Goodacre, 2005a, p.235.
12. Dalyell, 1834, p.550.
13. Davies, 2011, p.21; Sharpe, 1884, p.48; McPherson, 1929, p.178.
14. Calderwood, 1843, pp.13–18.
15. Scot, 1872, p.91.
16. Allan, 2005, p.31.
17. Maxwell-Stuart, 2001, p.144.
18. Goodacre, Julian, 2009, p.153.
19. Normand and Roberts, 2000, p.309.
20. Ibid., p.312.
21. Ibid., p.328.
22. Ibid., pp.319–20.
23. Murray, 1918, p.320.
24. King James VI, *The Demonology*, in Normand and Roberts, 2000, pp.205–7, pp.224–30.
25. Ibid., p.381.
26. Normand and Roberts, 2000, p.41.
27. Scot, 1872, p.104.
28. Calderwood, 1844, p.148.

29. Maxwell-Stuart, 2001, p.118.
30. Ibid., p.153.
31. Cowan, 1983, p.130.
32. Melville, 1929, pp.352-4.
33. Maxwell–Stuart, 2001, p.160.
34. Ibid., p.169.
35. Normand and Roberts, 2000, 77-78.
36. *Calendar State Papers* 10, p.510.
37. Reported by the Englishman Robert Carey, August 12, 1593; Bain, 1894, p.488.
38. Maxwell–Stuart, p.153; Bain, 1894, p.487.
39. Normand and Roberts, 2000, p.42.
40. Maxwell-Stuart, 2001, pp.176–7.
41. Maxwell-Stuart, 1997, p.221.
42. Stafford, Helen, 1953, p.106.
43. Contemporary pamphlet, *Gowrie's Conspiracy* (1600), reprinted in Anon. *Harleian Misc.*, 2, 1809, p.345.
44. Ibid., p.86; Lang, 1902, p.255.
45. Panton, 1812, p.168.
46. Mackenzie, 1713, p.xiii.
47. Cowan, 1912, p.157; Scott, 1818, p.310.
48. Anon., *Harl. Misc.* 3, 1809, p.85; Cowan, 1902, p.98; Pitcairn, 1833, p.219.
49. Elizabeth to James, September 14, 1600. *Cal. State Papers Scotland*, 2, p.787.
50. Sanderson, 1656, p.226.
51. Panton, 1812, p.168.
52. Arbuckle, 1957, p.106.
53. Collingwood, 1849, p.165, p.169.

Chapter 3. Andro Man and the Fairy Tradition

1. Stuart, 1841, p.124.
2. Ibid., pp.137–38.
3. Maxwell-Stuart, 2001, pp.203–5.
4. Map reference NJ 396 448. Both Canmore National Record of the Historic Environment and Moray Historic Environment Record state

the mound is natural, though it has not been excavated. The *Ordnance Survey Banffshire Name Book*, 1867–9 (volume 6, OS1/4/6/33, Scotland's Places https://scotlandsplaces.gov.uk/digital-volumes/ordnance-survey-name-books/banffshire-os-name-books-1867-1869/banffshire-volume-06/33) describes the feature as a natural grass knowe formed in the centre of solid rock. It is noted the place was reputedly the resort of fairies, but sadly no story of the site was given. There was another Elf Hillock, long vanished, at Upper Dallachy, Boyndie parish, possibly representing Pictish settlements.

5. Henderson and Cowan, Edinburgh, 2001, p.66.
6. George Mann, died 1884, aged 15. Bishop, 2005, p.37. There was also William Mann born illegitimately in Rathven on 6 September 1866, plus others in the Banff census records for 1881.
7. Davies, 2007, p.197.
8. Stuart, 1841, p.122.
9. Ibid., p.120.
10. Purkiss, 2003, p.136.
11. Stuart, 1841, p.120.
12. Bessie Dunlop consulted by Lady Blackwall and Lady Thirdpart.
13. There are rare instances of others travelling great distances to see magical workers. William Fourd, South Leith, travelled to Newcastle to see a warlock in 1597 and was brought before the session.
14. Munro, Robert, 1981, pp.98–100.
15. Paterson, Laura, 2012, pp.371–412, p.392.
16. McCabe Allan, 2016, pp.112–113.
17. Macdonald, 1997, pp.112–16; Smith, 1986, pp.221–4.
18. Macfarlane, 1971, p.115.
19. Reid, 1899, p.69.
20. Hume Brown, 1900, p.536.
21. Reid, 1899, p.70.
22. Hume Brown, 1908, pp.454–5.
23. Law, 1818, p.liv.
24. Survey of Scottish Witchcraft, https://witches.hca.ed.ac.uk/case/C/EGD/1094.
25. Hughes, 2003, pp.85–86.
26. Gilmore, 1948, p.253.
27. Davies, 2007, p.191.
28. Hall, 2006, p,17.

29. Hunter, 1917, p.62; Meikle, 1935, p.151.
30. Meikle, 1935, p.152.
31. Meikle, 1935, p.153.
32. Hunter, 1917, p.61.
33. Hume Brown, 1901, p.222.
34. Robertson, 2013, p.28. James Reid of Musselburgh, condemned in 1603, also gained healing powers from Satan.
35. Coleman, 2019.
36. Chambers, 1870, p.220.
37. Purkiss, 2003, p.134.
38. Goodacre, 2008, pp.26–50, p.42.
39. Maxwell-Stuart, 2001, 211.
40. Cowan, 2008, pp.71–94.
41. Buchanan, 1978, p.98.
42. Scott, 1884, p.108.
43. Gilmore, 1948, p.183.
44. Stuart, 1841, p.177.
45. Wilby, Emma, 2005, p.56, p.106.
46. Maxwell-Stuart, 2001, p.115.
47. Henderson, and Cowan, 2007, p.46; Macculloch, 1921, pp.227–44.
48. Pitcairn, volume one, part two, 1833, p.52.
49. Hutton, 2017, p.234.
50. Campbell, 1900, p.94.
51. Stuart, 1846, p.184.
52. Todd, 2002, p.256.
53. Maxwell-Stuart, 2005, p.133.
54. Hall, 2007, p.160.
55. Maxwell-Stuart, 2001, p.206; Spalding, 1841, pp.170–4.
56. Stuart, 1841, p.124.
57. Hume Brown, 1902, pp.637–9.
58. Ibid., p.637.
59. Ibid., p.638.
60. Ibid., 179, pp.565–6, p.570, pp.574–5.
61. MacPhail, 1920, pp.36–38.
62. Henderson, 1997, p.57; Henderson and Cowan, 2001, p.43.
63. Scott, 1884, pp.134–5, pp.255–64.
64. Maxwell-Stuart, 2005, pp.213–14.
65. Bell, 1897, pp.257–9.

66. Scott, 1884, pp.256–7.
67. Ibid., p.260.
68. Larner, Lee, McLachlan, 1977, pp.245–6.
69. Schulte, 2009, p.1.
70. Henderson, 2009, pp.141–66, p.142.
71. Dudley and Goodacre, 2013, pp.121–39, pp.128–9.
72. Wilby, 2005, pp.215–16 citing Kassin and Wrightsman, 1985, pp.76–78.
73. Ginzburg, 1991, pp.96–97.
74. Wilby, 2005, pp.239–378.
75. Goodacre, Julian, 2020, pp.37–54.
76. Donaldson, 1794, p.416.
77. Stuart, 1843, p.103, p.141, pp.143–5, p.174, p.180.
78. Maxwell-Stuart, 2004, p.88.

Chapter 4. The Anti-Witches: Prickers and Persecutors

1. Rowlands, 2009, pp.13–14.
2. Martin, 2013, p.71.
3. Neill, 1922, p.206.
4. Hume Brown, 1902, p.433.
5. Sinclair, 1871, p.110.
6. Larner, 1981, pp.110–11.
7. Hughes, 94; Maxwell-Stuart, 2003, p.106.
8. Maxwell-Stuart, 2003, 98–122 and Robertson, 2013, pp.63–72 document his career.
9. Maxwell-Stuart, 2005, p.147.
10. 'Declaration of John Kincaid, Pricker,' in *A Collection of Rare and Curious Tracts* Anon., 1820, pp.111–12.
11. Gilmore, 1948, pp.228–9.
12. Dalyell, 1834, p.640.
13. Survey of Scottish Witchcraft C/EGD/503, https://witches.hca.ed.ac.uk/index.cfm/case/C/EGD/503.
14. Henderson, Basingstoke, 2016, p.148.
15. Mather, 1693, pp.26–27.
16. Gardiner, 1796, p.114.
17. Lauder, Edinburgh, 1900, p.xl.

18. Mackenzie, 1678, p.91.
19. McDonald, 1997.
20. Fraser, 1905, pp.446–7.
21. Neill, 1922, p.208.
22. Borman, 2014, p.105.
23. Hickes, 1680, p.35.
24. Yeoman, 2009, p.29–46.
25. Gilmore, 1948, pp.254–6.
26. Todd, 2002, p.395.
27. Kirkton, 1703, p.25.
28. Wodrow, 1842, pp.102–4.
29. Miller, 1869, p.31.
30. Henderson, 2016, p.90.
31. Goodacre and Miller, 2008, p.4.
32. Goodacre, 2009, p.154.
33. Lang, 1909, p.46.
34. Ibid., p.40.
35. Mackenzie, 1673, pp.185–6.
36. Mackenzie, 1678, p.86.
37. Anon, *Diurnal of Occurrences*, 1845, pp.93–93.
38. Mackenzie, 1673, p.193.
39. Dalyell, 1834, p.279.
40. Henderson, 2001, pp.60–63.

Chapter 5. Major Weir

1. Sinclair, 1871, pp.225–51.
2. Law, 1818, p.23.
3. Fraser, James, 1977, p.261.
4. Lamont, 1830, p.218.
5. Law, 1818, 27; Scott-Moncrieff, 1905, pp.11–12.
6. Lamont, 1830, p.218.
7. Hickes, 1678, pp.60–73.
8. Wilson, 1875, p.336.
9. Fraser, 1977, p.264.
10. Scott-Moncrieff, 1905, p.10.
11. Hickes, 1678, p.63.

12. Ibid., p.64.
13. Fraser, 1977, p.266; Hickes, 1678, p.66.
14. Scott-Moncrieff, 1905, p.14.
15. Hume Brown, 1900, p.516.
16. Fraser, 1977, p.262.
17. Ibid., p.265.
18. Hickes, 1678, p.66.
19. Quoted by Wilson, 1875, p.337.
20. Chambers, 1847, p.35–36.
21. Roughead, 1913 p.61.
22. Hickes, 1678, p.72.
23. Cited by Roughead, William, 1913, p.42.
24. Stevenson, 1879, p.16.
25. Chambers, 1847, p.34.
26. Brock, 2016, p.60.
27. Ibid., pp.62–63.
28. Hume Brown, 1902, p.24.
29. Lauder, p.198.
30. Atkinson, 2013, p.247.

Chapter 6. Twilight People: Marginal Lives and the Modern Age

1. Chambers, 1861, pp.449–52.
2. Chambers, 1827, pp.128–9.
3. Bovet, 1684, pp.172–5.
4. Briggs, 1971, p.182.
5. Todd, 2002, p.358.
6. Henderson, 2016, p.285.
7. Alexander, 1877, pp.192–9.
8. Shaw, 2002.
9. Henderson, 1893, pp.98–100; Hume Brown, 1904, p.360; Ribton-Turner, 1887, p.340, p.346.
10. Shaw, 1992, pp.141–58.
11. Dalyell, 1834, pp.235–6.
12. Thomas, 1991, p.608.
13. Murray, Margaret, 1921–22, pp.50–51.

14. Dye, 2016, p.67.
15. Dalyell, 1834, pp.74–75, p.379; Pitcairn, volume two, part two, p.478.
16. Larner, 1981, p.149; Murray, 1921, p.45; Pitcairn, volume two part two, pp.477–9. The Devil also appeared to William Barton of Kirkliston in the shape of a woman and slept with him. Sinclair, 1871, p.160. Major Weir slept with the Devil in female form.
17. Sinclair, 1871, pp.122–7.
18. Ibid., p.123.
19. Robertson, 2013, p.33.
20. Bolin, 2020, p.279.
21. Robertson, 2013, pp.33.
22. Robertson, 2009, pp.12–16.
23. Black, 1903, p.125; Dalyell, 1834, p.109.
24. Pitcairn, Criminal Trials, volume 2, part two, pp.535–6.
25. Dye, 2016, p.99.
26. Fergusson, 1899, p.263; Millar, 1999, p.175.
27. Told by J. MacLeod, Laxford, Dempster, 1888, pp.230–1. A summary of different versions is given in Beith, 2004, pp.51–53.
28. Bannerman, 1986, p.93.
29. Beith, 2004, p.66.
30. Fraser, 1905, p.258.
31. Rorie, 1994, pp.27–30.
32. Ibid., pp.51–52.
33. Presbytery records quoted in Miller, 1999, p.99.
34. Pettigrew, 1844, p.73.
35. Summers, 1946, p.148.
36. Campbell, 1900, p.293.
37. Cheape, 1993, pp.111–23.
38. Kirk, 2001, p.67.
39. Hanford, 1995, p.144. One version related by William Matheson, Bruford and Macdonald, 1994, pp.395–6.
40. Marwick, 1986, p.57.
41. Curran, 2001, p.12.
42. Campbell, 1900, p.274.
43. Tobar an Dualchais. https://www.tobarandualchais.co.uk/track/57977?l=en; https://www.tobarandualchais.co.uk/track/65142?l=en; https://www.tobarandualchais.co.uk/track/57976?l=en; https://www.tobarandualchais.co.uk/track/44221?l=en; https://www.tobarandualchais.co.uk/track/65140?l=en

Chapter 7. Men of the Black School: The Wizard Lairds

1. Watt, 1980, p.3.
2. Hanford, 1995, pp.89–91.
3. Ibid., p.89.
4. Macdonald, 1893–94, p.278.
5. Campbell, 1900, p.286.
6. Chambers, 1870, p.386.
7. Jervise, 1882, p.244.
8. Sharpe, 1884, p.148.
9. Lamont, 1830, p.68.
10. Fraser, 1867, pp.141–2.
11. Anon, *The Witty and Entertaining Exploits of George Buchanan*. 'George Buchanan and the Dogs,' in Mclellan, 1997, pp.53–54. Duncan Williamson, 'How Buchanan Became the King's Fool'. Tobar an Dualchais https://www.tobarandualchais.co.uk/track/33243?l=en.
12. Laing, 1865, p.52.
13. Westwood and Kingshill, 2009, p.338.
14. Swire, 1963, p.79.
15. Westwood and Kingshill, 2009, p.354.
16. Dempster, 1888, pp.149–189.
17. Hanford, 1995, p.99.
18. Fergusson, 1886, p.7.
19. Napier, 1834, p.215.
20. Gray, 1987, pp.68–79.
21. Sinton, 1906, p.517; Wiseman, The Callum Maclean Project.
22. Gray, 1987, p.74.
23. 'Mac Iain', 1878, p.119.
24. Campbell, 1900, p.291; Sinton, 1906, p.516.
25. Shaw, 2007, pp.170–79.
26. Sinton, 1906, p.514; Wiseman, 2002, p.339.
27. Wiseman, The Calum Maclean Project.

Chapter 8. The Highland Experience

1. Carswell, 1873, p.19.
2. MacPhail, JRN, 1914, p.167; Stiùbhart, 2020, pp.185–7, who also cites Diarmid Campbell, 'Was Bishop Carswell's Widow a Witch?', *West Highland Notes & Queries*, series 4, 13 (June 2020).

3. Bolin, 2020, p.251.
4. Thomas and Thoresby, 1892, p.35.
5. Brochard, 2015, p.47.
6. Brochard, 2014, p.50.
7. Henderson, 2008; Henderson, 2016, p.99.
8. Larner, 1981, p.80.
9. Henderson, 2016, p.225.
10. Campbell, 1902, p.4; MacInnes, 2009, pp.189–91.
11. Hutton, 2017, p.246.
12. Campbell, 1902, p.20.
13. Oral tradition related by Angus MacKinnon, Eigg. https://www. tobarandualchais.co.uk/track/45728?l=en.
14. Campbell, 1902, p.50, p.53.
15. Campbell, 1900, p.291.
16. Henderson, 2016, p.127.
17. Hutton, 2017, p.244.
18. Maclagan, 1902, p.24.
19. Farquharson, n.d., p.84.
20. MacInnes, 2009, p.191.
21. Campbell, Glasgow, 1902, p.60.
22. Cameron, 1928, 77; Maclagan, 1902, p.127.
23. Hutton, 2017, p.247.
24. Sneddon, 2015, pp.13–14.
25. Kirk, 2001, p.79, p.88, p.94.
26. Ibid., p.90.
27. Macpherson, 1929, p.285.
28. Rutkowski, 2013, p.192.
29. Bolin, 2020, p.204.
30. Martin, 1698, pp.156–7; Martin, 1712, pp.288–9.
31. Kirk, 2001, p.86.
32. Adams, 1882, p.317.
33. Ross, 1990, p.49; Sutherland, Elizabeth, 1987, pp.44–45.
34. Sutherland, 2005, p.49.
35. Matheson, 1969–70, p.68.
36. Sutherland, 1977, p.138.
37. Sutherland, 2005, p.52.
38. Ibid., 131; Sutherland, 1987, p.31, pp.197.
39. Sutherland, 1987, p.199.

40. Matheson, 1969–70, pp.73–74.
41. MacInnes, 1989, p.15.
42. Burnett, 2010, pp.71–74.
43. Sutherland, 2005, p.98.
44. Bolin, 2020, p.270.
45. MacInnes, 1989, pp.12–13.
46. Ibid., p.18.
47. Kirk, 2001, p.89.
48. MacInnes, 1989, p.20.
49. Busst, 1995.

Chapter 9. The Last Magicians: Gregor Willox and Other Cunning Men

1. Grant, 1869, pp.63–76.
2. Callander, 2000, pp.13–14.
3. Jervise, 1872, p.282.
4. Farquharson, n.d., pp.44–46.
5. Gaffney, 1970, p.18.
6. Letter of Robert and James Grant. Cowie, 1999, p.40.
7. Cramond, 1897, pp.329–30.
8. Grant, 1980, p.3.
9. Anon, 'Willox the Wizard', 1888.
10. Lauder, 1841, pp.13–24.
11. Gregor, 1881, p.38.
12. Gray, 1987, pp.229–31.
13. Hall, 1807, p.438; McGregor, 1994, pp.19–24. Stewart, 1823, pp.216–23.
14. Macgregor, 1993, p.41; Stewart, 1823, p.221.
15. Sinclair, 1982, p.305.
16. Gray, 1987, p.233.
17. Mitchell, 1825, p.635.
18. McGregor, 1994, p.6.
19. McPherson, 1929, p.164.
20. Hall, 1807, p.439.
21. Grewar, 1910, p.205.
22. Lauder, 1837, pp.298–306.

23. Lauder, 1841, p.9.
24. Davies, 2011, p.148.
25. Murdoch, 1905, p.6, p.40.
26. Campbell, 1902, p.10.
27. Carmichael 1909, pp.341–5.
28. Gregor, 1881, p.185.
29. Waters, 2019, p.110.
30. Tobar an Dualchais. https://www.tobarandualchais.co.uk/track/63657?l=en.
31. Tobar an Dualchais, https://www.tobarandualchais.co.uk/track/63656?l=en.
32. McAldowie, 1896, p.313.
33. McPherson, 1929, p.223, p.243.

Chapter 10. Final Embers: The Goodman's Croft and the Horseman's Word

1. Lyle, 2013, p.111.
2. Bell, 1897, p.144.
3. Stuart, 1841, p.93.
4. Calderwood, 1849, p.326; Laing, 1845, p.834.
5. Cramond, 1897, p.96.
6. Spence, 1948, p.329.
7. Craigie and Aitken, 1974, p.190.
8. Purkiss, 2003, p.136.
9. Giraldus Cambrensis, 2005, p.286.
10. Davidson, 1955, p.21; McPherson, 1929, p.138.
11. McPherson, 1929, p.136, p.137.
12. Stuart, 1843, pp.xxiv–xxv, p.71.
13. McPherson, 1929, p.137.
14. McPherson, 1929, pp.138–9; Rogers, 1869, p.244; Spence, 1948, p.328.
15. Lyle, 2013, p.107.
16. Youngblood, 1995, p.27.
17. McNeill, 1989, p.58.
18. Lyle, 2013, p.105; Mcpherson, 1929, p.141.
19. Henderson, 2016, p.115.

20. Pitcairn, Criminal Trials 2, part 2, p.422.
21. Simpson, 1861, p.48.
22. Goldstein, 1964, p.68.
23. G. W. Anderson, *The Lays of Strathbogie*, p.220, cited by Munro, Robert, 1981, pp.142–3.
24. Goodacre, 2008, p.34.
25. McPherson, 1929, p.136.
26. Henderson, 1856, p.111.
27. Napier, 1879, p.140.
28. Gregor, 1898, pp.494–5.
29. Mactaggart, London, 1876, p.20; Watson, 1951, pp.179–85, 185. A secondary meaning is 'contemptible person'.
30. Henderson, 2016, p.138.
31. Davidson, 1955, p.24.
32. Warburton, 1896, p.160.
33. Henderson, 1879, p.278. The site at Lew Trenchard may have been no more mysterious than a sluice gate, see *Never Completely Submerged*, Ron Wawman, Guildford, 2009, p.259.
34. Cited by Spence, 1948, p.329.
35. Gunnell, 2018.
36. Stevenson, 1990, pp.26–51.
37. Stiùbhart, 2020, p.190.
38. Childe, 1940, p.180.
39. Westwood, 1985, p.230.
40. McPherson, 1929, p.258.
41. Henderson, 2016, p.279.
42. Reported by Dalyell, 1834, p.234.
43. Beith, 2004, p.116.
44. Miller, 1999, p.232.
45. A. Robb, *Memories of Mormondside*, MS, *c*.1920, cited by Munro, 1981, p.145.
46. Dalyell, 1834, p.524.
47. Gregor, 1894, pp.16–18.
48. Todd, 2002, p.358.
49. McAldowie, 1896, p.312.
50. Carter, 1997, p.154.
51. Cramond, 1897, p.98.
52. Maxwell-Stuart, 2005, p.23.

53. Davidson, 1956, p.68.
54. Allan, 1974, p.189. Lyon, 2003, p.25.
55. Hamish Henderson, cited by Munro, 1981, p.151.
56. Munro, 1981, p.152.
57. Carter, 1976, p.117.
58. Adams, 1992, pp.63–65.
59. Hood, 'Folk Culture in North East Scotland'.
60. Davidson, 1956, p.69.
61. Simpkins, 1912, pp.356–7.
62. Davidson, 1956, p.73.
63. Hutton, 1999b, p.64.
64. Lyon, 2003, p.33.
65. Bever, 2008, p.313.
66. Hutton, 1999a, pp.1–80. Hutton, 1999b, p.62.
67. Cameron, 1928, pp.114–15.

Bibliography

Adams, David G., *Bothy Nichts and Days*, Edinburgh, 1992.

Adams, W. H. Davenport, *Curiosities of Superstition, and Sketches of Some Unrevealed Religion*, London, 1882.

Albrecht, William P., *The Loathly Lady in 'Thomas of Erceldoune', With a Text of the Poem Printed in 1652*, Albuquerque, 1954.

Alexander, William, *Notes and Sketches Illustrative of Northern Life in the Eighteenth Century*, Edinburgh, 1877.

Allan, Annemarie, *81 Witches of Prestonpans*, Prestonpans, 2005.

Allan, John R., *North-East Lowlands of Scotland*, 2nd edition, London, 1974.

Anderson, Joseph, 'The Confessions of the Forfar Witches', *Proceedings of the Society of Antiquaries of Scotland* 22, 1888, pp.241–263.

Anon., *The Chronicle of Perth, A Register of Remarkable Occurrences Connected with That City, from the Year 1210 to 1668*, Edinburgh, 1831.

Anon., *A Collection of Rare and Curious Tracts on Witchcraft and the Second Sight*, Edinburgh, 1820.

Anon., 'The Diurnal of Occurrences, Chiefly in Scotland, Commencing 21st August 1652, and Ending April 13, 1654', in *The Spottiswoode Miscellany*, volume 2, Edinburgh, 1845, pp.72–208.

Anon., *The Harleian Miscellany*, volume 2, London, 1809.

Anon., *The Harleian Miscellany*, volume 3, London, 1809.

Anon., *The Historie and Life of King James the Sext*, Edinburgh, 1804.

Anon, 'Willox the Wizard', *Transactions of the Inverness Scientific Society and Field Club* 4, 1888, p.66.

Anon, *The Witty and Entertaining Exploits of George Buchanan, Commonly Called the King's Fool,* Stirling, n.d.

Arbuckle, W. F., 'The Gowrie Conspiracy', part 2, *The Scottish Historical Review* 36, No. 122, part 2, October 1957, pp.89–110.

Atkinson, Roark, 'Satan in the Pulpit: Popular Christianity During the Scottish Great Awakening, 1680–1750', *Journal of Social History* 47, no. 2, Winter 2013, pp.344–370.

Bain, Joseph (ed.), *Calendar of Letters and Papers Relating to the Borders of England and Scotland, volume 1, 1560–1594*, Edinburgh, 1894.

Balfour, Sir James, *The Historical Works of Sir James Balfour*, volume 1, Edinburgh, 1824.

Bannerman, John, *The Beatons: A Medical Kindred in the Classical Gaelic Tradition*, Edinburgh, 1986.

Beith, Mary, *Healing Threads, Traditional Medicines of the Highlands and Islands*, 1995, reprinted Edinburgh, 2004.

Bell, Rev. Thomas (ed.), *Records of the Meeting of the Exercise of Alford, 1672–1688*, Aberdeen, 1897.

Bever, Edward, *The Realities of Witchcraft and Popular Magic in Early Modern Europe, Edward Bever*, Basingstoke, 2008.

Bishop, Bruce B. (ed.), *Monumental Inscriptions, Botriphnie*, Aberdeen, 2005.

Black, George Fraser, *Examples of Printed Folk-Lore Concerning the Orkney Islands*, London, 1903.

Bolin, Jilian A., *Second Sight in Early Modern Scotland*, Ph.D. Thesis, San Diego, 2020.

Borman, Tracy, *Witches: James I and the English Witch Hunts*, London, 2014.

Bovet, Richard, *Pandæmonium, or The Devil's Cloyster*, London, 1684.

Bower, Walter, *The Scotichronicon*, volume 5, books 9 and 10, (ed.) Simon Taylor, D. E. R. Watt, Brian Scott, Aberdeen, 1990.

Briggs, Katharine M., *British Folk Tales in the English Language, Part B, Folk Legends*, volume 1, Bloomington, 1971.

Brochard, Thomas, 'Scottish Witchcraft in a Regional and Northern European Context: The Northern Highlands, 1563–1660', *Magic, Ritual, and Witchcraft* 10, number 1, Summer 2015, pp.41–74.

Brock, Michelle, *Satan and the Scots: The Devil in Post Reformation Scotland, c.1560–1700*, London, 2016.

Brown, Rev. James Wood, *An Enquiry into the Life and Legend of Michael Scot*, Edinburgh, 1897.

Bruford, A. J. and MacDonald, D. A. (ed.), *Scottish Traditional Tales*, Edinburgh, 1994.

Buchanan, George, *The Tyrannous Reign of Mary Stewart*, (ed.) W. A. Gatherer, 1958, reprinted Westport, 1978.

Burnett, Linda Andersson, 'Abode of Satan: The Appeal of the Magical and Superstitious North in Eighteenth Century Britain', *Northern Studies: The Journal of the Scottish Society for Northern Studies* 41, 2010, pp.67–77.

Burnham, Josephine, 'A Study of Thomas of Erceldoune', *Publications of the Modern Language Society of America* 23, new series 16, 1908, pp.375–420.

Burton, John Hill, *Criminal Trials in Scotland*, volume 2, London, 1852.

Busst, A. J. L., 'Scottish Second Sight: The Rise and Fall of A European Myth', *European Romantic Review* 5:2, 1995, pp.149–77.

Calderwood, David, *The History of the Kirk of Scotland*, volume 3, Edinburgh, 1843.

Calderwood, David, *The History of the Kirk of Scotland*, volume 5, Edinburgh, 1844.

Calderwood, David (ed.), Thomas Thomson, *The History of the Kirk of Scotland*, volume 8, Edinburgh, 1849.

Calendar of the State Papers Relating to Scotland, volume 2, (ed.) John Thorpe Markham, London, 1858.

Calendar of the State Papers Relating to Scotland and Mary Queen of Scots, 1547–1603, volume 10, (ed.) W. K. Boyd and H. W. Meikle, Edinburgh, 1936.

Callander, Robin, *History in Birse*, volumes 1–4, Banchory, 2000.

Cameron, Isabel, *A Highland Chapbook*, Stirling, 1928.

Campbell, Lord Archibald (ed.), *Waifs and Strays of Celtic Tradition* 1, Argyllshire Series, London, 1889.

Campbell, John Gregorson, *Superstitions of the Highlands and Islands of Scotland*, Glasgow, 1900.

Campbell, John Gregorson, *Witchcraft and Second Sight in the Highlands and Islands of Scotland*, Glasgow, 1902.

Carmichael, Alexander, 'Some Unrecorded Incidents of the Jacobite Risings', *The Celtic Review* 6, 1909, pp.334–48.

Carswell, John, *The Book of Common Order, Commonly Called John Knox's Liturgy*, Edinburgh, 1873.

Carter, Ian, 'Class and Culture Among Farm Servants in the North-East, 1840–1914', in *Social Class in Scotland: Past and Present*, (ed.) A. Allan MacLaren, Edinburgh, 1976, pp.105–27.

Carter, Ian R., *Farm Life in Northeast Scotland, 1890–1914: the Poor Man's Country*, Edinburgh, 1997.

Chambers, Robert, *Domestic Annals of Scotland, From the Revolution to the Rebellion of 1745*, Edinburgh, 1861.

Chambers, Robert, *The Picture of Scotland*, volume 1, Edinburgh, 1827.

Chambers, Robert, *The Popular Rhymes of Scotland*, 3rd edition, 1870.

Chambers, Robert, *Traditions of Edinburgh*, 1824, revised edition, Edinburgh, 1847.

Cheape, Hugh, 'Evidence and Artefact: Utility for Protohistory and Archaeology in Thomas the Rhymer Legends', in *Ancient Lives, Object, People and Places in Early Scotland*, (ed.) Fraser Hunter and Alison Sheridan, Leiden, 2016, pp.151–64.

Cheape, Hugh, 'The Red Book of Appin: Medicine as Magic and Magic as Medicine', *Folklore* 104, no 1/2 ,1993, pp.111–23.

Childe, V. Gordon, *Prehistoric Communities of the British Isles*, London, 1940.

Cohn, Norman, *Europe's Inner Demons, The Demonization of Christians in Medieval Christendom*, revised edition, Chicago, 2000.

Coleman, Keith, *The Afterlife of King James IV: Otherworld Legends of the Scottish King*, London, 2019.

Collingwood, Bruce J., 'Observations on the Trial and Death of William Earl of Gowrie', *Archaeologia* 33, 1849, pp.143–73.

Cowan, Edward J., 'The Darker Vision of the Scottish Renaissance: the Devil and Francis Stewart', in Ian B. Cowan and Duncan Shaw (ed.), *The Renaissance and Reformation in Scotland*, Edinburgh, 1983, pp.125–40.

Cowan, Edward J., 'Witch Persecution and Folk Belief in Lowland Scotland: The Devil's Decade', in *Witchcraft and Belief in Early Modern Scotland*, (ed.) Julien Goodacre, Lauren Martin and Joyce Miller, Basingstoke, 2008, pp.71–94.

Cowan, Samuel, (ed.), *The Ruthven Version of the Conspiracy and Assassination at Gowrie House, Perth, 5th August 1600*, London, 1912.

Cowie, Moyra, *The Life and Times of William Marshall, 1748–1833, Composer of Scottish Traditional Fiddle Music, Clock Maker, and Butler to the 4th Duke of Gordon*, Elgin, 1999.

Craigie, Sir William and Aitken, A. J., (ed.), *Dictionary of the Older Scots Tongue*, volume 3, Chicago, 1974.

Cramond, William (ed.), *Records of the Kirk Session of Elgin, 1567–1897*, Elgin, 1897.

Curran, Dr Bob, *The Dark Spirit: Sinister Portraits from Celtic Folklore*, London, 2001.

Dalyell, John Graham, *The Darker Superstitions of Scotland Illustrated from History and Practice*, Edinburgh, 1834.

Davidson, Hilda Ellis (ed.), *The Seer in Celtic and Other Traditions*, Edinburgh, 1989.

Davidson, Thomas, 'The Horseman's Word: A Rural Initiation Ceremony', *Gwerin: A Half-Yearly Journal of Folk Life* 1:2, 1956, pp.67–74.

Davidson, T. D., 'The Untilled Field', *The Agricultural History Review*, volume 3 part 1, 1955, pp.20–25.

Davies, Owen, 'A Comparative Perspective on Scottish Cunning-Folk and Charmers', in *Witchcraft and Belief in Early Modern Scotland*, (eds.) Julian Goodacre, Lauren Martin and Joyce Miller, Basingstoke, 2007, pp.185–205.

Davies, Owen, *Grimoires, A History of Magic Books*, Oxford, 2009.

Davies, R. Trevor, *Four Centuries of Witchcraft Belief, With Special Reference to the Great Rebellion*, volume 2, 1947, reprinted Abingdon, 2011.

Dempster, Miss, 'The Folklore of Sutherland-shire (Continued)', *The Folk-Lore Journal* 6, number 4, 1888, pp.215–252.

Denham Aislabie, Michael, *The Denham Tracts*, volume one, London, 1891, volume 2, London, 1895.

Donaldson, Rev. George, *County of Banff, Old Statistical Account*, volume 13, 1794; https://stataccscot.ed.ac.uk/static/statacc/dist/viewer/osa-vol13-Parish_record_for_Rathven_in_the_county_of_Banff_in_volume_13_of_account_1/.

Dudley, Margaret and Goodacre, Julian, 'Outside in or Inside Out: Sleep Paralysis and Scottish Witchcraft', in Martin Goodacre, (ed.), *Scottish Witches and Witch-Hunters*, Basingstoke, 2013, pp.121–39.

Dye, Sierra, *'Devilische Wordis:' Speech As Evidence in Scotland's Witch Trials, 1563–1736*, PhD. Thesis, Guelph, 2016.

Flood, Victoria, *Prophecy, Politics and Places in Medieval England From Geoffrey of Monmouth to Thomas of Erceldoune*, Woodbridge, 2016.

Gardiner, Ralph, *England's Grievance Against the Coal Trade Discovered, In Relation to the Coal Trade*, 1655, reprinted Newcastle, 1796.

Giraldus Cambrensis, 'Topographia Hibernie', (trans.) Philip Freeman, in *The Celtic Heroic Age*, (ed.) John Koch, 4th edition, Aberystwyth, 2005, p.286.

Grewar, David, 'Gregor Willox', *Aberdeen Journal Notes and Queries* 3, 1910, pp.204–205.

Egger, Ruth, *Fairies, Witches and the Devil: The Interface Between Elite Demonology and Folk Belief in Early Scottish Witchcraft Trials*, Mag. Thesis, Vienna, 2014.

Farquharson, Donald Robert, *Tales and Memories of Cromar and Canada*, Chatham, Ontario, n.d.

Fergusson, Robert Menzies, *Alexander Hume, An Early Pastor-Poet of Logie, and His Intimates*, Paisley 1899.

Fergusson, *The Laird of Lag*, Edinburgh, 1886.

Fraser, James, 'A Collection of Provincial Passages Antient and Modern Forreign and Domestick', in *A Source Book of Scottish Witchcraft*, (eds.) Christina Larner, Christopher Hyde Lee, and Hugh V McLagan, Glasgow, 1977, pp.261–8.

Fraser, James, *Chronicles of the Frasers, The Wardlaw Manuscript*, Edinburgh, 1905.

Fraser, James, 'A Collection of Provincial Passages Antient and Modern Forreign and Domestick', in *A Source Book of Scottish Witchcraft*, (eds.),Christina Larner, Christopher Hyde Lee, and Hugh V McLagan, Glasgow, 1977, 261–8.

Fraser, William, *History of the Carnegies, Earls of Southesk, and of their Kindred*, volume one, Edinburgh, 1867.

Gaffney, Victor, Tomintoul, *Its Glens and Its People*, Golspie, 1970.

Ginzburg, Carlo, *Ecstasies*, (trans.) Raymond Rosenthal, London, 1991.

Ginzburg, Carlo, *The Night Battles, Witchcraft and Agrarian Cults in the Sixteenth and Seventeenth Centuries*, (trans.) John and Anne Tedeschi, Abingdon, 2011.

Goldstein, Kenneth G., *A Guide for Fieldworkers in Folklore*, Hatboro, 1964.

Goodacre, Julian, 'Away With The Fairies: the Psychopathology of Visionary Encounters in Early Modern Scotland', *History of Psychology* 31, 2020, pp.37–54.

Goodacre, Julian, 'The Cult of the Seely Wights in Scotland', *Folklore* 123:2, 2012, pp.198–219.

Goodacre, Julian, 'John Knox on Demonology and Witchcraft', *Archiv für Reformationsgeschichte* 96, 2005a, pp.221–245.

Goodacre, Julian, 'Men and the Witch-Hunt in Scotland', in Alison Rowlands (ed.), *Witchcraft and Masculinities in Early Modern Europe*, Basingstoke, 2009, pp.149–70.

Goodacre, Julian, 'The Scottish Witchcraft Act Author(s)', *Church History* 74, no. 1, March 2005b, pp.39–67.

Goodacre, Julian, 'Scottish Witchcraft in its European Context', in Julian Goodacre, Lauren Martin and Joyce Miller (eds.), *Witchcraft and Belief in Early Modern Scotland*, Basingstoke, 2008, pp.26–50.

Grant, Isobel, Frances, *Along A Highland Road*, London, 1980.

Grant, Joseph, *Tales of the Glens, With Ballads and Songs*, Stonehaven, 1869.

Gray, Affleck, *Legends of the Cairngorms*, Edinburgh, 1987.

Gregor, Rev. Walter, 'Further Report on Folklore in Scotland', in *Report of the Sixty-Seventh Meeting of the British Association for the Advancement of Science*, London, 1898, pp.456–500.

Gregor, Rev. Walter, *Kilns, Mills, Millers, Meal and Bread*, London, 1894.

Gregor, Rev. Walter, *Notes On The Folk-Lore of the North-east of Scotland*, London, 1881.

Grewar, David, *Aberdeen Journal Notes and Queries*, volume 3, 1910, pp.204–5.

Gunnell, Terry, 'The Power in the Place: Icelandic *Álagablettir* Legends in a Comparative Context', in *Storied and Supernatural Places, Studies in Spatial and Social Dimensions*, (eds.) Ülo Valk and Daniel Sävborg, Helsinki, 2018, pp.27–41.

Hall, Alaric, *Elves in Anglo Saxon England: Matters of Belief, Health, Gender and Identity*, Woodbridge, 2007.

Hall, Alaric, 'Folk-healing, Fairies and Witchcraft: the Trial of Stein Maltman, Stirling, 1628', *Studia Celtica Fennica* 3, 2006, pp.10–25.

Hall, Rev. James, *Travels in Scotland By An Unusual Route*, London, 1807.

Hanford, Mark Carlton, *The Role of the Wizard in Scottish and Icelandic Folk Legend*, Ph.D. Thesis, Edinburgh, 1995.

Hay, Alexander, *The Diary of Alexander Hay of Craignethan, 1659–1660*, Edinburgh, 1901.

Henderson, E. (ed.), *Extracts from the Kirk-Session Records of Dunfermline, from AD 1640 to 1689 Inclusive*, Edinburgh, 1865.

Henderson, George, *The Popular Rhymes, Sayings and Proverbs of the County of Berwick*, Newcastle, 1856.

Henderson, Jan-Andrew, *The Ghost That Haunted Itself, The Story of the Mackenzie Poltergeist*, Edinburgh, 2001.

Henderson, Lizanne, *The Guid Neighbours, Fairy Belief in Early Modern Scotland, 1500–1800*, Ph.D. Thesis, St John's, Newfoundland, 1997.

Henderson, Lizanne, 'Witch, Fairy and Folk Tale Narratives in the Trial of Bessie Dunlop', in Lizanne Henderson (ed.), *Fantastical Imaginations, The Supernatural in Scottish History and Culture*, Edinburgh, 2009, pp.141–66.

Henderson, Lizanne, 'Witch-Hunting and Witch Belief in the Gàidhealtachd,' in J. Goodacre, L. Martin, J. Miller (eds.), *Witchcraft and Belief in Early Modern Scotland*, Basingstoke, 2008, pp.95–118.

Henderson, Lizanne, *Witchcraft and Folk Belief in the Age of Enlightenment, Scotland, 1640–1740*, Basingstoke, 2016.

Henderson, Lizanne and Cowan, Edward J., *Scottish Fairy Belief, A History*, Edinburgh, 2001.

Henderson, T. F., *Old World Scotland, Glimpses of its Modes and Manners*, London, 1893.

Henderson, William, *Notes on the Folk-Lore of the Northern Counties of England and the Borders*, London, second edition, 1879.

Hickes, George, *Ravillac Redivivus, Being a Narrative of the Late Tryal of the Preacher James Mitchell*, London, 1678.

Hickes, George, *The Spirit of Popery Speaking Out of the Mouths of Phanatical Protestants*, London, 1680.

Hill, Alexandra, 'Decline and Survival in Scottish Witch-Hunting, 1701–1727', in *Scottish Witches and Witch-Hunters*, (ed.) J. Goodacre, Basingstoke, 2013, pp.215–233.

Hood, David W., 'Folk Culture in North East Scotland: An overview', The North East Folklore Archive: http://www.nefa.net/archive/peopleandlife/customs/folk.htm.

Hughes, Paula, 'Witch-Hunting in Scotland, 1649–1650', in *Scottish Witches and Witch-Hunters*, (ed.) Jonathan Goodare, Basingstoke, 2013, pp.85–102.

Hume Brown, P. (ed.), *Register of the Privy Council of Scotland*, second series, volume 2, 1627–1628, Edinburgh, 1900.

Hume Brown, P. (ed.), *Register of the Privy Council of Scotland*, second series, volume 3, 1629–1630, Edinburgh, 1901.

Hume Brown, P. (ed.), *Register of the Privy Council of Scotland*, second series, volume 4, 1630–1632, Edinburgh, 1902.

Hume Brown, P. (ed.), *Register of the Privy Council of Scotland*, second series, volume 5, 1633–1635, Edinburgh, 1904.

Hume Brown, P. (ed.), *Register of the Privy Council of Scotland*, second series, volume 8, 1544–1660, Edinburgh, 1908.

Hunter, Rev. John., *The Diocese and Presbytery of Dunkeld, 1660–1689*, volume 2, London, 1917.

Hunter, Michael (ed.), *The Occult Laboratory. Magic, Science, and Second Sight in Late Seventeenth-Century Scotland*, Woodbridge, 2001.

Hutton, Ronald, 'Modern Pagan Witchcraft', in *Witchcraft and Magic in Europe in the Twentieth Century*, (eds.) Bengt Ankarloo and Stuart Clark, Philadelphia, 1999a, pp.1–80.

Hutton, Ronald, *The Triumph of the Moon*, Oxford, 1999b.

Hutton Ronald, *The Witch, A History of Fear from Ancient Times to the Present*, New Haven, 2017.

James VI, King, *The Demonology, in Witchcraft in Early Modern Scotland, James VI's Demonology and the North Berwick Witches*, (eds.) Lawrence Normand and Gareth Roberts, Exter, 2000, pp.353–425.

Jacob, Violet, *The Lairds of Dun*, London, 1931.

Jervise, Andrew, *Epitaphs and Inscriptions from Burial Grounds and Old Buildings in the North-East of Scotland*, volume 1, Edinburgh, 1875.

Jervise, Andrew, *The Land of the Lindsays in Angus and the Mearns*, second edition, Edinburgh, 1882.

Jessop, J. C., *Education in Angus*, London, 1931.

Kassin, Saul M. and Wrightsman, Lawrence S. (eds.), *The Psychology of Evidence and Trial Procedure*, Beverley Hills, 1985.

Kay, Richard, 'The Spare Ribs of Dante's Michael Scot', *Dante Studies/ The Annual Report of the Dante Society* 103, 1985, pp.1–14.

Kidd, William, *Extracts from the Records of the Presbytery of Brechin from 1639 to 1669*, Dundee, 1877.

Kirk, Robert, *The Secret Common-Wealth*, in Hunter, (ed.), *The Occult Laboratory*, Woodbridge, 2001, pp.77–106.

Kirk, Thomas and Thoresby, Ralph, *Tours in Scotland, 1677 and 1681*, (ed.) P. Hume Brown, Edinburgh, 1892.

Kirkton, James, *The History of the Life and Sufferings of Mr John Welsh, Minister of the Gospel at Aire*, Edinburgh, 1703.

Laing, David (ed.), *The Book of the Universall Kirk of Scotland: Acts and Proceedings of the General Assemblies of the Kirk of Scotland from the Year MDLX*, 1845, part 3, Edinburgh, 1845.

Laing, Jeanie M., *Notes on Superstition and Folklore*, Brechin, 1865.

Lamont, John, *The Diary of Mr John Lamont of Newton, 1649–1671*, Edinburgh, 1830.

Lang, Andrew, *James VI and the Gowrie Mystery*, London, 1902.

Lang, Andrew, *Sir George Mackenzie*, London, 1909.

Larner, Christina, *Enemies of God: The Witch Hunt in Scotland*, London, 1981.

Larner, Christina, Lee, Christopher Hyde and McLachlan, Hugh V., *A Source Book of Scottish Witchcraft*, Glasgow, 1977.

Lauder, Sir John, *Historical Notices of Scottish Affairs, volume one, 1661–1683*, Edinburgh, 1848.

Lauder, Sir John, *Lauder of Fountainhall's Journals*, Edinburgh, 1900.

Lauder, Sir Thomas Dick, *Highland Rambles and Long Legends to Shorten the Way*, volume 2, Edinburgh, 1837.

Lauder, Sir Thomas Dick, *Legendary Tales of the Highlands*, volume 1, London, 1841.

Law, Rev. Robert, *Memorialls, or The Memorable Things that Fell Out in the Island of Britain from 1638 to 1684*, (ed.) Charles Kirkpatrick Sharpe, Edinburgh, 1818.

Levack, Brian P., 'Crime and the Law', in *Palgrave Advances in Witchcraft Historiography*, (eds.) Jonathan Barry and Owen Davies, Basingstoke, 2007, pp.146–163.

Levack, Brian P., *Witch Hunting in Scotland: Law, Politics, and Religion*, London, 2008.

Levack, Brian P. (ed.), *The Witchcraft Sourcebook*, London, 2004.

Lyle, Emily, (ed.) 'The Good Man's Croft,' *Scottish Studies* 36, 2013, pp.103–24.

Lyle, E. B., 'Thomas of Erceldoune: The Prophet and the Prophesied', *Folklore* 79, number 2, 1968, pp.111–21.

Lyon, Russell, *The Quest for the Original Horse Whisperers*, Edinburgh, 2003.

Macculloch, Canon J. A., 'The Mingling of Fairy and Witch Beliefs in Sixteenth and Seventeenth Century Scotland', *Folklore* 32, number 4, December 1921, pp.227–44.

Macdonald, Rev. James, 'Stray Customs and Legends', *Transactions of the Gaelic Society of Inverness* 19, 1893–94, pp.272–286.

Macdonald, Stuart, *Threats to a Godly Society: The Witch-Hunt in Fife, Scotland 1560–1710*, Phd Thesis, University of Guelph, 1997.

Macdougall, Norman, *James III, A Political Study*, Edinburgh, 1982.

Macfarlane, Alan, *Witchcraft in Tudor and Stuart England*, London, 1971.

'Mac Iain', 'The Black Captain – An T'Offigeach Dubh', *The Celtic Magazine* 3, issue 27, 1878, pp.112–119.

MacInnes, John, 'The Seer in Gaelic Tradition', in *The Seer in Celtic and Other Traditions*, (ed.) Hilda Ellis Davidson, Edinburgh, 1989, pp.10–24.

MacInnes, John, 'The Church and Traditional Belief in Gaelic Society', in *Fantastical Imaginations, The Supernatural in Scottish History and Culture*, (ed.) Lizanne Henderson, Edinburgh, 2009, pp.185–195.

Mackay, William (ed.), *Records of the Presbyteries of Inverness and Dingwall, 1643–1688*, Edinburgh, 1896.

Mackenzie, Alexander, *The Prophecies of the Brahan Seer, Coinneach Odhar Fiosaiche*, (ed.) Elizabeth Sutherland, London, 1977 (1877).

Mackenzie, George, *Pleadings in Some Remarkable Cases Before the Supreme Courts of Scotland Since the Year 1661*, Edinburgh, 1673.

Mackenzie, George, Edinburgh, *The Law and Custome of Scotland in Matters Criminal*, Edinburgh, 1878.

Mackenzie, George, Earl of Cromarty, *An Historical Account of the Conspiracies of the Earls of Gowry*, Edinburgh, 1713.

Mackie, R. L., *King James IV of Scotland*, Edinburgh and London, 1958.

Maclagan, Robert C., *Evil Eye in the Western Highlands*, London, 1902.

Maclellan, Angus, *Stories from South Uist*, (trans.) John Lorne Campbell, Edinburgh, 1997.

MacPhail, J. R. N., *Highland Papers*, volume 1, Edinburgh, 1914.

MacPhail, J. R. N., *Highland Papers*, volume 3, Edinburgh, 1920.

Mactaggart, John, *The Scottish Gallovidian Encyclopedia*, second edition, London, 1876.

Martin, Lauren, 'The Witch, the Household and the Community: Isobel Young in East Barns, 1580–1629', in *Scottish Witches and Witch-Hunters*, (ed.) Julian Goodacre, Basingstoke, 2013, pp.67–84.

Martin Martin, *A Journey to the Western Isles*, London, 1712.

Martin, Martin, *A Late Voyage to St Kilda*, London, 1698.

Marwick, Ernest, *The Folklore of Orkney and Shetland*, London, 1975, reprinted 1986.

Mather, Increase, *Cases of Conscience Concerning Evil Spirits*, Boston, 1693.

Matheson, William, 'The Historical Coinneach Odhar and Some Prophecies Attributed to Him', in *Transactions of the Gaelic Society of Inverness* 46, 1969–70, pp.66–88.

Maxwell, Sir Herbert (trans.), *The Chronicle of Lanercost, 1272–1346*, Glasgow, 1913.

Maxwell-Stuart, P. G., *An Abundance of Witches, The Great Scottish Witch Hunt*, Stroud, 2005.

Maxwell-Stuart, P. G., 'The Fear of the King is Death: James VI and the Witches of East Lothian', in *Fear in Early Modern Society*, (ed.) William P. Naphy and Penny Roberts, Mancher, 1997, pp.209–25.

Maxwell-Stuart, P. G., 'Witchcraft and Magic in Eighteenth-Century Scotland', in *Beyond the Witch Trials, Witchcraft and Magic in Enlightenment Europe*, (ed.) Owen Davies and Willem de Blécourt, Manchester, 2004, pp.81–99.

Maxwell-Stuart, P. G., *Satan's Conspiracy, Magic and Witchcraft in Sixteenth–Century Scotland*, East Linton, 2001.

McAldowie, Alex, 'Personal Experiences in Witchcraft', *Folklore* 7, no. 3, September 1896, pp.209–14.

McCabe Allan, Morgana Elizabeth, *The Difference Of Being In The Early Modern World: A Relational-Material Approach To Life In Scotland In The Period Of The Witch Trials*, Ph.D. Thesis, Glasgow, 2016.

McDonald, S. W., 'The Devil's Mark and the Witch-Prickers of Scotland', *Journal of the Royal Society of Medicine* 90, 1997, pp.507–11.

McGregor, Richard E., *Gregor Willox the Warlock*, Aberdeen, 1994.

McNeill, F. Marian, *The Silver Bough*, 1956, reprinted Edinburgh, 1989.

McPherson, J. M., *Primitive Beliefs of the Northeast of Scotland*, London, 1929.

Meikle, James, 'The Seventeenth Century Presbytery of Meigle', *Records of the Scottish Church Society* 5, part 2, 1935, pp.145–56.

Melville, Sir James, *Memoirs of Sir James Melville of Halhill, 1535–1617*, (ed.) A. Francis Steuart, London, 1929.

Michel, Francisque, *Les Écossaise en France, Les Française en Écosse*, volume 1, London, 1862.

Miller, Hugh, *My Schools and Schoolmasters*, 1854, 14th edition, Edinburgh, 1869.

Miller, Joyce, *Cantrips and Carlins: Magic, Medicine and Society in the Presbyteries of Haddington and Stirling, 1603–88*, Ph.D. Thesis, Edinburgh, 1999.

Mitchell, James, *The Scotsman's Library: Being a Collection of Anecdotes and Facts Illustrative of Scotland and Scotsmen*, Edinburgh, 1825.

Mitchell, John and Dickie, John, *The Philosophy of Witchcraft*, Paisley, 1839.

Monteath, John, *Traditions of Dunblane*, Stirling, 1887.

Munro, Robert, Folklore and Society in North-East Scotland, Ph.D. Thesis, Edinburgh, 1981.

Murdoch, Robert, 'Macgregors of Gaulrig', *Scottish Notes and Queries*, second series, 7, June 1905–June 1906, p.40.

Murray, James A. H., *The Romance and Prophecies of Thomas of Erceldoune*, London, 1875.

Murray, Margaret A, 'The "Devil" of North Berwick', *The Scottish Historical Review* 15, number 60, July 1918, pp.310–21.

Murray, Margaret A., 'The Devil's Officers and the Witches' Covens', *Man* 19, September 1919, pp.137–40.

Murray, Margaret A., *The God of the Witches*, New York, 1960.

Murray, Margaret A., *The Witch-Cult in Western Europe, A Study in Anthropology*, Oxford, 1921.

Murray, Margaret A., 'Two Trials for Witchcraft', in *Proceedings of the Society of Antiquaries of Scotland* 56, 1921–1922, pp.46–64.

Napier, James, *Folk Lore, or Superstitious Beliefs in the West of Scotland Within This Century*, Paisley, 1879.

Napier, Mark, *Memoirs of John Napier of Merchiston*, Edinburgh, 1834.

Neill, Rev. W. N., 'The Professional Pricker and his Test for Witchcraft', *Scottish Historical Review* 19, 1922, pp.205–13.

Newton, Michael, 'Prophecy and Cultural Conflict in Gaelic Tradition', *Scottish Studies* 35, 2010, pp.144–73.

Normand, Lawrence and Roberts, Gareth (ed.), *Witchcraft in Early Modern Scotland, James VI's Demonology and the North Berwick Witches*, Exeter, 2000.

Panton, William, *A Dissertation on that Portion of Scottish History Termed the Gowrie Conspiracy*, Perth, 1812.

Paterson, Laura, 'The Witches' Sabbath in Scotland', *Proceedings of the Society of Antiquaries of Scotland* 142, 2012, pp.371–412.

Pettigrew, Thomas, *On Superstitions Connected with the History and Practice of Medicine and Surgery*, London, 1844.

Philip, Neil (ed.), *The Penguin Book of Scottish Folk Tales*, London, 1995.

Pitcairn, Robert, *Criminal Trials in Scotland*, volume 1, part 1 and part 2, Edinburgh, 1833.

Pitcairn, Robert, *Criminal Trials in Scotland*, volume 2, part 1 and part 2, Edinburgh, 1833.

Preston, Kathleen, *Cumbria Lore and Legend*, Kendal, 1979.

Purkiss, Diane, *At the Bottom of the Garden, A Dark History of Fairies, Hobgoblins, and Other Troublesome Things*, New York, 2003.

Reid, Alexander George, *The Annals of Auchterarder and Memorials of Strathearn*, Crieff, 1899.

Ribton-Turner, C. J., *A History of Vagrants and Vagrancy, Beggars and Begging*, London, 1887.

Robertson, David McK., *Wise Wives and Warlocks, A Rogue's Gallery of East Lothian Witchcraft*, Kilkerran, 2013.

Robertson, Elizabeth, *Panic and Persecution: Witch-Hunting in East Lothian, 1628–1631*, MSc. Thesis, Edinburgh, 2009.

Rogers, Rev. Charles, *Memorials of Life and Manners in North Britain*, London, 1869.

Rorie, Davie, *Folk Tradition and Folk Medicine in Scotland, The Writings of David Rorie*, (ed.) David Buchan, Edinburgh, 1994.

Rose, Elliot, *A Razor For A Goat, A Discussion of Certain Problems in the History of Witchcraft and Diabolism*, 1962, reprinted Toronto, 2003.

Ross, Anne, *The Folklore of the Scottish Highlands*, London, 1976, reprinted 1990.

Roughead, William, *Twelve Scottish Trials*, Edinburgh, 1913.

Rowlands, Alison, 'Not "the Usual Suspects"? Males Witches, Witchcraft, and Masculinities in Early Modern Europe', in *Witchcraft and Masculinities in Early Modern Europe*, (ed.) Alison Rowlands, Basingstoke, 2009, pp.1–30.

Russell, Jeffrey Burton, *Witchcraft in the Middle Ages*, London, 1972.

Rutkowski, Pawel, 'Scotland as a Land of Seers: the Scottish Second Sight at the Turn of the Eighteenth Century', in *Facets of Scottish Identity*, (ed.) Izabela Szymańska and Aniela Korzeniowska, Warsaw, 2013, pp.186–194.

Sanderson, Sir William, *A Compleat History of the Lives and Reigns of Mary, Queen of Scotland, and her Son and Successor, James the Sixth*, London, 1656.

Scarre, Geoffrey, *Witchcraft and Magic in Sixteenth and Seventeenth Century Europe*, Basingstoke, 1987.

Scot, Sir John, *The Staggering State of Scottish Statesmen*, Edinburgh, 1872.

Scot, Walter, *Metrical History of the Honourable Families of the Name of Scot and Elliot in the Shires of Roxburgh and Selkirk*, Edinburgh, 1892.

Scott, Hew, *Fasti Ecclesiæ Scoticanæ*, new edition, volume 5, Edinburgh, 1925.

Scott, Rev. James, *A History of the Life and Death of John Ruthven, Earl of Gowrie*, Perth, 1818.

Scott, Sir Walter, *Letters on Demonology and Witchcraft*, 1830, reprinted London, 1884.

Scott-Moncrieff, W. G., *The Records of the Justiciary Court of Edinburgh, 1661–1678*, volume 2, Edinburgh, 1905.

Schulte, Rolf, *Man As Witch, Male Witches in Central Europe*, Basingstoke, 2009.

Sharpe, Charles Kirkpatrick, *A Historical Account of Witchcraft in Scotland*, London, 1884.

Shaw, John (trans. and ed.), *The Blue Mountains and Other Gaelic Stories from Cape Breton*, Montreal, 2007.

Shaw, John, 'Scottish Gaelic Traditions of the Cliar Sheanchain', *in Celtic Languages and Celtic Peoples: Proceedings of the Second North American Congress of Celtic Studies held in Halifax August 16–19, 1989*, (ed.) Cyril J. Byrne, Margaret Harry, Pádraig Ó Siadhail, Halifax, Nova Scotia, 1992, pp.141–58.

Shaw, John, 'What Alexander Carmichael Did Not Print: The "Cliar Sheanchain", "Clanranald's Fool" and Related Traditions', *Béaloideas* 70, 2002, pp.99–126.

Simpkins, John Ewart, *County Folklore VII: Fife, Clackmannan, Kinross-shire*, London, 1912.

Simpson, Jacqueline, 'Witches and Witchbusters', *Folklore* 107, 1–2, 1996, pp.5–18.

Simpson, Sir James Young, *Archaeology: its past and its future work; being the annual address to the Society of Antiquaries of Scotland, given January 28, 1861*, Edinburgh, 1861.

Sinclair, *Satan's Invisible World Discovered*, 1685, reprinted Edinburgh, 1871.

Sinton, Rev. Thomas, *The Poetry of Badenoch*, Inverness, 1906.

Sinclair, Sir John (ed.), *The Statistical Account of Scotland*, 1791–1799, volume 16, Banffshire, Moray and Nairnshire, reprinted Wakefield, 1982.

Smith, Mark C., *The Presbytery of St Andrews 1586–1605: A Study and Annotated Edition of the Register of the Minutes of the Presbytery of St Andrews*, Ph.D. Thesis, St Andrews, 1986.

Sneddon, Andrew, *Witchcraft and Magic in Ireland*, Basingstoke, 2015.

Somerset, Lady Anne, *Unnatural Murder: Poison in the Court of James I: The Overbury Murder*, London, 1997.

Spence, Lewis, *The Fairy Tradition in Britain*, London, 1948.

Stafford, Helen, 'Notes On Scottish Witchcraft Cases, 1590–91', in *Essays in Honor of Conyers Read*, (ed.) Norton Downs, Chicago, 1953, pp.96–118.

Stevenson, David, *The Origins of Freemasonry*, paperback edition, Cambridge, 1990.

Stevenson, *Robert Louis, Edinburgh: Picturesque Notes*, Edinburgh, 1879.

Stewart, W. Grant, *The Popular Superstitions and Festive Amusements of the Highlanders of Scotland*, W. Grant Stewart, Edinburgh, 1823.

Stiùbhart, Dòmhnall Uilleam, 'The Invention of Highland Second Sight', in *The Supernatural in Early Modern Scotland*, (ed.) Julian Goodacre and Martha McGill, Manchester, 2020, pp.178–203.

Stiùbhart, Dòmhnall Uilleam, 'Some Heathenish and Superstitious Rites, A Letter from Lewis, 1700', *Scottish Studies* 34:203, December 2006, pp.203–224.

Stuart, John (ed.), *Extracts from the Presbytery Book of Strathbogie*, Aberdeen, 1843.

Stuart, John (ed.), *The Miscellany of the Spalding Club*. volume one, Aberdeen, 1841.

Stuart, John (ed.), *Selections from the Kirk Session, Presbytery and Synod of Aberdeen*, Aberdeen, 1846.

Summers, Montague, *Witchcraft and Black Magic*, London, 1946.

Sutherland, Alexander Mackenzie Sutherland, *The Brahan Seer, The Making of A Legend, c.1570–2001*, Ph,D. Thesis, Aberdeen, 2005.

Sutherland, Elizabeth, *Ravens and Black Rain, The Story of Highland Second Sight*, London, 1985, reprinted 1987.

Sutherland, Elizabeth, 'Who Was the Brahan Seer?' in Mackenzie, Alexander, *The Prophecies of the Brahan Seer, Coinneach Odhar Fiosaiche*, (ed.) Elizabeth Sutherland, London, 1977, pp.135–48.

Swire, Otta F., *The Highlands and Their Legends*, Edinburgh, 1963.

Thomas, Charles, 'Present Day Charmers in Cornwall', *Folklore* 64, number 1, March 1953, pp.204–5.

Thomas, Keith, *Religion and the Decline of Magic. Studies in Popular Beliefs in Sixteenth and Seventeenth Century England*, 1971, reprinted London, 1991.

Thorndike, Lynn, *Michael Scot*, Lynn Thorndike, London, 1965.

Tobar an Dualchais, Kist o Riches, https://www.tobarandualchais.co.uk/.

Todd, Margo, *The Culture of Protestantism in Early Modern Scotland*, New Haven, 2002.

Truckell, A. E.. 'Unpublished Witchcraft Trials', *Transactions of the Dumfriesshire and Galloway Natural History and Antiquarian Society*, third series, 51, 1975, pp.48–58.

Tveit, Miriam, 'Bearded Women and Sea-Monsters: European Representations of the Far North in the Early and High Middle Ages', in *Myths and Magic in the Medieval Far North, Realities and Representations of a Region on the Edge of Europe*, (ed.) Stefan Figenschow and Richard Holt, Turnhout, 2020, pp.19–38.

Warburton, Rev. William, 'Notes on Altcar Parish', *Transactions of the Historic Society of Lancashire and Cheshire* 47, new series 11, 1896, pp.157–206.

Wasser, Michael, 'Scotland's First Witch-Hunt: The Eastern Witch-Hunt of 1568–9', in Julian Goodacre (ed.), *Scottish Witches and Witch-Hunters*, London, 2013, pp.17–33.

Waters, Thomas, *Cursed Britain, A History of Witchcraft and Black Magic in Modern Times* New Haven, 2019.

Watson, George, '"The Goodman's Croft" and its relation to "Aploch"', *Proceedings of the Dumfriesshire and Galloway Natural History and Antiquarian Society* 28, 1951, pp.179–85.

Watt, D. E. R., 'Scottish Student Life Abroad in the Fourteenth Century', *The Scottish Historical Review* 59, number 167, part 1, April 1980, pp.3–21.

Westwood, Jennifer, *Albion, A Guide to Legendary Britain*, London, 1985.

Westwood, Jennifer and Kingshill, Sophie, *The Lore of Scotland, A Guide to Scottish Legends*, London, 2009.

Wilby, Emma, *Cunning Folk and Familiar Spirits, Shamanistic Visionary Traditions in Early Modern British Witchcraft and Magic*, Eastbourne, 2005.

Willumsen, Liv Helene, 'Seventeenth Witchcraft Trials in Scotland and Northern Norway: Comparative Aspects', *Historical Research* 1, number 1, December 2011, pp.61–74.

Willumsen, Liv Helene, *Witches of the North, Scotland and Finnmark*, Leiden, 2013.

Wilson, Sir Daniel, *Memorials of Edinburgh in the Olden Time*, third edition, Edinburgh, 1875.

Wiseman, Andrew, 'The Black Captain and the Catastrophe of Gaick', The Callum Maclean Project, https://calumimaclean.blogspot.com/2018/09/the-black-capain-and-catastrophe-of.html

Wiseman, Anndra E. M., 'Call Ghàdhaig ann am Fiscean is ann am Fìrinn', *Transactions of the Gaelic Society of Inverness* 60–62, 2002, pp.298–346.

Wodrow, Rev. Robert, *Analecta: or Materials for a History of Remarkable Providences*, volume one, Glasgow, 1842.

Wood, James Maxwell, *Witchcraft and Superstitious Record in the South-Western District of Scotland*, Dumfries, 1911.

Yeoman, Louise, 'Away With The Fairies', in Lizanne Henderson (ed.), *Fantastical Imaginations, The Supernatural in Scottish History and Culture*, Edinburgh, 2009, pp.29–46.

Youngblood, Marian, *Bourtree Kirk: 800 Years*, Inverurie, 1995.

Index

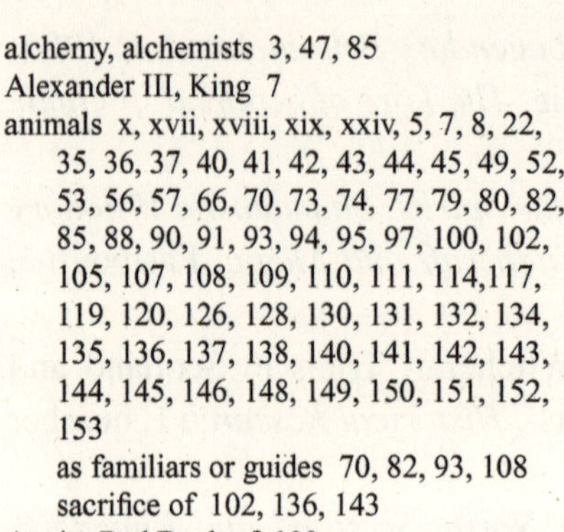